# Visit IHOP-KC at www.IHOP.org

The International House of Prayer Missions Base website has been designed for easy browsing. The following branches of the missions base have been incorporated into one cohesive website:

- IHOP-KC
- Onething
- Children's Equipping Center
- Forerunner School of Ministry
- Forerunner Music Academy
- Joseph Company
- Events & Conferences
- Internships & Training Programs
- Omega Course

The website also offers a variety of services. Whether you are interested in visiting IHOP-KC, receiving the Missions Base Podcast, browsing the bookstore, watching live Webcasts, or enrolling in FSM's online eSchool, the website delivers the information you need. With login capabilities that allow you access to more comprehensive IHOP-KC materials, we hope our site will be a valuable resource for you. Website features include:

- Podcasting
- Mp3 Downloads
- Forums
- Free & subscription-based webcasts
- Sermon and teaching notes
- eSchool distance learning
- Internship applications
- Prayer room blogs
- Online bookstore
- And more!

## *Visit us soon at www.IHOP.org!*

## RELENTLESS — *NEW CD by Misty Edwards*

This new CD reveals Misty's genuine heart cry to search out the depths of God, which fuels her intimate lyrics and illuminates her mature vocals. More than just another good worship album, *Relentless* is a prophetic message declaring the soon return of Christ.

The rock-induced arrangements and unconventional melodies call the listener to enter into divine worship. David Brymer joins Misty in poetic duets that release the spirit of desire in "My Soul Longs for You" and apprehend the beauty of Song of Songs in "You Won't Relent." Music created during hours in prayer and worship pour out as the theme of the album mingles between God's incessant pursuit of man's heart, and in return our response to tirelessly seek Him out.

*Purchase this and other Forerunner Music CDs at www.ihop.org/store or purchase and download the MP3 files at www.ihopmp3store.com.*

# Table of Contents

## Session 1 Introduction to the Song of Solomon

### I. INTRODUCTION

A. In this session, we will give introductory information about the Song of Solomon and principles of interpretation. This will give us a road map so as to understand the big picture in the Song.

B. King Solomon is the author of this eight chapter love Song in approximately 900 BC. It was probably written before his spiritual decline (1 Kings 11:3-4).

C. The two primary sections of the Song are Song 1-4 and Song 5-8.

    1. The first four chapters of the Song focus on the Bride understanding and enjoying her inheritance in Christ. These chapters emphasize how God views and desires her.

    2. The last four chapters focus on Jesus' inheritance in the Bride. We seek something from Him, but He also seeks something from us. He wants us to love Him with all our heart (Mt. 22:37). The focus of the book completely shifts in the middle (4:16-5:1).

### II. MY PERSONAL MANDATE AND JOURNEY WITH THE SONG

A. The Lord spoke to me by His audible voice in July 1988. I was in my office and I was reading Song of Solomon 8:6 and began to pray, "Let Jesus seal my heart with the seal of His love."

B. The Lord said that He would release grace to walk in Song 8:6-7 across the Body of Christ worldwide and that I was to focus on this theme throughout my ministry.

C. My first response was to be perplexed after I read the Song of Solomon that day. My next response was to study the Song by faith without enjoying it. I was initially intimidated by the symbolic terminology. I soon began to find much delight and pleasure in studying the Song as I encountered Jesus the Bridegroom and felt the power of His love.

### III. THE SONG REVEALS THE PATTERN OF HOLY PASSION

A. This Song reveals God's pattern in how we grow in passion for Jesus. It touches the significant principles and practical realities needed to develop mature love for God.

B. Understanding this Song helps us identify the issues that God is specifically dealing with in our lives. It equips us to discern what God is doing in the different seasons in our lives. Through our life, we ebb and flow in and out of the testing and blessing described throughout the Song. People often find themselves in two different places in this Song in the seasons of their life. I revisit the same place in the Song again and again.

## IV.   HOW TO INTERPRET THE SONG OF SOLOMON

A.   ***Natural interpretation***: this view depicts a natural love story between King Solomon and his bride, the Shulamite maiden. It emphasizes biblical principles that honor the beauty of love within marriage. This view has grown in popularity in the last 100 years and has many good commentaries. There are two basic story lines when interpreting the Song as a natural love story.

   1.   The first tells of a Shulamite maiden who was wooed by the handsome and wealthy King Solomon who progressively wins her heart as the storyline unfolds.

   2.   The second is the story of a godly Shulamite maiden who deeply loves a poor shepherd in her hometown (Shunem). King Solomon passed through her town and noticed her working in a vineyard. He was struck by her extraordinary beauty. Thus, he sought to steal her heart away from the poor shepherd that she loved. She remained loyal to the poor shepherd in the midst of the temptations of King Solomon's wealth and power.

B.   ***Spiritual interpretation***: this is a symbolic interpretation to see the spiritual truths in our relationship with Jesus behind the natural love story. This is the approach I will use in this study course. We study the Song to gain deeper understanding of our relationship with Jesus. This is the most common interpretation over the last 3000 years (since Solomon wrote this Song).

   1.   Jesus is exalted in the Song. He spoke of Himself from <u>all</u> the Scriptures to the disciples on the Emmaus road. He went through all 39 books of the OT to speak of Himself.

   *[27] He expounded…in <u>all the Scriptures</u> the things <u>concerning Himself</u>. (Lk. 24:27)*

   2.   The Spirit inspired all Scripture (2 Tim. 3:16) and exalts Jesus in all that He does.

   *[14] He will <u>glorify Me</u>, for He will take of <u>what is Mine</u> and declare it to you. (Jn. 16:14)*

   3.   The Spirit has deep friendship with Jesus and a fierce loyalty to fill people with love for Jesus. They have been together from eternity past. Thus, it is inconceivable for the Spirit to inspire a book in the Bible without Jesus being the predominant theme.

## V.   THE SPIRITUAL INTERPRETATION: 3 COMMON APPROACHES

A.   First, is the relationship between Jesus and the <u>individual believer</u>. This approach gives spiritual principles that aid us in our progression of holy passion. This is the way we approach this study.

B.   Second, is the relationship between Jesus and His <u>corporate Church</u> throughout history.

C.   Third, is the relationship between God as the Bridegroom and <u>ethnic Israel</u> as His Bride (Jer. 2:2; Hos. 2:16-20; Ezek. 16:8-14, 20-21, 32, 38; Is. 54:5-6). This was the primary approach of the scribes in OT times as well as Jewish rabbis today.

*Studies in the Song of Solomon: Progression of Holy Passion (2007) – MIKE BICKLE*
Session 1 Introduction to the Song of Solomon
PAGE 3

D. We bless different interpretations as long as they exhort others to grow in love for Jesus.

## VI. ALL BELIEVERS ARE INCLUDED IN THE BRIDE

A. Theologically, all believers on earth are betrothed (engaged) to Jesus. In Hebrew tradition, an engaged couple was legally married and needed to be divorced if they broke their engagement.

*² For I have __betrothed__ you to one husband, that I may present you as a chaste virgin to Christ. (2 Cor. 11:2)*

B. The consummation of the marriage relationship occurs in the age to come (Rev. 19:7).

*⁷ Let us be glad and rejoice and give Him glory, for the marriage of the Lamb has come, and His wife has made herself ready. (Rev. 19:7)*

C. A working definition of the Bride is one that includes all those who are mature in love.

D. I believe that the Bride of Christ is the entire Church from history that is filled with mature love. In the resurrection, the Spirit will bring God's work to completion in the whole church. In other words, every believer will experience a mature bridal relationship with Jesus.

E. First, the maturity of the Bride is ultimately the fruit of Jesus' work on the cross.

*³¹ If God is for us, who can be against us? 32 He who did not spare His own Son, but delivered Him up for us all, __how shall He not with Him also freely give us all things?__ (Rom. 8:31-32)*

F. Second, in heaven there will be only one unified people, rather than two classes of believers. Jesus prayed that His people would be unified like the Father and the Son.

*²¹ That they __all__ may be __one__, as You, Father, are in Me, and I in You... (Jn. 17:21)*

G. Third, we will be like Jesus when we see Him in glory. The impact of seeing God will release great power that will transform all believers in the age-to-come.

*² When He is revealed __we shall be like Him__, for we shall see Him as He is. (1 John 3:2)*

H. Fourth, the Bride's destiny is ensured by God's ravished heart for her. His heart is ravished for all of His people. God's heart is ravished for all the redeemed, not just for those who are spiritually mature during their brief time on the earth. Jesus is not more ravished for one group in the Church than He is for another group.

*⁹ You have __ravished__ My heart, My sister, My spouse… (Song 4:9).*

I. Summary: the maturity of the Bride is based primarily upon Jesus' work on the cross, His intercession, the revelation of His glory and His ravished heart for us.

## VII.   THE THREE MAIN CHARACTERS OF THE BOOK

A.   ***King Solomon***: in the spiritual interpretation he is a picture of the triumphant resurrected Jesus Christ who is King of Kings.

B.   ***Shulamite maiden***: in the spiritual interpretation she is a picture of the Bride of Christ. She is introduced as a young maiden who grows up to become a Bride in mature partnership with King Jesus. The Shulamite is mentioned once by name (6:13). She lived in Shunam (north of Jezreel).

C.   ***Daughters of Jerusalem***: in the spiritual interpretation they speak of sincere yet spiritually immature believers. They look to the Shulamite for answers on how to grow close to the King. They are not an actual group that we can identify in history (but personify immature believers).

## VIII.   COMPARING ECCLESIASTES AND SONG OF SONGS

A.   Solomon wrote 3 books in the Old Testament: Proverbs, Ecclesiastes and Song of Solomon. It was common for the Jewish fathers to relate the 3 books of Solomon to the temple he built.
1. They related the book of <u>Proverbs</u> to the **outer court** of Solomon's temple.
2. They related the book of <u>Ecclesiastes</u> to the **inner court** of Solomon's temple.
3. They related the <u>Song</u> to the **Holy of Holies** in Solomon's temple.

B.   In Ecclesiastes, he wrote, "Vanity of vanities, all is vanity." This book proclaims that life without obedience to God is vanity. Therefore, it is impossible to be satisfied with even the most desirable circumstances. This book speaks of man's endless wanderings until he finds rest in God. We can have everything but if we lack reality with God then in reality we have nothing.

C.   In the Song of Solomon, Solomon shows forth the joy of life that can be attained without regard to how our circumstances are going. In this book, the Holy Spirit is calling us to make intimacy with God the goal of our life. The Song highlights how full our life is when our consuming passion is to love and know Jesus. Even with hard circumstances, our spirit can be alive in God.

D.   Ecclesiastes teaches us that no matter how great our accomplishments are in man's eyes they will not ultimately have any value if they are not pleasing to God. When Ecclesiastes is understood it awakens us to the fervency that begins the journey in Song 1:5. Thus, Ecclesiastes prepares us to understand the Song of Solomon.

E.   The philosophy in Ecclesiastes tells us to "assert ourselves to gain more worldly experience as the way to enjoy life." Song of Solomon speaks of entering fulfillment through humility, obedience and the impartation of God's love.

F.   Ecclesiastes speaks of the vanity of pursuing the best things found in earthly life, while Song of Solomon speaks of the spiritual pleasure of pursuing the best things found in heavenly life.

## IX.  THE CANTICLES OR A SERIES OF SONGS

A.   The Song of Songs is sometimes referred to as the Canticles. The Latin noun "canticum" means "a Song". Canticles mean a series of Songs.

B.   The Vulgate was a popular Bible translation written in the 4th century by Jerome who translated the Scripture into Latin so that the common people could understand it.

C.   In the Vulgate, the Song of Solomon is called the Canticles. The following references may be rightfully used: Cant. 4:9 or Song 4:9 or SS 4:9 or SOS 4:9.

## X.  ALLEGORICAL INTERPRETATION

*23 But he who was of the bondwoman was born according to the flesh, and he of the freewoman through promise, 24 which things are <u>symbolic</u> (figurative in NIV; <u>allegorically speaking</u> in NAS). For these are the two covenants: the one from Mount Sinai which gives birth to bondage, which is Hagar-- 25 for this Hagar is Mount Sinai…and corresponds to Jerusalem which now is, and is in bondage with her children—26 but the Jerusalem above is free, which is the mother of us all. (Gal. 4:23-26)*

A.   The allegorical interpretation has been used in different ways through history. Paul's treatment of the Hagar-Sarah story "is described by Paul as symbolic by the NKJV, as figurative by the NIV and as an allegory by NAS.

B.   Paul's use of the Sarah-Hagar story in Gal. 4:21-31 is more "figurative" (typology) instead of an "allegory." Paul's use of allegory differed greatly from Alexandrian allegory (first-century Philo as well as the third and fourth century Origen and Chrysostom).

C.   The Alexandrians used allegory in a way that ignored its historical context and meaning. In 1 Cor. 9:9-10, Paul used an allegorical interpretation of the "muzzled ox" (Deut 25:4) to apply to the full-time workers in the gospel receiving finances.

D.   An allegory is a fictional story with symbolic meaning without historical facts as its basis. An experience of this type of an allegory is seen in the book, <u>The Chronicles of Narnia</u>.

E.   An allegory is a literary form where people or objects symbolically represent truths. Allegories illustrate truths to make them easier to understand. Our primary interpretation of Scripture must be the historical grammatical that takes the Scripture at face value. We approach the Scripture this way unless the Scripture indicates otherwise (Gal. 4:24; Jn. 15:1-6; Rev. 11:8; Isa. 5:1-7; Hos. 2:1-14; Ezek. 16; Dan. 7:2-8, 16).

F.   Allegorical interpretations are helpful if we only use them to illustrate truths that are clearly established throughout the New Testament.

*Studies in the Song of Solomon: Progression of Holy Passion (2007) – MIKE BICKLE*
*Session 1 Introduction to the Song of Solomon*

PAGE 6

# Session 2: Encountering Jesus in the Greatest Song (Song 1:1)

## I.   THE GREATEST SONG

A.   Solomon was a prolific Songwriter, writing 1005 Songs (1 Kings 4:32). The Holy Spirit inspired him to name this Song using the ultimate superlative (i.e., King of Kings, Lord of Lords, Holy of Holies). The Song of Solomon is the greatest song in redemptive history. I refer to it as the Song.

> *¹ The __Song of Songs__, which is Solomon's. (Song1:1).*

B.   There will be a great interest in the Song of Solomon in the generation in which the Lord returns. The Spirit is raising up many, young and old who proclaim it, sing it, write about it and pray it. Arise prophetic singers of God's new song. Arise songwriters to take your place before the Lord.

C.   I will offer practical advice to songwriters who are inspired by the Song of Solomon in writing new songs. Some write songs using the exact language of the Song of Solomon, rather than interpreting its meaning. We receive edification from symbolic language if we understand it.

D.   I recommend only taking a small portion of the Song of Solomon to write a new song. It is the longest Song in the Bible and is in a "concentrated" form.

## II.   FOUR DISTINTIVES OF THE SONG OF SOLOMON

A.   We seek to love God with all our heart because God loves us with all His heart and strength. Our whole heart has a vast and mysterious capacity. It is like a diamond with many facets. The reason we have deep and diverse emotions is because God does. We are made in His image. There are aspects of our heart that are best and most touched by *God's holy poetic affection*.

B.   The Song emphasizes the emotional side of Jesus' activity. Why did Jesus created in Gen. 1 and why did He go to the cross for us.

C.   These four distinctives are found in many places in Scripture. The uniqueness of the Song is not the fact that it contains these truths. Rather, it is in the focused concentration of them.

   1.   First, is the revelation of <u>Jesus' passionate affections and enjoyment of His people</u>.

   2.   Second, is the revelation of the <u>beauty of Jesus</u>, especially as a Bridegroom King.

   3.   Third, is the revelation of the <u>beauty of the individual believer to Jesus</u>, even in our weakness. If you want to know what you look like to God then study the Song.

   4.   Fourth, are the principles needed to <u>grow in love and mature partnership with Jesus</u>.

D.    The Church needs to be equipped with this revelation because of the significant increase of emotional wounding and sexual brokenness. Jesus wants to fascinate us with His beauty and to enthrall our heart with the beauty that He has given to us. The Song of Solomon is one of God's holy laser beams of revelation of Jesus' heart and desire.

## III.    THE 3-FOLD INHERITANCE—PS. 2:11-12

A.    King David described God's 3-fold inheritance as being a people who tremble, rejoice and kiss the Son of God. This is one of most excellent descriptions of the mature Bride.

> *⁸ Ask of Me, and I will give You the nations for Your <u>inheritance</u>…10 Be wise, O kings…11 Serve the LORD with <u>fear</u>, and <u>rejoice with trembling</u>. 12 <u>Kiss the Son</u>…. (Ps. 2:8-12)*

B.    David showed us the three sides of our redemption.
1. *Trembling* – we tremble in the fear of God by seeing the eternal majesty of Jesus.
2. *Rejoicing* – we rejoice by seeing who we are in Christ and the legal benefits of the cross.
3. *Kissing* – we figuratively "kiss the Son" or we love Him with all our heart as expressed by holy affections. In this, we touch the emotional and passionate side of our redemption

C.    There are three books of the bible that focus on these three sides of our redemption.
1. *Revelation*: the majestic eternal side that causes us to tremble before God
2. *Romans*: the legal practical side that causes us to rejoice in our benefits of the cross
3. *Song of Solomon*: the passionate emotional side that empowers us to love God

D.    Luther wrote of the legal side of our redemption, yet avoided the passionate and emotional side.

## IV.    TURNING THE SONG INTO AN AFFECTIONATE PRAYER DIALOGUE WITH JESUS

A.    We must engage in long and loving meditation on the Song with a hungry and honest heart before God. One of the Spirit's purposes in the Song is to fill us with the Father's love for Jesus.

> *²⁶ I have declared to them Your name, and will declare it, <u>that the love with which You loved</u> <sup>Me</sup> <u>may be in them</u>, and I in them. (Jn. 17:26)*

B.    If we are to receive the full benefit of the Song, we must turn it into an on-going affectionate prayerful dialogue with Jesus. It is not enough to only study the Song without going to the next step of turning it into a prayer dialogue. The language of the Song must get into our prayer life and thought life before it will transform our emotions.

C.    We approach the Song as more than an academic exercise as seen in Bible research. Informing our intellect is significant but it is only a starting point. No one would go to a famous restaurant to merely study the menu. The menu is there to help them obtain a good meal. It is not enough to be a connoisseur of the Song of Solomon, we must allow this book to fill our heart.

D.    I have about 10 phrases that have become deeply personal to me. In my early days, I wrote them on postcards to use when I drove or took a walk. I slowly whispered them to Jesus. For example, "Father, let Him kiss me with His Word" or "Spirit, sustain me, refresh me" (Song 1:2; 2:5).

E.    As you read through the these study notes, pray specific phrases from the Song back to God. By doing this, we use the Song as a springboard to launch into the depths of God's love.

## V.    ENCOUNTERING JESUS: PRAY-READING THE SONG OF SOLOMON

A.    I define two general categories of truth related to meditating on the Word. The first category is related to truths that exhort us "*to believe*" something about God, ourselves or the Kingdom. The second category is related to truths that exhort us "*to obey*" God's Word.

B.    Below are two ways to pray-read the Scriptures that exhort us "*to believe*" God's Word.

   1.    First, we **thank God** for the particular truth set forth in the passage. We turn the truth into a dialogue that includes taking time to say "Thank You, Jesus" in a specific way.

      a.    For example, when reading, "*You have ravished My heart,*" (Song 4:9) we respond by thanking God for this truth by praying, "Thank you Jesus, that I ravish Your heart."

      b.    For example, when Jesus says to the Bride, "*Your love is better than wine*" (Song 4:10), we respond by praying "I thank You Jesus that You esteem my love for You as better than the wine (the glory and pleasure) of this world."

      *¹⁰ How fair is your love…How much better than wine is your love… (Song 4:10)*

   2.    Second, we **ask for understanding** of the truth as we seek to believe more. Ask God to release revelation that causes us to know and feel the power of specific truths (Eph. 1:17).

      a.    For example, when reading, "*You have ravished My heart, My bride.*" ask Jesus for heart revelation by praying, "Jesus, show me more how *I have ravished Your heart.*"

      b.    For example, when reading that Jesus says to the Bride, "*Your love is better than wine,*" respond by asking for understanding by praying, "Jesus, show me more about the truth that "*My love for You is better to You than all the wine of this world.*"

C.    Below are two ways to pray-read the Scriptures with truths that exhort us "*to obey*" God's Word.

   1.    First, we **commit to obey** Jesus in the specific way described in the passage. We turn a particular truth into a simple dialogue with God that includes declaring our intention or commitment to obey Him (according the particular exhortation in that passage).

a. For example, when Jesus exhorts the Bride to *"rise up in obedience to leave the comfort zone to follow Him"* (costly obedience; Song 2:10), we respond by simply committing to obey this truth by praying, "Jesus, I will rise from the comfort zone to meet You on the mountains of costly obedience (Song 4:6)."

*¹⁰ My Beloved…said to me: "Rise up, My love…and come away. (Song 2:10)*

b. For example, when Jesus honors the Bride's heart for being like *"an enclosed garden whose springs of water are undefiled"* (a king's garden was enclosed or locked, in contrast to public garden. This points to having a pure heart that is as an enclosed garden or fully reserved for Jesus). We respond by committing to obey this truth by praying, "Jesus, my heart is locked to all compromise. I am fully Yours."

*¹² A garden enclosed is…My spouse, a spring shut up… (Song 4:12)*

2. Second, we **ask for God's manifest power to obey** a particular truth in a passage. Ask the Spirit for help to obey specific exhortations in a passage.

a. For example, when the Lord exhorts the Bride to *"arise in obedience to follow Him to the mountains,"* we ask the Spirit to help us obey by praying, "Jesus, empower me to obey You as I arise from the comfort zone to meet you in costly obedience."

b. For example, when the Lord honors the Bride's heart for being like *"an enclosed garden…"* we respond by asking God for help to obey this truth by praying, "Jesus, empower me to live with a locked heart that resists all compromise for You."

## VI.   THE NECESSITY OF JOURNALING

A.   Take time to journal by writing down your thoughts, prayers and meditations as you "pray-read" through the Song. This will help you to capture the truths that the Lord puts on your heart. The simple exercise of writing your ideas will help you take this magnificent Song and turn it into a glorious prayer dialogue between your heart and Jesus.

B.   Be patient, speak slowly and softly, then journal your thoughts. You may be surprised how the Spirit will give you more revelation, strengthen your obedience and tenderize your heart by this.

# Session 3 The Divine Kiss: Transformed by the Word (Bridal Paradigm)

## I. INTRODUCTION

*² Let Him kiss me with the <u>kisses of His mouth</u> (Word) -- for Your love is better than wine. (Song 1:2)*

A. What is a Bridal paradigm? A paradigm is a point of view or a perspective. It is the lens through which we interpret our worldview. In July 1988, the Lord began to lead me to see the Kingdom of God through the eyes of a cherished Bride who is to be fascinated with the beauty of Jesus as the Bridegroom God. I began to see Jesus' beauty in a whole new way, even in familiar passages.

B. The dominant theme in the Song is the King's emotions or affections for His Bride. We must make it a priority to study and meditate on the subject of God's emotions. This is important to our own emotional health. We are transformed as we understand the way God thinks and feels about us, especially in our weakness. This revelation causes us to run to Him instead of from Him. It causes us to have confidence in His love and to open our spirit to Him in our weakness. Many sincere believers seek God with a condemned heart or a closed and guarded spirit.

C. In the grace of God, our experience of God's love is not to be quenched nor drowned by any flood. Many have a quenched heart in which their ability to experience God's love has been drowned. The truths of the Song unlock our heart by the fire of God.

*⁶ Set Me (Jesus) as a seal upon your heart…for love (God's love in us) is as strong as death…its flames are <u>flames of fire</u>…7 Many waters (persecution, sin, condemnation, pressures, etc.) cannot <u>quench</u> love, nor can the floods <u>drown</u> it. (Song 8:6-7)*

## II. THE KISS OF GOD'S WORD

A. The focus of this session is to understand the Divine kiss of God's Word. The eight chapter love Song unfolds the implications of receiving the Divine kiss. This is the theme of the Bride's life.

*² Let Him kiss me with the kisses of His mouth (Word) wine. (Song 1:2)*

B. There are different types of kisses in Scripture. Examples are the kiss on the cheek of a friend, or the kiss on the feet of a servant. The kiss of the mouth speaks of holy married love or intimacy.

C. The maiden requests the kisses of the King's mouth. The Word of God is what proceeds from God's mouth. Our heart can only live by that which comes from the mouth of God. Jesus quoted Deut. 8:3 in His wilderness temptation (Mt. 4:4). For 3,000 years, rabbis have referred to the "kisses of the mouth" in this verse as the "kiss of the Torah".

*³ That He might make you know that man shall not live by bread alone; but man <u>lives</u> by <u>every word that proceeds from the mouth of the LORD</u>. (Deut. 8:3)*

D.  The Divine kiss is a metaphor for intimacy with God. We are to think of God's hand touching our heart by the Holy Spirit to expand our capacity to receive His love and to give ourselves back to Him in love. It speaks God's invitation to go deep with Jesus. The kisses of His mouth speak of the release of the Word of God that tenderizes our hearts in the love of God. We are NOT to think of kissing Jesus on the mouth. This is entirely outside the boundaries of God's Word. We renounce all interpretations of the "kisses of the Word" that come from sensual imagination.

E.  The Song of Solomon was written to extol the beauty of married love and to give us insight into our relationship to Jesus as our Bridegroom God. All that the Spirit teaches motivates us to love Jesus more. It is inconceivable that the Spirit would inspire Scripture that did not point to Jesus.

*¹⁴ He will __glorify__ Me, for He will take of what is Mine and declare it to you. (Jn. 16:14)*

F.  The Word of God covers many different subjects such as relationship skills, ministry skills or apostolic strategies for outreach (Book of Acts). The Word as it pertains to growing in these skills and insights is very valuable to us. However, in Song 1:2, the Bride cried out specifically to receive the Word of God in a way that would reveal and impart God's love to her heart.

G.  There are three metaphors of intimacy with God in the Song. They are the Divine kiss (1:2), the Divine seal (8:6), and the Divine embrace (2:5; 8:4).

H.  The Bride's journey started with a longing for the kisses of His Word (Song 1:2) and up ended up encountering Jesus in His holy jealous love (Song 8:6-7). He came to seal her heart with holy jealous love which is the ultimate expression of maturity in the Song.

## III.  THE DIVINE KISS: THE BRIDE'S SUPREME REQUEST

A.  The maiden made her request to One with authority over the King instead of directly to the King. She said, "Let Him..." She asks One who could influence the King in personal matters.

B.  Solomon writes this love Song in a way that is reminiscent of his own experience with God. In Solomon's early years as king of Israel, God visited him in a dream to test him (2 Chr. 1; 1 Kg. 3). The Lord tested Solomon by allowing him to make one supreme request or to ask God for anything. He asked for a supernatural impartation of wisdom and knowledge to serve God better.

*⁷ God appeared to Solomon, and said to him, "Ask! __What shall I give you__?"...10 Now give me wisdom and knowledge...for who can judge this great people of Yours?" 11 God said to Solomon: "Because this was in your heart, and you have not asked __riches__ or wealth or __honor__ or the life of your __enemies__, nor have you asked __long life__--but have asked wisdom and knowledge for yourself, that you may judge My people...12 wisdom and knowledge are granted to you; and I will give you riches and wealth and honor, such as none of the kings have had who were before you, nor shall any after you have the like." (2 Chron. 1:7-12)*

C.     In a similar way, the Lord has invited the Church to ask for anything in His will. As the Bride, we stand in the Father's presence to ask for what we want most. We cry "Father, let Him kiss me with the kisses of His Word." We ask for the deepest things that God will give the human spirit.

*²² And <u>whatever things you ask</u> in prayer, believing, you will receive. (Mt. 21:22)*

*²³ Whoever…does not doubt in his heart, but believes that those things he says will come to pass, <u>he will have whatever he says</u>. (Mk. 11:23)*

*¹³ <u>Whatever</u> you ask in My name, that I will do, that the Father may be glorified in the Son. 14 If you ask <u>anything</u> in My name, I will do it. (Jn. 14:13-14)*

D.     God continues to test His people by allowing them to ask for anything. The Bride's supreme request from the Father is the Divine kiss of the Word. She wants this more than power, prominence and earthly comforts. God is raising up a people who long for the kisses of God's Word as their supreme request. There are many necessary things to ask for. They are secondary. The greatest prayer of faith is to receive grace to love God with all our heart and strength.

## IV.     THE 3-FOLD NATURE OF THE CRY FOR THE KISS OF GOD'S WORD

A.     First, this is the great *prophetic cry* that expresses *where* the Spirit is leading the Church in the nations. The Spirit will restore the First Commandment to first place before Jesus returns. God promised Moses that in the End-Times, He would circumcise the heart of His people so that they would love God with all their heart. The Church will cry out with a bride's love, "Come, Jesus!"

*³⁷ Jesus said to him, "You shall <u>love</u> the LORD your God with <u>all your heart</u>…" (Mt. 22:37)*

*⁶ The LORD your God will circumcise…the heart of your descendants, <u>to love the LORD your God with all your heart</u> and with all your soul, that you may live. (Deut. 30:6)*

*¹⁷ The Spirit and the Bride say, "Come!" (Rev. 22:17)*

B.     Second, this is the great *philosophical cry* of the human spirit that answers *why* we exist in time and eternity. The ultimate purpose and meaning of our life is to experience intimacy with God. The absolute definition of success is to a wholehearted lover of God. When we know that we are loved by God and desire to be a wholehearted lover of God, then we are truly successful.

C.     Third, this is the great *psychological cry* that answers *how* our heart functions. It answers the mystery of how our heart experiences true happiness and is satisfied. God designed us so that experiencing His love is the most pleasurable reality available to the human make-up. We were created to love God with all our heart. When we do not love God with a passionate heart, then our emotional life is out of balance. Life does not work without pursuing this. We were created in such a way that we can not live in wholeness without the pursuit of being wholehearted for God. If we have nothing to die for, then we have nothing to live for. Many in the Body of Christ are suffering from spiritual boredom because they are not passionate in their pursuit to love God.

## V.     THE 2-FOLD SPIRITUAL REST OF THE BELIEVER

A.     *The rest of forgiveness*: we experience this with the knowledge that we are fully forgiven as a free gift in Jesus. We rest in receiving forgiveness because of Jesus' finished work on the cross.

B.     *The rest of intimacy*: we experience this as we pursue intimacy with God. There is no rest until we conclude the highest purpose of our life is intimacy with God. Augustine (354-430 AD) wrote, "Man does not rest until he finds his rest in God." We only find our ultimate purpose for life in being wholehearted in our love for God. This is our highest life purpose that brings us peace and happiness in this life. Many believers who have the assurance of being forgiven are striving to find purpose and happiness. It is not an issue of going to heaven but how and why they live on earth.

C.     There is a God-shaped vacuum in our hearts that can only be fulfilled in the rest of intimacy. Without resting in this area of our lives, we are far more vulnerable to sexual bondage, addictions and bitterness, etc.

## VI.     LIVING BEFORE AN AUDIENCE OF ONE

A.     I heard the story of a concert pianist in the last century that longed to play in the great concert hall in Vienna. When he finished his first concert before thousands, the people gave him a long standing ovation. Afterwards, he was asked, "Was it the greatest moment in your life to receive this long applause?" The concert pianist replied, "No! I liked it, but it was not the most important thing to me." He said, "When the people all sat down, an elderly man who sat in the top corner of the balcony simply nodded his head at me. That was the greatest moment of my life because he is the master who taught me for 30 years. One nod from him was worth much more than the long applause of the masses."

B.     We must learn to live before an audience of One. Receiving the nod from our Master has great power in the hearts of those who love Him. It has more power than the approval of all others.

## VII.     PRACTICAL APPLICATION: SEEKING THE KISSES OF GOD'S WORD

A.     The cry for the kisses of God's Word is the same reality as living before the audience of One.

B.     We receive the kisses of God's Word by pray-reading God's Word or in meditation on it (as covered in session 2) as we set our heart to receive the deepest things that God will give us.

C.     In times of temptation, we speak this truth before the Lord. We say, "I will not yield to sin. Father let Him kiss me. My life is about receiving the kisses of God's Word. This is who I am." When people mistreat us. We declare, "My life is not primarily about being more popular, I live for the kisses of God's Word."

# Session 4 An Overview of the Storyline in the Song of Solomon

## I. SONG OF SOLOMON: THE DIVINE KISS & THE BRIDE'S LIFE VISION (SONG 1:2-4)

A. The theme of the Song of Solomon is the Bride's spiritual journey to be drawn near to Jesus in intimacy and then to run in deep partnership with Him in ministry. She matures in these two realities as she experiences the kisses of God's word touching her heart.

> *² Let Him kiss me with the <u>kisses of His mouth</u> (Word). For Your love is better than wine… 4 <u>Draw me away</u> (intimacy)! <u>We will run after you</u> (ministry). (Song 1:2-4)*

B. The Song of Solomon has two main sections. First, Song 1-4 is focused on receiving <u>**our inheritance**</u> in God. Second, Song 5-8 is focused on God receiving <u>**His inheritance**</u> in us.

## II. HER JOURNEY BEGINS WITH THE PARADOX OF GRACE (SONG 1:5-11)

> *⁵ I am dark (in heart), but <u>lovely</u> (to God)…⁶ my own vineyard (heart) I have not kept. (Song 1:5-6)*

A. The paradox of our faith is that we are dark in our heart yet we are lovely to God. Both truths must be held in tension to understand who we are before God. Some emphasize how sinful we are (darkness of our heart) and others emphasize how beautiful we are to God (lovely in Christ).

B. We are lovely before God even in our weakness for four reasons.

1. <u>God's personality</u>: is filled with tender loving emotions for His people. God sees us through His heart that is filled with tender love. Beauty is in the eyes of the beholder.

2. <u>The gift of righteousness</u>: we receive the beauty of Jesus' righteousness as a free gift.
> *²¹ For He made Him who knew no sin to be sin for us, <u>that we might become the righteousness of God</u> in Him. (2 Cor. 5:21)*

3. <u>The Spirit's impartation</u>: of a sincere and willing spirit of obedience that cries for God.
> *¹⁵ You received the Spirit of adoption by whom <u>we cry</u>, "Abba, Father." (Rom. 8:15)*

4. <u>Our eternal destiny</u>: as Jesus' Bride. God sees the end from the beginning. He sees us in light of the billions of years in which we will be perfect in obedience.

C. She has a desperate cry to have more of Jesus. She wants Him to personally feed her spirit.
> *⁷ Tell me, O You whom I love, <u>where You feed your flock</u>…For why should I be as one who veils herself by the flocks of Your companions? (Song 1:7)*

D. Jesus tenderly reveals His heart for her. Then He reaffirms her sincerity (1:8-11).
> *⁸ …O fairest (most beautiful) among women… (Song 1:8)*

III.     **UNDERSTANDING HER IDENTITY IN GOD'S BEAUTY (SONG 1:12-2:7)**

A.     She has an initial revelation of the beauty of Jesus and the pleasure of knowing Him (Ps. 27:4).

*<sup>16</sup> Behold, You are <u>handsome</u> (beautiful), my Beloved! Yes, <u>pleasant</u>! (Song 1:16)*

B.     She receives revelation of her identity in Christ as a beautiful rose in God's sight.

*<sup>1</sup> I am the <u>rose of Sharon, and the <u>lily</u> of the valleys. (Song 2:1)*

C.     Jesus is sweet to her heart as she rests under the shade of the finished work of the cross. She experiences the <u>superior pleasures</u> of knowing God as she feeds at His table and lives under the banner of His excellent leadership. In this she becomes <u>lovesick</u>. The goal of her life is her own spiritual happiness. This happens best when she experiences God's Presence. In the future, her goal will be to walk as His inheritance regardless of the cost.

*<sup>3</sup> I <u>sat down</u> in His shade (resting in the finished work of the cross) with <u>great delight</u>, and His fruit was <u>sweet</u> to my taste. <sup>4</sup> He brought me to the banqueting House, and <u>His banner (leadership) over me was love</u>. <sup>5</sup> Sustain me…refresh me…for I am <u>lovesick</u>. (Song 2:3-5)*

IV.     **CHALLENGING THE COMFORT ZONE (SONG 2:8-17)**

*<sup>8</sup> The voice of my Beloved! He comes <u>leaping</u> upon the mountains, <u>skipping</u> upon the hills. <sup>9</sup> My beloved is like a gazelle…<sup>10</sup> My Beloved spoke, "<u>Rise up</u>, My love…and <u>come away</u>. <sup>14</sup> Let Me see your face, let Me hear your voice; for your voice is <u>sweet</u>, and your face is <u>lovely</u>." <sup>17</sup> Until the day breaks and the shadows flee away, <u>Turn, my Beloved</u>… (Song 2:8-17)*

A.     Jesus is pictured as effortlessly skipping and leaping over the mountains or as working to fulfill the Great Commission. The mountains speak of obstacles (human, demonic). Jesus has power over all of them. She is accustomed to eating apples at His table, under the shade tree (2:3-5).

B.     She refuses Him by telling Him to <u>turn</u> and go to the mountain without her (2:17). Her painful compromise is due to her immaturity and fear <u>not rebellion</u>. She fears that total obedience will be too difficult and costly. She loves Him, but does not think she has the strength to fully obey Him.

V.     **SHE EXPERIENCES GOD'S LOVING DISCIPLINE (SONG 3:1-5)**

*<sup>1</sup> By night on my bed I sought the One I love…but <u>I did not find Him</u>. <sup>2</sup> <u>I will rise now</u>…I will seek the one I love. <sup>4</sup>…When I found the One I love. I held Him and would not let Him go… (Song 3:1-4)*

A.     She experiences the discipline of God as He hides His face from her. The sweetness of Song 2 is gone. He disciplines us out of His affection (Heb. 12:5-12). God's correction is not the same thing as His rejection. The Father promises to pry our fingers off what holds us in bondage. The Father loves us too much to allow us to come up short of partnering with Jesus as His Bride.

B.     She soon "arises" to obey the call to leave her comfort (3:2). Jesus' manifest presence returns in response to her obedience (3:4).

## VI.   A FRESH REVELATION OF JESUS AS A "SAFE SAVIOR" (SONG 3:6-11)

Jesus reveals Himself as one who is safe to obey 100%. She believes that "100% obedience is the only safe place in life. Walking with Jesus on the water is far safer than being in the boat without Him.

## VII.   THE PROPHETIC HEART OF THE BRIDEGROOM GOD (SONG 4:1-8)

*¹ Behold, <u>you are fair</u> (beautiful), My love! Behold, you are fair (Song 4:1)*

A.   The King reveals how beautiful the maiden is to Him. He describes 8 distinct virtues of her beauty that He sees emerging in her life. (4:1-5). Jesus prophetically proclaims her "budding virtues". He calls things that are not as though they were (Rom. 4:17). He sees the cry in her spirit, not just her failures. God defines us by the cries in our spirit not just by our struggles.

B.   A life of total commitment is foundational for all who are to be mature in ministry (4:6). Initially, she refused His call to come to the mountain (2:9-10). However, in this season she commits to go to the mountain. She is only in the initial stages of her obedience. Later she becomes mature.

*⁶ <u>I will go</u> my way to <u>the mountain</u> of myrrh... (Song 4:6)*

## VIII.   THE RAVISHED HEART OF THE BRIDEGROOM GOD (SONG 4:9-5:1)

A.   The King is now revealed as a Bridegroom. His heart is ravished with desire for her. Jesus has passionate affection for His Bride. This revelation of His heart, equips her to fully embrace the cross (Song 4:9). Jesus describes His pleasure over her character (4:10d-11).

*⁹ You have <u>ravished My heart</u>…My spouse…with one look of your eyes…10 How fair (beautiful) is your love…How <u>much better</u> than wine is your love... (Song 4:9-10)*

B.   Jesus gives her a 7-fold description of her purity (4:12-15). A king's garden was private. This is in contrast to a public one with defiled water. We can speak this to Jesus in our desire for purity.

*¹² A garden <u>enclosed</u> is My sister, My spouse, a spring <u>shut up</u>, a fountain <u>sealed</u>. (Song 4:12)*

C.   Her garden speaks of her heart before God. She wants the fragrance of God's <u>spices</u> to increase in her life. The <u>north wind</u> speaks of the cold bitter winds of winter. The <u>south wind</u> speaks of the warm refreshing winds of the summer. She is no longer afraid of the testings of God. She desires that Jesus receive <u>His inheritance in her</u> and cries, "Let my Beloved come to His garden."

*¹⁶ Awake, O <u>north wind</u>, and come, O south! Blow upon my garden, <u>that its spices may flow out</u>. Let my Beloved come to <u>His garden</u> and eat its pleasant fruits. (Song 4:16 )*

D.   In the first 4 chapters she was concerned with <u>her inheritance</u> (her garden). However, in the last 4 chapters, <u>Jesus' inheritance</u> in her is her focus. From now on, her heart is <u>His garden</u> not hers. She now defines her life radically different. Nine times He uses the ownership word "My".

*¹ I have come to <u>My</u> garden, <u>My</u> sister, <u>My</u> spouse; I have gathered <u>My</u> myrrh with <u>My</u> spice; I have eaten <u>My</u> honeycomb with <u>My</u> honey; I have drunk <u>My</u> wine with <u>My</u> milk. (Song 5:1).*

## IX.    THE ULTIMATE 2-FOLD TEST OF MATURITY (SONG 5:2-8)

*² The voice of my Beloved! He knocks, saying, "<u>Open</u> for Me…My love…My perfect one; for My head is covered with dew, <u>My locks with the drops of the night</u>." (Song 5:2)*

A.    Jesus embraced the cross in the long and lonely night in Gethsemane. Jesus comes to her as the man of sorrows in Gethsemane (5:2) and invites her to share His sufferings (Phil. 3:10).

   *¹⁰ That I may know Him, he power of His resurrection, and the <u>fellowship of His sufferings</u>, (Phil. 3:10)*

B.    Jesus asks her to, "Open up that He may come to her as the Man of Gethsemane." Jesus wants to be the <u>goal of her life</u>, and not just the stepping stone to her agenda of success and happiness.

C.    She responds in obedience saying she took off her dirty robes and washed her feet in His grace (5:3). She is not afraid of obeying Jesus and thus, asked for the bitter north winds (Song 4:16). She rises immediately with a heart yearning in love for Him. The locks of her heart have myrrh on them, which speak of her heart commitment to embrace death in her pursuit of Jesus.

   *⁴ My <u>heart yearned</u> for Him. ⁵ I <u>arose</u> to <u>open</u> for my Beloved, and my hands dripped with <u>myrrh</u>…on the handles of the lock. (Song 5:4-5)*

D.    She experiences her first test as God <u>withdraws His presence</u> (5:6). This affects her ability to experience intimacy with God. In this passage, His presence leaves her for the second time in the Song (3:1). However, this time it is not related to disobedience (as in 3:1-2), but rather to her mature obedience. Some medieval teachers called this "the dark night of the soul."

   *⁶ I <u>opened</u> for my Beloved, but my Beloved had <u>turned away</u> and was <u>gone</u>. My heart leaped up when He spoke. I sought Him, but <u>I could not find Him</u>… <u>He gave me no answer</u>. (Song 5:6)*

E.    She experiences her second test as her <u>ministry is rejected</u> (5:7). The watchmen or the leaders strike and wound her taking her veil (spiritual covering) so she can no longer function in ministry in the Body. Her ministry is gone. How will she respond to Him now?

   *⁷ The watchman…<u>struck me</u>, they <u>wounded me</u>; the keepers of the walls <u>took my veil</u> away from me. (Song 5:7)*

F.    The Lord is asking her, "Will you be Mine even if I withhold the things you deeply desire? Are you Mine when you cannot feel My Presence? Will you still love and trust Me when you are disappointed by circumstances?" She responds, "I am Yours, at the deepest level of love. She responds in humility by asking for help from the daughters of Jerusalem (who are less spiritual).

   *⁸ O daughters of Jerusalem, if you find my Beloved…tell Him I am <u>lovesick</u>! (Song 5:8)*

G.    <u>Summary</u>: Jesus called her to join Him in Gethsemane. She responded in obedience. He gave her a 2-fold test related to her life vision to be drawn near Him and to run with Him (Song 1:2-4).

   *² Let Him kiss me with the <u>kisses of His mouth</u> (Word). For Your love is better than wine… 4 <u>Draw me away</u> (intimacy)! <u>We will run after you</u> (ministry). (Song 1:2-4)*

## X.     THE BRIDE'S RESPONSE TO THE 2-FOLD TEST (SONG 5:9-6:5)

A.     The daughters of Jerusalem ask the Bride a question. In essence, they ask, "Why do you love Him so much that you charge us to go find Him? He has abandoned you. He took His presence away from you (v. 6) and lets the elders wound you as they took their ministry from you (5:7).

*⁹ What is your Beloved more than another Beloved, O fairest among women? (Song 5:9)*

B.     Her answer reveals her love for Jesus. She gives 10 descriptions of Jesus' majestic beauty (5:10-16). This is one of the greatest proclamations on Jesus' beauty in the Scripture.

*¹⁰ My beloved is white (dazzling, NAS)…and chief among ten thousand. ¹¹ His head is like the finest gold; His locks are wavy…and black as a raven. ¹² His eyes are like doves by the rivers of waters…¹³ His cheeks are like a bed of spices…His lips are lilies, dripping liquid myrrh. ¹⁴ His hands are rods of gold set with beryl. His body is carved ivory inlaid with sapphires. ¹⁵ His legs are pillars of marble set on bases of fine gold. His countenance is like Lebanon, excellent as the cedars. ¹⁶ His mouth is most sweet, Yes, He is altogether lovely. This is my Beloved, and this is my friend… (Song 5:10-16)*

## XI.    JESUS PRAISES HER AFTER THE SEASON OF TESTING (SONG 6:4-10)

A.     Her 2-fold test is now over. Jesus breaks the silence as He lavishes affection on her and describes her beauty. He declares that she is as beautiful as *Tirzah* (became the capital city of the northern kingdom of Israel) and as lovely as *Jerusalem* (the capital of Israel, spiritually and politically). He proclaimed that she was as awesome as a victorious army with banners. When an army in the ancient world returned victorious from battle, they displayed their banners in a military procession. She defeated her greatest enemies, those found in her heart.

*⁴ O My love, you are as beautiful as Tirzah, lovely as Jerusalem, awesome as an army with banners! (Song 6:4)*

B.     Jesus is "conquered" only by His Bride's extravagant love. Our eyes of devotion deeply touch the King's heart. All the armies in hell cannot conquer Jesus, but the eyes of His Bride "conquer" Him when they are true to Him in times of testing.

*⁵ Turn your eyes away from Me, for they have overcome Me. (Song 6:5)*

C.     Jesus describes the Bride's maturity and devotion (6:5c-7).

D.     Jesus describes the Bride's pre-eminence in the King's court. Jesus' attendants around His heavenly court are seraphim, cherubim, archangels and angels without number.

*⁸ There are 60 queens and 80 concubines, and virgins without number. ⁹ My dove, my perfect one, is the…only one of her mother, the favorite of the one who bore her... (Song 6:8-9)*

E.     The Holy Spirit describes the Bride's crown of glory (6:10).

*¹⁰ Who is she who looks forth as the morning, fair as the moon, clear as the sun, awesome as an army with banners? (Song 6:10)*

**XII.    THE VINDICATION OF THE PERSECUTED BRIDE (SONG 6:11-7:9A).**

   A.    As the Bride walks in this revelation of who she is before the Lord, she is persecuted. Mature love and commitment to serve the whole church (6:11) overcomes her (6:12).

   B.    She receives a sincere response from some in the church (6:13a,b) yet a hostile response from others (6:13c,d).

   *13 Return, return, O Shulamite; Return, return, that we may look upon you! What would you see in the Shulamite-- As it were, the <u>dance of the two camps</u>? (Song 6:11-13)*

   C.    The Bride is vindicated by discerning saints (7:1-5). The Bride is vindicated by Jesus (7:6-9a).

**XIII.   THE BRIDE'S MATURE PARTNERSHIP WITH JESUS (SONG 7:9B-8:4).**

She walks out mature bridal partnership with Jesus which is expressed in obedience (7:9b-10). She expresses Bridal partnership in her intercession for more power (7:11-13). She expresses partnership in her boldness in public ministry (8:1-2). She expresses Bridal partnership in their full union (8:3-4).

**XIV.   THE BRIDAL SEAL OF MATURE LOVE (SONG 8:5-7)**

Jesus invites her to receive the seal of fire upon her heart and to walk with Him in holy jealous love. God is a consuming fire and desires to impart His fire into our hearts. This is His supernatural love that seals our heart. It empowers us to live without the fire of our love being quenched.

**XV.    THE BRIDE'S FINAL INTERCESSION AND REVELATION (SONG 8:8-14)**

   A.    The Bride intercedes for the church (8:8–9) and for Jesus' return (8:14). In Song 8:8–9, her apostolic passion for the church is seen.

   B.    In Song 8:10, her 3-fold confidence is as a wall (selfless motives), as a tower (her supernatural abilities to nurture) and as one with peace (emotional hindrances are removed).

   C.    In Song 8:11-12, she experiences the power and enjoyment of living before His eyes instead of before the eyes of men. Her sense of importance is rooted in eternity as she has revelation of giving account before God (8:11). The Bride has a revelation of her own spiritual maturity before God (8:12).

   D.    Jesus' final commission to the Bride (8:13-14). The Bride's urgency is expressed in intercession.

   *13 You who dwell in the gardens (the Bride), the companions listen for your voice-- Let Me (Jesus) hear it! 14 <u>Make haste</u>, my Beloved (Jesus), and be like a gazelle or a young stag on the mountains of spices. (Song 8:13-14)*

   *17 The Spirit and the Bride say, "<u>Come!</u>" (Rev. 22:17)*

# Session 5 God's Love is Better than the Wine of this World (Song 1:2)

## I. REVIEW: UNDERSTANDING THE KISSES OF GOD'S WORD

*² Let Him kiss me with the <u>kisses</u> of His mouth (Word) - For Your love is better than wine. (Song 1:2)*

A. The Bride made her request to the One with authority over the King. She said, "Let Him..." She asks the One who could influence the King in personal matters. We cry "Father, let Him kiss me with the kisses of His Word." In this, we pray the prayer of faith asking for grace to love Jesus with all our heart. The commandment to love God is God's first priority in our lives.

*³⁷ Jesus said to him, "You shall <u>love</u> the LORD your God with <u>all your heart</u>, with all your soul, and with all your mind." 38 This is the <u>first</u> and great commandment. (Mt. 22:37-38)*

B. The Word of God is what proceeds from God's mouth. For 3,000 years, rabbis have referred to the "kisses of the mouth" in this verse as the "kiss of the Torah".

*³ That He might make you know that man shall not live by bread alone; but man <u>lives</u> by <u>every word that proceeds from the mouth of the LORD</u>. (Deut. 8:3)*

C. The theme of the Song is the Bride's cry for the kiss of God's Word to touch the deepest place in her heart. This refers to encountering the Word in the deepest and most intimate way. In other words, the Word as it reveals the King's emotions for His Bride and awakens our heart in the 3-fold love of God (love from God then for God which overflows to others).

## II. THE SUPERIOR PLEASURES IN THE GRACE OF GOD

A. After asking the Father for the kisses of God's Word. She gives her reason for wanting the kisses of the Word. She speaks directly to Jesus in the second person, "For Your love (affection) is better than wine." We can use the word "because" in place of the word "for." She is saying that experiencing Jesus' affection is better than the wine of this fallen world.

*² Let Him kiss me with the kisses of His mouth-- for Your love <u>is better than</u> wine (Song 1:2).*

B. She uses the wine metaphor because wine "exhilarates" the heart. Wine, in the context of this marriage metaphor is "the drink of earthly celebration." It is the drink of gladness that makes people happy. It speaks of the intoxicating things of this world, both good and bad.

  1. There is the "good wine" of God's blessing and also the "bad wine" of our sin. She is saying more than, "Your love is better than sin." That is obvious. She is saying, "Experiencing Your love is better than all the other privileges in this life.

  2. The good blessings of God in our circumstances include financial increase, favor in relationships, physical health, new spheres of influence in ministry, etc. The wine speaks of the best experiences that we can have in the natural realm (in this age).

*Studies in the Song of Solomon: Progression of Holy Passion (2007) – MIKE BICKLE*
*Session 5 God's Love is Better than the Wine of this World (Song 1:2)*
PAGE 22

C.   As wonderful as God's blessings are, they are not to be the primary focus of our heart. Many experience God's blessing in the increase of finances or prominence, etc. without their hearts being enlarged in the love of God. Many who increase in God's blessing in their circumstances often gradually decrease in their love for Jesus (Rev. 2:4-5).

*³ You have persevered…and have labored for My name's sake…4 Nevertheless I have this against you, that you have left your first love. 5 Remember therefore from where you have fallen; repent and do the first works, or else I will…remove your lampstand. (Rev. 2:3-5)*

D.   The Bride introduces the priority that the "superior pleasures" of gospel have in her life. This reveals her theology of her life and her pursuit of holiness.

*² Let Him kiss me with the kisses of His mouth-- for Your love is better than wine (Song 1:2).*

*² …with the kisses of His mouth- for Your love is more delightful than wine. (Song 1:2, NIV)*

E.   "Is better than" or "is superior to" or "is more delightful than" points to the superior pleasures that come from growing in revelation of God's heart (affection). These superior pleasures are in contrast to the inferior pleasures of sin. God frees us from the dominion of the inferior pleasures of sin by allowing us to experience superior pleasures that are more powerful.

F.   There are many different categories of pleasures that we are to celebrate under the leadership of Jesus. There are physical, emotional, and mental pleasures. God is the author of these. God made us spiritually, physically and emotionally hungry or needy. We long for happiness. We yearn deeply for pleasure because we are designed by God to be pleasure seekers. This in itself is not sinful; finding our pleasure in unrighteousness is what is sinful.

G.   God created the human spirit with seven longings that draw us to Him and reflect His glory in us. These longings are common in all of us. They give insight into the way God designed our spirit. Each longing is a reflection of God's personality. We are made in His image, thus, we have these longings. We feel delight because He is filled with delight, we have happiness because He has happiness. (see the book: *7 Longings of the Human Heart* by M. Bickle and Deborah Hiebert).

H.   They are the longing for the assurance that we are enjoyed by God, the longing to be fascinated, the longing to be beautiful, the longing to be great, the longing for intimacy without shame, the longing to be wholehearted and passionate, and the longing to make a deep and lasting impact.

I.   They are cravings put into us strategically by God. They will never ever go away. The reason food is so good is because we were created to be hungry. The reason God satisfies us with pleasure is because He created a hunger for pleasure in us. They each have an element of delight, pain and ache as they woo us into God's presence. The enemy uses these cravings to woo us into darkness as well. When these longings are not touched in the grace of God they leave us empty; they leave us with pain, mourning, and dissatisfaction. God created us with a "God shaped vacuum" (gnawing emptiness) in our heart that can only be filled by God.

J.     Satan counterfeits the pleasures that God created so that he might draw us away from God. Sin produces immediate pleasure. No one sins out of obligation. We sin because we believe that it will provide a pleasure that is superior to obeying God. The power of temptation rests on a deceptive promise that sin will bring more satisfaction than living for God, thus, it is referred to as the deceitfulness of sin or as deceitful lusts.

*²² Put off…the old man which grows corrupt according to the <u>deceitful lusts</u>… (Eph. 4:22)*

*¹³ Lest any of you be hardened through the <u>deceitfulness of sin</u>. (Heb. 3:13)*

K.     The greatest "pleasures" that we can experience are spiritual ones. These are best experienced by encountering Jesus as the Bridegroom God. This intoxicates our heart and makes us lovesick. God does not call us to holiness so that He can test us by keeping us from a life of pleasure. Holiness is not drudgery. It is a call to pleasure that is perfect and eternal.

*¹¹ In Your presence is <u>fullness of joy</u>…Your right hand are <u>pleasures</u> forevermore. (Ps. 16:11)*

L.     The Bride develops the theme of the superior pleasure in God throughout the Song.

*³ I sat down in His shade with <u>great delight</u>, and his fruit was <u>sweet</u> to my taste. (Song 2:3)*

M.     Sin is pleasurable and sin appears to be the most pleasurable thing that the human spirit can experience until we experience the full truth of the gospel. The superior pleasures of the Spirit, are far more powerful than the inferior pleasure of sin. God's main strategy in producing a holy people and restoring the first commandment to first place in the generation in which the Lord returns is to introduce into our experience the superior pleasures of the gospel.

N.     The End-Time saints will come up victorious over the Antichrist singing about Jesus as they marvel at His greatness. The martyrs are <u>victorious in love</u> because their love never diminished in the midst of temptation and persecution.

*³ I saw…those who have the <u>victory</u> over the beast (Antichrist)…standing on the sea of glass... 3 They sing…saying: "Great and <u>marvelous</u> are Your works..." (Rev. 15:3-4)*

O.     This truth is seen later in the song when Jesus says that the waters of temptation and persecution cannot quench or drown God's love in us as we truly experience it. Our experience of God's love is not to be quenched nor drowned by the flood of condemnation or compromise. Many have a quenched heart in which their ability to experience God's love has been drowned.

*⁷ Many waters cannot <u>quench</u> love, nor can the floods <u>drown</u> it. If a man would <u>give for love</u> all the wealth of his house, it would be utterly despised. (Song 8:7)*

P.     Paul spoke of experiencing Jesus as surpassing any privilege in this age.

*⁸ I count all things loss for the <u>excellence</u> of the knowledge of Christ Jesus…for whom I have suffered the loss of all things, and count them as <u>rubbish</u>, that I may gain Christ… (Phil. 3:8)*

Q.    The reward of a lover is the power to love. A lover does twice as much as the worker and does not care for any reward except for the power to love. Do you know what happens when the worker becomes a lover? They throw away the check list! The lover does not need a check list and every now and then a worker becomes a lover and it is a glorious thing to watch.

R.    We are wise to exert our strength for the rest of our life to answer the question, "How much better is the affection of God than the wine of other blessings?

## III.    AFFECTION BASED OBEDIENCE: MOTIVATED BY SATISFACTION IN JESUS

A.    "Affection-based obedience" is obedience that flows from experiencing Jesus' love (affection). We understand He has affection for us and we experience an impartation of it back to Him. It is the strongest kind of obedience because it results in the deepest and most consistent obedience. A lovesick person will embrace and endure anything for the sake of love.

B.    "Obedience by faith" or obedience without feeling God's presence is still required in God's Word. In other words, we must continue to obey God when we do not feel like it.

C.    "Fear-based obedience" or "shame-based obedience" is obedience that flows from fear of being put to shame or the fear of suffering negative consequences. This is biblical. However, it is not enough to motivate us to consistently resist the pleasures of sin for many years. In other words, it is not the most effective approach to obedience.

D.    Experiencing God is more effective in motivating us to resist sin than the fear of consequences. Why? Because the temptation to experience the immediate pleasure of sin is usually more powerful than the fear of punishment. This fear of sin's consequences does not overpower the tendency in our hearts to sin. Instead, it will cause us to sin in secret, in more creative ways. We sin because we enjoy the pleasure it brings. We sin when our heart is hungry and unsatisfied with God. Our struggle for holiness must be set in context to our pursuit to live satisfied in God.

E.    Picture giving a homeless boy a ticket for a vacation by the sea in which he would stay at a resort hotel, eat excellent food and sleep on a clean bed. Imagine the hungry little boy placing the ticket in his cardboard box hidden under the shelter that he sleeps in to keep out of the rain and cold. Instead of enjoying the hotel, he continues to eat rotten meat that he gathered from the trash.

F.    C. S. Lewis said: "We are half-hearted creatures fooling about with alcohol and sex and ambition when infinite joy is offered to us. We are like an ignorant child who wants to go on making mud pies in a slum because we cannot imagine what is meant by an offer of a holiday at the sea."

G.     That's the choice we make when we are tempted with sin. It looks as if it will satisfy us, when in fact it is spoiled meat. The pleasures of God are a banquet set before us, a table of spiritual delights that can deliver us from the emptiness of seeking pleasure in sin. The way to free the heart from the domination of sin is by delighting in God. Encountering Jesus is a superior pleasure that transcends anything that sin can offer us.

H.     Holiness has often been presented in a negative way with endless lists of threats and warnings of the consequences of sin. The Word of God teaches about the consequences of deliberate, sinful rebellion. The Bible is full of don'ts and prohibitions, but these laws and rules were never designed by God to supernaturally transform the human heart.

I.     The approach of many is to only use shame and fear to motivate people into keeping a list of dos and don'ts. But in the end, the allure of the immediate pleasure of sin is often more powerful than the fear of long-term consequences. Yes, we must continue to present the consequences of sin, but we must do so realizing that this alone is not sufficient. Something more is needed. Warning people about the social and spiritual consequences of sin does not often cause them to reject pornography, greed, lying and cheating.

J.     Moses had experienced the pleasures of the flesh that accompanied the riches and power of his position in Egypt, but he chose greater riches. He experienced something more pleasurable and beautiful than Egypt, something supernaturally attractive and altogether satisfying. As you press into the pleasures of holiness, like Moses, you will discover that none can fill the soul like Jesus.

*²⁴ By faith Moses…25 choosing rather to suffer affliction with the people of God than to enjoy the <u>passing pleasures of sin</u>, 26 esteeming the reproach of Christ <u>greater riches</u> than the treasures in Egypt; for he looked to the reward. (Heb. 11:24-26)*

*¹⁸ I consider that the sufferings of this present time are <u>not worthy to be compared</u> with the glory which shall be revealed in us. (Rom. 8:18)*

*¹⁷ Our light affliction, which is but for a moment, is working for us a <u>far more exceeding</u> and eternal weight of glory… (2 Cor. 4:17)*

## IV.     GOD LOVES US IN THE SAME WAY THAT GOD LOVES GOD

A.     At the Last Supper, Jesus emphasized that the measure of the Father's love (affection) for Jesus is the same measure of His love for His people. Jesus emphasized this three times (John 14-17). This single truth gives every believer the right to view themselves as "God's favorite."

*⁹ <u>As the Father loved Me, I <u>also</u> have loved you;</u> abide (live) in My love. (Jn. 15:9)*

*²³ That the world may know that You…have loved them <u>as</u> You have loved Me. (Jn 17:23)*

*²⁶ I declared Your name…that the <u>love with which You loved Me</u> may be <u>in them</u>… (Jn 17:26)*

B.      The ultimate statement about our worth and value is that Jesus has the same measure of love (affection) towards us that His Father has towards Him.

C.      The way that the Father loves Jesus is the only accurate measure in which we can understand how Jesus feels about us. God's love is a powerful reality that includes deep desire, enjoyment, pleasure and longing. It is not a sterile religious idea devoid of passion. Ponder the vast implications of how much the Father loves Jesus. Such a truth had never been spoke before.

D.      Oh! the mystery of the vastness of the ocean of God's love for us. The gospel is a call to live in the vast ocean of divine love. We will know the pleasure of loving God in the way that God loves God as we are loved in the way God loves God.

*¹⁷ You being <u>rooted and grounded in love</u>, 18 may be able to comprehend…the width, length, depth and height-- 19 to know the love of Christ which <u>passes knowledge</u>… (Eph. 3:17-19)*

E.      The disciples were sincere but yet still spiritually immature. Jesus' affirmations of love were spoken to weak believers that He knew would betray Him that very night (Mt. 26:31). They would feel great condemnation and shame. God felt great passion even for these ambitious immature young apostles who would betray Jesus that very night. Jesus knew that the only thing what would stabilize them was by knowing how God felt about them. This the strongest revelation that can touch the human heart.

F.      Jesus gave them the revelation of His love to prepare them to love God under the pressures of condemnation, disappointment, temptation, disillusionment, persecution and their future service.

G.      Jesus knew they would be devastated with disappointment when the Pharisees and Romans seemed to win by killing John the Baptist and Jesus. Their movement seemed to be over. In the days to come they would be beaten and thrown in prison. How could God still be with them?

H.      We best win the battle against temptation by enjoying God. The best way to overcome sin is in experiencing that His love is better than wine or in being satisfied in God. Turning the Song of Solomon into devotional prayer is how we experience this

I.      We must make it a priority to meditate on the truths about God's emotions for us. This is important to our emotional health. We are transformed most as we understand how God feels about us, especially in our weakness. ***This revelation causes us to run to Him instead of from Him***. It causes us to have confidence in His love and to open our spirit to Him in our weakness. Many sincere believers seek God with a condemned heart or a closed and guarded spirit.

J.      I wrote a book called Passion For Jesus, thus, I am often asked, "How can we have more passion for Jesus?" It takes God to love God, or it takes the power of God on our heart to love God back. When God wants to empower us to love Him, He reveals Himself as One who loves us. We love (enjoy or pursue) Him because we understand that He first loved (enjoy or pursue) us.

*¹⁹ We love Him <u>because</u> (we understand that) He first loved us. (1 Jn. 4:19)*

# Session 6 God's Superior Love: How God Feels about Us (Song 1:2)

## I. REVIEW: THE SUPERIOR PLEASURES IN THE GRACE OF GOD

A. The Bride referred to the "superior pleasures" of the Word. This reveals her theology related to holiness. She points to the superior pleasures that come from growing in revelation of God's heart (affection). God created us with 7 longings that draw us to Him and reflect His glory in us.

*² Let Him kiss me with the kisses of His mouth-- for Your love is **better than** wine (Song 1:2).*

B. In this session, we will look at seven principles of "Jesus' love that is better than the wine." These are foundational principles that are essential in helping us understand God's affection for us in our weakness (this 8 chapter love Song develops these principles in the Bride's journey). It is not difficult to imagine God loving perfected believers in heaven. The difficulty comes with believing that He has affection for weak and broken people in this age.

*¹ Behold **what manner of love** the Father has bestowed on us… (1 Jn. 3:1)*

C. God loves us in the same way that God loves God. The Father's love (affection) for Jesus is the same measure of His love for His people.

*⁹ **As the Father loved Me, I also** have loved you; abide (live) in My love. (Jn. 15:9)*

*²³ That the world may know that You…have loved them **as** You have loved Me. (Jn 17:23)*

D. We love God because we understand that God first loved us.

*¹⁹ We love Him **because** (we understand that) He first loved us. (1 Jn. 4:19)*

## II. FOUNDATIONAL PREMISE: SPIRITUAL IMMATURITY IS NOT REBELLION

A. God feels different emotions related to how people respond to Him. Some live confused without knowing whether God is mad, sad or glad when relating to them. We do not want to think God is mad when He is delighting over us, thus living in condemnation. Nor do we want to think He delights in us if He is grieved because of our compromise, thus living in presumption.

B. We receive God's righteousness and favor because of what Jesus did on the cross not because of what we do (Rom. 3:21-31). It is necessary to sincerely repent to receive God's saving grace.

C. Repentance is a change of the attitude of the heart that turns ***from sin*** and ***to God*** according to the "light of understanding" that we have at each season of our spiritual journey. Repentance is breaking our agreement with darkness and agreeing with God in our thoughts, words and deeds.

D. Spiritual immaturity is not the same as rebellion. Many are confused about this. At times they look the same outwardly yet inwardly they arise from very different heart responses. Our actions do matter to God, however, God looks at our heart <u>more</u> than our actions.

E.   A genuine lover of Jesus sincerely pursues to obey Him with a willing spirit. A sincere yet still immature believer repents in each area of failure that they receive light on. The rebellious says "No" to God without immediate plans to obey. Pre-meditated sin is sin that is planned beforehand. This is much more serious to God than sinning in our spiritual immaturity.

*⁴¹ The spirit indeed is willing, but the flesh is weak. (Mt. 26:41)*

F.   Our repentance, obedience and love for God are sincere even while they are weak and flawed. Weak love is not false love, therefore, Jesus values our love for Him even when it is weak.

G.   The sincere intention to obey God is distinct from the attainment of mature obedience. The pursuit of full obedience is different than attaining it. The Lord is pleased with us from the time we repent (by setting our heart to obey Him) which is long before our obedience matures. As genuine lovers of God we do not immediately attain to all that we seek to walk in.

H.   The believer who sins, shows their sincerity by quickly repenting and renewing their war against that sin. Sincere repentance is not the same as attaining "sinless perfection" in this life. Do not write yourself off as rebellious if in fact you are spiritually immature.

I.   A hypocrite is somebody who says one thing but does not pursue or seek to obey it. Struggling in weakness (immaturity) is not the same thing as being a hopeless hypocrite (rebellious).

J.   God delights in the sincere desire or cry in our spirit to obey Him. Our sincere desire to obey God is a substantial beginning of our victory over sin. It is part of God's work in you.

K.   God does not confuse spiritual immaturity with rebellion (the OT law spoke of clean and unclean animals: sheep and swine which both become stuck in the mud). The illustration of clean and unclean animals helps us understand this because both sheep and swine become stuck in mud.

L.   If we confuse this, we will bring others under condemnation. This can injure their faith. This is the opposite of the conviction of the Spirit, which gives us confidence to go deep in God.

M.   God viewed the spiritual immaturity of the apostles very differently than the rebellion of the Pharisees. David seemed to commit more serious sins than Saul, but God's favor continued with David. Why? When David sinned his heart was wounded because he grieved God's heart. He cared more about his relationship with God than the consequences of getting caught. When Saul sinned he planned to continue in it until caught and confronted. He only gave an outward show of repentance as he continued in rebellion (1 Sam. 15:22-23).

*⁶ Surely goodness and mercy shall follow me all the days of my life? (Ps. 23:6)*

N.   God's mercy gives us confidence that we can have a new beginning with God as a first class citizen after we repent. We are defined by God's passion for us, receiving the gift of righteousness, and by our sincere heart cry to be a wholehearted lover of God.

O.     We "push delete" after we have sincerely repented. Jesus paid the price that we might stand before God with confidence of having His favor. This is very different from "pushing delete" on our need to understand the process and mindset that contributed to a stronghold of sin in our life.

P.     Our identity is as a genuine lover of God. Guilt says that our actions are wrong. Shame says we (our whole personhood) are wrong. **Question**: are you a slave of sin who struggles to love God or a lover of God who still struggles with sin? Many define themselves by their failure. Because of Jesus, we are much better in God's sight than the worst thing we have done.

## III.    PRINCIPLE #1: GOD LOVES AND BLESSES UNBELIEVERS

A.     God loves unbelievers even when they rebel against Him and have no regard for Him (Mt. 5:45).

*16 God so loved the world that He gave His only…Son that whoever believes… (Jn. 3:16)*

*8 God demonstrates His love…in that while we were still sinners, Christ died for us. (Rom. 5:8)*

B.     God blesses evil people. We are not to mistake His blessings on them as His approval of them.

*45 Makes His sun rise on the evil and the good…sends rain on the just and unjust. (Mt. 5:45)*

C.     God is angry at their rebellion and refuses to forgive those who will not repent (Esau, Saul, etc.).

*22 Many will say to Me in that day, 'Lord, Lord, have we not prophesied in Your name…?' 23 "I will declare to them, 'I never knew you; depart from Me!" (Mt. 7:22-23)*

## IV.    PRINCIPLE #2: GOD ENJOYS AND DELIGHTS IN IMMATURE BELIEVERS

A.     God loves unbelievers, yet He only enjoys believers. Jesus immediately rejoices over us at the time of our repentance. He smiles over us when we begin the growth process with sincere repentance, long before we attain spiritual maturity.

*4 What man…having a hundred sheep…does not leave the ninety-nine…and go after the one…? 5 When he has found it, he lays it on his shoulders, rejoicing…6 he calls together his friends…saying to them, 'Rejoice with me, for I have found my sheep which was lost!' 7 There will be more joy in heaven over one sinner who repents… (Lk. 15:4-7)*

B.     Jesus feels compassion over the prodigals on the day they repent. God revealed His enjoyment of the prodigal son by the father giving him the best robes (Lk. 15:22). This newly repentant yet immature prodigal son had many areas of his life that still needed transformation.

*18 I will…say to him, "Father, I have sinned…" 20 He arose and came to his father. When he was still a great way off, his father saw him and had compassion, and ran and fell on his neck and kissed him. 22 The father said to his servants, "Bring out the best robe and put it on him, and put a ring on his hand and sandals on his feet…" (Lk. 15:18-22)*

C.     God enjoys us even in our immaturity. He delighted in David on the day of his repentance.

*19 He delivered me (David) because He delighted in me… (Ps. 18:19)*

D.     Our most sincere efforts to love God are flawed. We are lovely to God even in our weakness.

*⁵ I am __dark__ (in my heart), __but lovely__ (to God because of Jesus)… (Song 1:5)*

E.     Jesus walked in the anointing of gladness more than any man in history. Gladness is at the center of His personality. Many think of God as being mostly mad or sad when they relate to Him.

*⁹ Your God, has anointed You with the __oil of gladness__ more than Your companions. (Heb. 1:9)*

F.     God __delights__ in showing us mercy. He wants us confident that He enjoys us (even in our weakness) as we walk in sincere repentance. Then we run to Him instead of from Him.

*¹⁸ He does not retain His anger forever, __because He delights in mercy.__ (Mic. 7:18)*

*²⁴ I am the LORD, exercising __lovingkindness__, judgment…for in these I __delight__. (Jer. 9:24)*

G.     God gives a repentant believer a __new beginning__ as a "first class citizen" each time they repent.

*²² Through the LORD's mercies we are not consumed, because His compassions fail not. 23 They are __new every morning__; great is Your faithfulness. (Lam. 3:22-23)*

H.     God remembers and understands our weaknesses far more than we do. He does not discipline us to the degree that we deserve nor does He change the way He feels about us in our weaknesses.

*¹⁰ He has not dealt with us according to our sins, nor __punished__ us according to our iniquities. 11 For as the heavens are high above the earth, so __great is His mercy__ toward those who fear Him…14 For He __knows__ our frame; He __remembers__ that we are dust. (Ps. 103:10-14)*

I.     __Summary__: God smiles over our life in a general sense, while He deals with __particular sins__ in us. Several areas of immaturity __do not define our entire relationship with God__. We are defined by God's passion for us, receiving the gift of righteousness and by our heart cry to obey Jesus.

## V.     PRINCIPLE #3: GOD'S ENJOYMENT IS NOT THE SAME AS HIS APPROVAL

A.     The fact that God enjoys us does not mean He overlooks the areas in us that need transformation. God's enjoyment of a believer is not the same as __His approval__ of all that they do. He corrects areas that He disapproves of so that He might remove all that hinders love (holiness) in us.

*¹⁰ He (disciplines us) for our profit, that we may be __partakers of His holiness.__ (Heb. 12:10)*

B.     God has __tender patience__ for a season with believers who do not repent. They must not confuse His patience with His __approval__. Jesus gave Jezebel and her disciples in Thyatira time to repent.

*²¹ I gave her (Jezebel) __time to repent__ of her immorality…22 I will cast her into a sickbed, and __those__ who commit adultery with her into great tribulation, unless they repent… (Rev. 2:21-22)*

*¹¹ Because the sentence against an evil work __is not executed speedily__, therefore the heart of the sons of men is fully set in them to do evil. (Ecc. 8:11)*

C.      When we neglect to honestly and thoroughly confront sin in our heart <u>we are not loved less by God</u> but we do suffer loss in several ways. We minimize our ability to experience the joy of our salvation, the spirit of revelation, godly fellowship and to receive eternal rewards.

D.      God patiently suffers long with us in His love as He works to lead us to repentance.

> *⁴ Do you despise the riches of His goodness, <u>forbearance</u>, and <u>longsuffering</u>, not knowing that the goodness of God <u>leads you to repentance</u>? (Rom. 2:4)*

> *⁴ Love <u>suffers long</u> and is kind…7 <u>bears</u> all things…<u>endures</u> all things. (1 Cor. 13:4-7)*

## VI.     PRINCIPLE #4: GOD'S DISCIPLINE IS NOT THE SAME AS HIS REJECTION OF US

A.      God's correction is not His rejection, rather it is proof of His love. God hates the sin yet delights in the person He disciplines.

> *¹² Whom the LORD <u>loves</u> He corrects, <u>just as</u> a father the son in whom he <u>delights.</u> (Prov. 3:12)*

> *⁶ Whom the LORD <u>loves</u> He chastens, and scourges every son whom <u>He receives</u>… (Heb. 12:6)*

B.      Jesus rebukes yet loves believers that are in need of repentance.

> *¹⁹ As many as I <u>love</u>, I <u>rebuke</u> and <u>chasten</u>. Therefore be zealous and <u>repent</u>. (Rev. 3:19)*

C.      To be disciplined means God cares and has not given up on us. It is a terrible thing to "get away with" sin long term because that means God is giving that person over to their sin. God's discipline is proof that He has not given up on us (Rom. 1:24-28).

> *²⁴ <u>God gave them up</u> to uncleanness, in the lusts of their hearts… (Rom. 1:24)*

> *³² When we are <u>judged</u>, we are <u>chastened</u> by the Lord, <u>that we may not be condemned</u> with the world. (1 Cor. 11:32)*

D.      God did not give up on His people Israel when even when they were in a season of disobedience.

> *³⁷ For their (children of Israel) heart was <u>not steadfast</u> with Him, nor were they faithful in His covenant. 38 But He, being full of compassion, forgave their iniquity, and did not destroy them. Yes, <u>many a time</u> He turned His anger away, and <u>did not stir up all His wrath</u>; 39 For He <u>remembered</u> that they were but flesh, a breath that passes away… (Ps. 78:37-39)*

## VII.    PRINCIPLE #5: GOD IS GRIEVED OVER THE PERSISTENT SIN OF HIS PEOPLE

A.      Jesus will vomit lukewarm believers out of His mouth. This does not speak of God casting them away, but of Him feeling sick at heart or grieved over their lives.

> *¹⁶ Because you are lukewarm…<u>I will vomit you out of My mouth.</u> (Rev. 3:16-17)*

> *³⁰ And do not <u>grieve</u> the Holy Spirit of God. (Eph. 4:30)*

> *¹⁹ Do not <u>quench</u> the Spirit. (1 Thes. 5:19)*

B.    God feels the pain of those He disciplines and continues to consider them as His dearly beloved.

*⁹ In __all__ their affliction __He was afflicted__…in His love and in His pity He redeemed them; and He bore them and carried them all the days of old. (Isa 63:9)*

*⁷ I have given the __dearly beloved__ of My soul into the hand of her enemies. (Jer. 12:7)*

C.    When we neglect to thoroughly confront sin in our heart we are not loved less by God but we do suffer loss in several ways. We minimize our ability to experience the joy of our salvation, the spirit of revelation, God's power, fellowship with God and others, and receiving eternal rewards. We can only fulfill our highest calling and destiny in this age and the age-to-come by walking in faithful obedience and with a history of diligently seeking God. Faithfulness does not earn our calling for us but it positions us to receive more grace that we might enter into it. The Spirit calls us to diligence that we might enter into our fullness of authority in this age and the age-to-come.

*¹¹ We also pray always for you that our God would __count you worthy__ of this calling, and fulfill all the good pleasure of His goodness and the work of faith with power, (2 Thes. 1:11)*

D.    We must be confident that God in His love for us will manifest His zeal or jealousy over us. God jealously requires that we live in wholehearted obedience. He zealously insists on that which deepens our relationship with Him and results in our greatness.

*⁵ Do you think the Scripture says in vain, "The Spirit…in us __yearns jealously__"? (Jas 4:5)*

## VIII.    PRINCIPLE #6: SPIRITUAL DISCIPLINES DO NOT EARN US GOD'S FAVOR

A.    Spiritual disciplines (prayer, fasting, meditation, etc.) are ordained by God as a necessary way to posture our heart to freely receive more grace. These activities do not earn us God's favor. The power is in the "bonfire of God's presence" not in our cold hearts that are positioned before it.

B.    God gives to our heart on the basis of how much we hunger for relationship with Him not on how much He loves us (Mt. 5:6). God honors the value we put on the relationship by giving us more according to our spiritual hunger (Gal. 6:8) but He does not love us more. God will not enjoy an obedient believer more in a billion years than He does now (Mal. 3:6).

## IX.    PRINCIPLE #7: MATURITY ALLOWS US TO RECEIVE MORE (NOT BE LOVED MORE)

A.    God loves us all yet He entrusts a greater measure of power to the mature. He determines the measure of power that He has planned for each to walk in. This measure is different for each believer (Mt. 25:15). Our obedience positions us to walk in whatever that full measure is.

B.    People with greater power in ministry or influence in business are not loved more by God. He will entrust more to us as we mature because it will not damage us nor others. The gifts of the Spirit are given to us by faith (Acts 3:11-12; Gal. 3:5). They are not earned by our discipline. However, our spiritual maturity provides added protection from the counterattack of Satan (Lk. 14:30-32) on those operating in the anointing. Four things increase as we experience more of the Holy Spirit's power (God's zeal, Satan's rage, man's demands, our emotional capacities).

## Session 7 The Fragrance of Jesus (Song 1:3)

I.  **REVIEW: JESUS' LOVE IS BETTER THAN THE WINE OF THIS FALLEN WORLD**

   A.  The theme of the Song is the Bride's cry for the kiss of God's Word to touch the deepest place in her heart. This refers to encountering the Word in the deepest and most intimate way. In other words, the Word reveals the King's emotions for His Bride and awakens our heart in the 3-fold love of God (love from God then for God which overflows to others).

   *² Let Him kiss me with the kisses of His mouth-- for Your love is better than wine (Song 1:2).*

   B.  She experiences the superior pleasure of encountering Jesus. His love (affection) "is better than" or "is more delightful than" (NIV) the inferior pleasures of sin (the wine of this fallen world).

   C.  "Affection-based obedience" is obedience that flows from experiencing Jesus' affection for us and then giving it back to Him. It is the strongest kind of obedience. It results in the deepest and most consistent obedience. A lovesick person endures anything for love.

   D.  "Duty-based obedience" is obedience that does not feel God's presence. God's Word requires that we obey God even when we do not feel inspired to do so.

   E.  "Fear-based obedience" or "shame-based obedience" is obedience that flows from the fear of being put to shame or the fear of suffering negative consequences. This is biblical. It is not enough to motivate us to consistently resist the pleasures of sin for many years.

II. **THE GOOD PERFUME OF CHRIST JESUS**

   *³ Because of the fragrance of Your good ointments (perfumes, NIV), Your Name is ointment (perfume, NIV) poured forth; therefore the virgins love You. (Song 1:3)*

   A.  The fragrance of a rose comes from its internal properties and qualities. In a similar way, the King's perfume in the Song speaks symbolically of His internal life or what He thinks and feels. God's perfume speaks of His thought life and emotional make-up, especially His affection for His people. The Bride enjoys the sweet perfume of God's affection. When perfume is in the air it can powerfully stir our heart. We feel its impact without being able to see it or take hold of it.

   B.  Paul spoke of the fragrance of Jesus. It is figurative for the knowledge of God. It is also literal. The fragrances around God's Throne are surely awesome. All heaven can smell them forever.

   *¹⁴ Now thanks be to God who always leads us in triumph in Christ, and through us diffuses the fragrance of His knowledge in every place. (2 Cor. 2:14)*

   C.  Its use of perfume in the Song is reasonable since it speaks of love in context to a bridal metaphor. She is saying, "Because of Your perfumes my heart is stirred. If a scientist was to express excitement in God, they might write, "Because You are so brilliant, my heart is stirred.""

D.   The Bride is saying, "Because of the fragrance of Jesus' good perfumes (His internal qualities) two significant things will occur throughout history.

E.   First, God will pour Jesus' Name forth or He will exalt and reveal it in the nations. God has chosen to pour forth only one Name. Why? Because Jesus' life is a good perfume before God. She understood that Jesus' name will ultimately be the supreme reality over all the earth.

*⁹ Therefore God also has <u>highly exalted Him</u> and <u>given Him the name</u> which is above every name, 10 that at the name of Jesus every knee should bow… (Phil. 2:9-10)*

1.   When God pours forth Jesus' name, He openly reveals it or draws attention to His beauty or character. God will highly exalt Jesus' name by filling the earth with it.

*¹⁴ The <u>earth will be filled</u> with the knowledge of the glory of the Lord… (Hab. 2:14)*

2.   God will pour forth Jesus' name in the Church by filling it with the knowledge of Jesus.

*¹¹ He Himself gave some to be apostles, some prophets…13 till we all come to the unity of the faith and of the <u>knowledge of the Son of God</u>… (Eph. 4:11-13)*

F.   Second, we will love Jesus more as God pours forth or reveals the beauty of His name to us.

## III.   WE LOVE JESUS MORE AS THE KNOWLEDGE OF GOD IS POURED FORTH

A.   The Church will love Jesus as the Father pours forth or reveals more of the beauty of His name. The Bride knows that the beauty of Jesus will cause all believers (virgins) to love Jesus. God's name is like good perfume. Its mystery, beauty and wonder powerfully impact us.

*³ Your Name is ointment (perfume) <u>poured forth</u>; <u>therefore the virgins love You</u>. (Song 1:3)*

B.   The virgins speak of the daughters of Jerusalem in the Song. They are genuine yet immature believers who seek Jesus throughout the Song but are never fully committed as the Bride is. All the Church will eventually become extravagant lovers of Jesus even if not so until eternity.

C.   She understands how God changes the human heart. There is only one "perfumed name" that effectively transforms us. Do you see Jesus' name is a "perfumed name" that can change the most broken and spiritually dull person to an extravagant lover of God? If you do, then you will do anything to know more about that Name. This is the only Name that causes us to love God.

*² In that day (End-Times) the Branch of the LORD (Jesus) shall be <u>beautiful</u>… (Isa. 4:2)*

D.   When God reveals God to the human spirit it exhilarates us. There is nothing more powerful or pleasurable than when God reveals God to the human spirit. To understand Jesus more is to love and enjoy Him more. Our zeal for Jesus is strengthened by receiving the knowledge of God. This motivated Paul to suffer loss and endure hardship.

*⁸ I count all things loss for the <u>excellence of the knowledge of Christ Jesus</u>… (Phil. 3:8)*

E.   Jesus declares the Father's name (personality) to awaken our hearts to love God. We will love Jesus with the love which the Father loves Him. Loving Jesus in the overflow of the Father's affection for Jesus is our inheritance, our destiny. There is nothing more glorious than loving God by the power of God. The Bride will love Jesus just as the Father loves Jesus.

*26 I have underlined to them Your name, and will declare it, that the love with which You loved Me may be in them, and I in them. (Jn. 17:26)*

F.   Jesus the "ultimate psychologist" gives us insight on how the human heart works. He explained to Simon that when people experience much forgiveness, they overflow with much love.

*47 I say to you, her sins, which are many, are forgiven, for she loved much. But to whom little is forgiven, the same loves little." (Luke 7:47)*

G.   Satan accuses God in people's hearts as he convinces them that God is like a cruel father. He tells many they are rejected by God so they run from God instead of to Him in weakness.

H.   The Christian life is a life of being loved and enjoyed by God. This is more exhilarating than any pleasure, position, or possession. She understands the impact of encountering God's emotions.

I.   The revelation of God's affections militates against our pride and religious formalism. It causes us to grow in gratitude instead of pride and it renews our love so we do not merely go through the motions or mechanics in our spiritual life.

J.   I wrote a book called Passion For Jesus, therefore, I am regularly asked, "How do we grow in passion for Jesus?" The answer is simple and straight forward. We do this by understanding the passion of God's heart for us. The revelation of God's desire empowers us to desire God. If you want to love God more then fill your mind with truths related to His love (affection) for you.

K.   The whole earth is currently full of the glory or beauty of Jesus. It takes the spirit of revelation to see the perfume or glory of God which is manifested in the natural in many places.

*3 One (seraphim) cried to another and said: "Holy, holy, holy is the LORD of hosts; the whole earth is full of His glory!" (Isa. 6:3)*

L.   David lived with a spirit of revelation so he saw God's beauty even when he looked at the sky.

*1 The heavens declare the glory of God…2 Day unto day utters speech, and night unto night reveals knowledge…4 Their line has gone out through all the earth… (Ps. 19:1-4)*

M.   Throughout the Song the perfume of God is imparted to the Bride. His perfume becomes her perfume. The turning point in the Song is in Song 4:16. The Bride prays for winds to blow on the garden of her heart that God's perfumes would be imparted to her, that she would feel like God feels. We may study the progression of God's perfume in the Bride throughout the Song. She discerns His perfumes and they are imparted to her in a progressive way.

*16 Awake, O north wind, And come, O south! Blow upon my garden, that its spices may flow out. Let my Beloved come to His garden and eat its pleasant fruits. (Song 4:16)*

IV.     THE SWEET PERFUME OF GOD'S PERSONALITY- 5 VERBS

A.      Jesus emphasized the sweet perfume of the Father's affection and personality (Lk. 15:20). This is one of the most comprehensive yet concise statements of God's emotional make up in Scripture. We rest in the God who sees, feels, runs and embraces and kisses our heart.

*²⁰ And he arose and came to his father. When he was still a great way off, his father <u>saw</u> him and had <u>compassion</u>, and <u>ran</u> and <u>fell on</u> (embraced) his neck and <u>kissed</u> him. (Lk. 15:20).*

B.      The father <u>saw</u> the prodigal son – God's view of His people

C.      The father <u>felt compassion</u> for the prodigal son – God's tenderness for His people

D.      The father <u>ran towards</u> the prodigal son – God's action and initiative for His people

E.      The father <u>embraced</u> the prodigal son – God's affection for His people

F.      The father <u>kissed</u> the prodigal son – God's desire for nearness with His people

V.      APPLYING THESE TO OUR LIVES

A.      First, we learn these truths. Informing our intellect is significant but it is only a starting point. No one would go to a famous restaurant to merely study the menu. It is not enough to be a connoisseur of the Song of Solomon, we must allow this book to fill our heart.

B.      Second, these become revelation in our heart as we speak them back to God. We must engage in long and loving meditation on the Song with a hungry and honest heart before God. If we are to receive the full benefit of the Song, we must turn it into an on-going affectionate prayerful dialogue with Jesus. It is not enough to only study the Song without going to the next step of turning it into a prayer dialogue. The language of the Song must get into our prayer life and thought life before it will transform our emotions.

C.      I have about 10 phrases that have become deeply personal to me. In my early days, I wrote them on postcards to use when I drove or took a walk. I slowly whispered them to Jesus. For example, "Father, let Him kiss me with His Word" or "Spirit, sustain me, refresh me" (Song 1:2; 2:5).

D.      Confess that His affections are better than the wine of this fallen world. Declare that the fragrance of His good perfumes (the personality of God) make you love Him.

E.      Take time to journal by writing down your thoughts, prayers and meditations as you "pray-read" through the Song. This will help you to capture the truths that the Lord puts on your heart.

## VI.     THE FRAGRANCE OF JESUS IN THE SONG

A.     In Song 1:3, she sees the reality of Jesus' fragrance as good perfume pointing to His emotions

B.     In Song 1:13-14, she develops her experience of the Song 1:3 fragrance in a more specific way with myrrh and henna blooms and in an abundant way with bundles and clusters (Song 8:14)

C.     In Song 2:3, Jesus has the refreshing scent of apples as in Song 8:5

D.     In Song 2:12-13, Jesus proclaims his own fragrance to woo the Bride. God woos the Bride by the fragrance of His son. She decides to go to the mountain.

E.     In Song 3:6, Jesus is as perfumed with myrrh, frankincense and fragrant powders (pomegranates are implied in the apples in Song 2:3, 5) and cedar (implied in Song 3:9; 8:9)

F.     In Song 4:6, she agrees to embrace suffering as the mountain of myrrh and the hill of frankincense (tokens of Song 8:14)

G.     In Song 5:13, Jesus' fragrance is found in His cheeks as beds of spices and banks of scented herbs and in His lips as lilies that drip with myrrh (2:12-13 smells like figs and grapes)

## VII.    THE FRAGRANCE OF THE BRIDE IN THE SONG

a.     The Bride drenched in fragrance is a result of the Mountain of Spices (Song 8:14)

b.     In Song 1:12, the Bride is first aware of the imparted fragrances that are manifested through her

c.     In Song 2:1, the Bride's identity is in Jesus' fragrance (lily/rose)

d.     In Song 2:2, we see Jesus' first affirmation of the Bride's fragrance

e.     In Song 2:16; 4:5; 6:3; and 7:2, the Bride is like a lily

f.     In Song 4:3, the fragrance of the believer is as pomegranates (Song 6:7)

g.     God's vineyard with the Song 8:13 gardens (Song 2:16; 6:3, 11; 7:2, 12-13) includes gardens, a valley, walnuts, grapes, pomegranates (Song 7:12), mandrakes (Song 7:13) and other fruits

# Session 8 The Bride's Life Vision (Song 1:4)

## I. INTRODUCTION

A. In this session, we will look at Song 1:4, as the Bride describes her spiritual goals and life vision.

> *⁴ __Draw__ me away! We will __run__ after You. The King has brought me into His chambers. We will be glad and rejoice in You. We will remember Your love more than wine. (Song 1:4)*

B. Review: Song 1:2-4 sums up the main themes and theology for the Song as the progression of holy passion. She cries for the kisses of God's Word knowing that Jesus' affection is better than anything this world has to offer. She declares the reality and effectiveness of the good perfumes of Jesus and then declares her life vision as one who wants to be drawn near to Jesus in intimacy and to receive grace to run with Him and the Body of Christ in ministry.

C. In Song 1:2-4, the Bride speaks in three different ways

   1. In Song 1:2a, she speaks to the Father, "Let Your Son kiss me with His Word."

   2. In Song 1:2b-4, she speaks to Jesus saying, "Your love is better than wine. Because of Your perfume, Your name will be poured forth and the virgins will love You." She asks Jesus to draw her to Himself in intimacy and to receive grace to run with Him in ministry.

   3. In Song 1:4c, she speaks to Jesus <u>with others</u> who are diligently running with her.

## II. THE EXPRESSION OF HER FERVENCY: 2-FOLD LIFE VISION

A. Her 2-fold life vision expresses her goals in the form of a prayer to God. A life vision is one that our short and long term goals for our family, vocation and ministry fit into. The NAS translates this as "draw me after You." The words "after You" modifies "draw me" in many Bible translations. In the NKJ the "after You" modifies the verb "running."

> *⁴ __Draw__ me away! We will __run__ after You. (Song 1:4)*

B. She prays, "Jesus, draw me away." She longs to be drawn close to God's heart in deep intimacy as an extravagant worshipper who loves God with all her heart.

> *³⁷ You shall <u>love the LORD</u> your God with all your heart, with all your soul… (Mt. 22:37)*

C. She prays, "We will run after You." The 'we' refers to running with Jesus and His people. Being drawn to God is singular but running with Him is plural. She longs to serve people in ministry partnership with Jesus and those who love Him. Running represents a life of service motivated by compassion for people. It involves obedience in action, reaching out to others, and stepping out in faith. We run behind Jesus who sets the pace and in relationship with other people.

> *³⁹ The second is like it: 'You shall <u>love your neighbor</u> as yourself.' (Mt. 22:39)*

D.  The balance is to have passion for Jesus and compassion for people. There is a constant tension throughout our entire spiritual journey between "drawing" and "running." At the beginning, most are focused on running in ministry without being drawn in intimacy.

   1.  Because running brings conflict, rejection, and persecution, many soon burn out even as the maiden did in Song 1:5-7. Some overreact, determining to focus only on being drawn without any vision to run in ministry.

   2.  As Jesus answered her prayer to "be drawn to Him" in intimacy, she temporarily refused to "run in ministry" (Song 2:8-13). She lost the balance of these 2 tensions. Jesus answers both parts of her prayer related to her life vision throughout the 8 chapter love Song.

E.  We are to both be drawn and run in each season. It is not enough to be only drawn near to God's heart in intimacy. Nor is it enough to only run in ministry. The Lord often emphasizes one over the different spiritual seasons in our lives. We are not to totally neglect either in any session. Do not be afraid of what others say when the Lord emphasizes one in a specific season in God.

F.  The general order of the Kingdom is to first be drawn in intimacy and then to run in ministry in the overflow of our close relationship with Jesus. The First Commandment focus to love God with all our heart empowers us to much more effectively walk out the Second Commandment focus to relate to and serve others. The 2-fold life vision of the Bride speaks of the two Great commandments (Mt. 22:37-40) and the Great Commission (Mt. 28:19-20). Our life vision should always contain both aspects of "drawing and running".

G.  I was taught to write out my life vision at about age 18. A life vision is established regardless of our occupation, family status, economic status, etc. I determined to be *an extravagant worshipper of God and an anointed deliverer of people* so as to fulfill the two Great Commandments in loving God and people (Mt. 22:37-39). I wanted to learn the Scripture and learn to live in the Spirit as an extravagant worshipper of God and an anointed deliver of people.

   [18] *Where there is no revelation, the people cast off restraint… (Pro. 29:18)*

   [18] *Where there is no vision, the people perish. (Pro. 29:18, KJV)*

H.  The components of a focused life include having an overall life vision with life goals in each of the main areas of our life such as our *spiritual life* (prayer time, fasting days, Bible study, etc.); *relationships* (family, friends, etc.); *vocation* (marketplace calling); *ministry* (in the church, outside the church); *economic* (earning, spending, giving, saving, investing); *physical* (exercise, health, diet, etc.); and *rest* (recreation, vacation, play, entertainment, sports, etc.).

I.  We must have an action plan for each long and short-term goal in every area of our life (long-term goals are over 10 years and short-term goals are from 3 months to 3 years). We must have a schedule for each action plan to help us focus or prioritize our time.

## III.  THE GROWTH OF FERVENCY: THE CHAMBER EXPERIENCES

*⁴ Draw me away! We will run after You. <u>The King has brought me into His chambers</u>… (Song 1:4)*

A.  The King's chamber is a bridal chamber. It refers to the times that she develops her secret life in God. We all have a secret history in God where Jesus draws us to Himself especially in His Word. The times in the chamber form and fashion our inner man. It is the times that the Lord woos and warns us and promises and confronts us so that we grow in the Spirit. The King's chamber is a time of preparation that we might love and obey Jesus with all our heart as He fashions us for future tasks to run with Him in active service.

B.  The young Bride asked the Lord to draw her (take the initiative to help her) and Jesus answered by carrying her into His chambers. He responds by carrying or bringing her into His chambers.

*⁴ He <u>brought</u> me to the banqueting house…. (Song 2:4)*

C.  Jesus described the good shepherd as <u>carrying</u> the lost sheep on His shoulders of grace.

*⁵ And when he has found it, <u>he lays it on his shoulders</u>, rejoicing. (Luke 15:5)*

D.  The chamber experiences refer to the times that God <u>carries</u> us to Himself by granting us unusual experiences in the Spirit (revelations, encounters and impartations). Two examples of my personal "chamber experiences" surprised me as a new believer. I was filled with the Holy Spirit in Feb. 1972 without any prior understanding of it and without seeking it. I also experienced a vision of the Judgment seat of Christ in Oct. 1978 that I did not seek.

## IV.  THE CERTAINTY OF FERVENCY: THE PROPHETIC ASSURANCE

A.  The Bride declares to the daughters of Jerusalem with the bold resolution and the certainty of faith that together they would, "Be glad and rejoice in God and remember His love through all the seasons of life." This was her resolute confession of faith through each season in life.

*⁴ The King has brought me into His chambers. <u>We will be glad and rejoice in You</u>. <u>We will remember Your love</u> (affection) more than wine. (Song 1:4)*

B.  We will be glad and rejoice in Jesus and remember His love in three ways. First, we rejoice in and remember His tender mercy in our weakness as we refuse condemnation. Second, we rejoice in and remember His excellencies and exhilarating affections that are superior to the wine of sin. Third, we rejoice in and remember His leadership over our lives in times of difficulty and testing.

*¹¹ We also <u>rejoice in God</u> through our Lord Jesus Christ… (Rom. 5:11)*

C.  This faith confession in times of despair and testing is an expression of spiritual warfare as we declare that God is good and the devil is a liar. This confession of faith foreshadows the Marriage Supper of the Lamb. We will use these very words on the great Wedding Day.

*⁷ Let us be <u>glad</u> and <u>rejoice</u> and give Him glory, for the marriage of the Lamb has come, and His wife has made herself ready. (Rev. 19:7)*

# V.   REMEMBERING CAUSES US TO LOVE GOD

A.   The goodness of Jesus' love powerfully causes us to love Him. When the Church remembers Jesus' love and goodness it awakens our heart in the 3-fold love of God (love from God, then for God which overflows to others). The Bride understands how God changes the human heart.

*⁴ We will remember Your love more than wine. Rightly do they love You. (Song 1:4)*

B.   The Bride is showing the way to maintain the fervency she received in the chamber experiences. In the chamber experiences we receive personal encouragement and assurances in God. It is not enough to have these experiences. God holds us accountable to remember them and to act on them by setting our soul to agree with what God spoke to us in these times.

C.   We engage in spiritual warfare by proclaiming God's Word as darkness assaults our heart. We must renew our mind as we refuse to lose anything that God gave us in the chamber experiences.

D.   There are two dimensions of gladness. First, the gladness that is by faith that requires the setting of the heart to remain in agreement with the confession of our faith in difficulty. Second, is the gladness by overflow that automatically rises up in our heart. She refers to both dimensions here.

E.   The gladness that is by faith remembers Jesus' love and refuses to draw back. We must regularly re-align our soul to God's Word. There is a place to set our soul to be glad by faith.

1.   In difficult circumstances, we actively rejoice in God and confess His loving leadership instead sinking in anxiety. We declare that we glad in His good leadership. In the darkness of the midnight hour, we remember the revelation He gave us in His chambers.

*⁴ His banner (leadership) over me was love. (Song 2:4)*

*²⁸ We know that all things work together for good to those who love God… (Rom. 8:28)*

2.   In temptation, actively rejoice in God and confess that His affections and promises are better than the wine of this fallen world.

*²⁴ By faith Moses…25 choosing rather to suffer affliction…than to enjoy the passing pleasures of sin 26…for he looked to the reward. (Heb. 11:20-30)*

3.   In failure, we confess His love as we believe in His tender mercy instead of wallowing in condemnation. We will not accept the accusations of the enemy. Satan tells many they are rejected by God so they run from God instead of to Him in weakness.

F.   In difficult circumstances, temptation and failure, we declare that the Lord is good and His mercy endures forever (1 Chr. 16:34, 41; 2 Chr. 5:13; 7:3, 6; 20:21; Ezra 3:11; Jer. 33:11; Ps. 52:1; 100:5; 106:1; 107:1; 117:2; 118:1-4, 29; 138).

*¹¹ They sang responsively…giving thanks to the LORD: "For He is good, for His mercy endures forever toward Israel." (Ezra 3:11)*

# Session 9 Dark in Heart but Lovely to God (Song 1:5)

### I.   OUR JOURNEY BEGINS WITH THE PARADOX OF GRACE: DARK BUT LOVELY

> *⁵ I am <u>dark</u> (in my heart), **but <u>lovely</u> (to God), O daughters of Jerusalem, like the tents of Kedar, like the curtains of Solomon. Do not look upon me, because I am dark… (Song 1:5-6).***

A.   The Bride's spiritual journey begins with a spiritual crisis common to every sincere believer as seen in her 2-fold confession of faith (Song 1:5). I refer to this as the "paradox of grace" because as she discovers her sin she also knows that she is lovely to God. The Holy Spirit allows her to see her sinfulness as well as her loveliness to God. This describes a sincere yet weak believer.

B.   It is essential for our spiritual growth to see that we are lovely as we see more of our sinfulness. The combination of these two truths causes us to grow in confidence and gratitude in our relationship with Jesus.

   1.   Some streams in the body of Christ focus on the darkness of our heart or on how sinful we are. To emphasize this without emphasizing how lovely we are to God destroys our confidence before the Lord and produces shame driven believers. They are sincere in their repentance but are emotionally paralyzed in their relationship with Jesus by shame.

   2.   We walk in the light in different measures. We are to walk in the fullness of the light that we have as God dwells in the fullness of the light that He has. As we walk in the light, God increases it so that we see more of the darkness that is in our heart. <u>Our most sincere efforts to love God are flawed and fragile.</u> Those who sincerely seek to obey Jesus need not fear that they will be <u>disqualified</u> from their calling because of weakness. We are lovely to God even in our weakness. He is tender towards us in our spiritual immaturity.

C.   Jeremiah had revelation of the depth and deceitfulness of sin in the human heart. We have a greater capacity for sin than we comprehend. No one fully grasps the depth of our unperceived areas of sin. They are below the surface like hidden fault lines before an earthquake.

> *⁹ The <u>heart is deceitful</u> above all things, and desperately wicked; who can know it? (Jer. 17:9)*

> *²² Put off…the old man which grows corrupt according to the <u>deceitful lusts</u>. (Eph. 4:22)*

D.   Paul, as a mature apostle described himself as chief among sinners. This was not an exaggerated statement with false humility. The more light we have, the more we see the darkness in our heart.

> *¹⁵ Jesus came into the world to save sinners, <u>of whom I am chief</u>. (1 Tim. 1:15)*

E.   Knowledge of our weak flesh is an important aspect of the truth about who we are, although it is not the whole truth of who we are. God knows about the depth of our sin before we are saved. He does not discover our sin because we do. He is aware of it when He declares His love for us. God did not over commit Himself to love us without first understanding the gravity of our sin.

F.     We are sometimes surprised when we sin. At such times, we can be overwhelmed with grief. We think that because we are surprised by our sin then surely God must also be surprised. If He is surprised with the new information about us then we fear that He may want to renegotiate our relationship with Him or that He is reconsidering His love for us.

G.     To consistently grow spiritually requires that we know that we are lovely to God while we are in the process of discovering the darkness of our heart. God's motivation to love us comes from within His heart not from our promises to never fail in a given area. He does not want us relating to Him on the presupposition that we motivate Him to take an interest in us. I have seen people who for many years emphasize only the darkness of their heart. They are extremely sincere in their repentance. They do not enter into the enjoyment or delight that God feels for them.

H.     They do not experience "the love that is better than wine." They have a sincere heart but a closed spirit before God. A closed spirit says, "Jesus, I love You but please forgive me and do not reject me. I swear I will never do this sin again." In other words, they continually negotiate their relationship with God while they worship Him. The issue is one of understanding God's affections and in what way He imparts beauty to us in the grace of God so that we can say, "I am dark, but lovely. I know I sin but You are ravished over me." This is a powerful place of confidence. It empowers us to run to God instead of from Him when we stumble.

## II.     WHY WE ARE BEAUTIFUL TO GOD EVEN IN OUR WEAKNESS: FOUR REASONS

A.     <u>We received the gift of righteousness</u>: Our loveliness comes by receiving the gift of righteousness or the same beautiful righteous garments that Jesus possesses. Sinful people are made lovely in God's sight because of what Jesus did not because of what we do.

*17 Therefore, if <u>anyone</u> is in Christ, he is a <u>new creation</u>; old things have <u>passed away</u>; behold, all things have become new. 18 Now <u>all things</u> are of God, who has <u>reconciled</u> us to Himself through Jesus…19 God was in Christ reconciling the world to Himself, <u>not imputing</u> (counting) their trespasses to them…21 For He made Him who knew no sin to be sin for us, that <u>we might become the righteousness of God</u> in Him. (2 Cor. 5:17-21)*

B.     <u>We have a willing spirit</u>: At the new birth, the Holy Spirit put a "Yes, in our spirit" to God. We agree to change our behavior before the change actually occurs. The "yes" in our spirit to God is beautiful to Him. Each movement of our heart to God is the work of the Spirit in us called a willing spirit. David prayed to be sustained by a willing spirit.

*12 Restore to me the joy of Thy salvation, and <u>sustain me with a willing spirit</u>. (Ps. 51:12, NAS)*

*41 The <u>spirit indeed is willing</u>, but the flesh is weak. (Mt. 26:41)*

C.   <u>The nature of God's personality</u>: Our beauty is related to God's emotional make up. The very affections and passions in God's heart determine how He feels towards us. <u>Beauty is in the eyes of the beholder</u>. It is because of the heart of the Beholder, that we are beautiful to God. If God was mostly angry, we would not be beautiful in His sight by virtue of having a willing spirit. The way He views people flows out of what is in His heart. His point of view is what determines who and what is beautiful. If someone else were looking at the exact same information about us, they would not call us beautiful. God views things very differently than man does.

*⁷ Do not look at his appearance…for <u>the LORD does not see as man sees</u>; for man looks at the outward appearance (performance), but the LORD looks at the heart. (1 Sam. 16:7)*

*⁷ "Let the wicked forsake his way, and the unrighteous man his thoughts; let him return to the LORD, and He will have mercy on him…for He will <u>abundantly pardon</u>. 8 For <u>My thoughts are not your thoughts</u>…," says the LORD. 9 "For as the heavens are higher than the earth, So are My ways higher than your ways, and <u>My thoughts</u> than your thoughts." (Isa. 55:7-9)*

D.   <u>Our eternal destiny as Jesus' bride</u>: God sees us through the lens of who we are and how we will live for billions of years in the grace of God as the enthroned Bride with Jesus. This is a significant part of who we are in God's sight.

## III.   PETER EARLY STRUGGLES: DARK BUT LOVELY OR WEAK BUT WILLING (MT. 26:41)

A.   Jesus warned Peter that he would deny Him (Lk. 22:31-34). Later that evening in the garden of Gethsemane, Jesus gave Peter a significant 2-fold description of how the heart of the redeemed operates in God's grace. Jesus told Peter that his spirit was willing but his flesh was weak.

*⁴¹ The <u>spirit indeed is willing</u>, but the <u>flesh is weak</u>. (Mt. 26:41)*

B.   Peter stumbled because of his "weak flesh" yet he longed to obey God with a "willing spirit." Most Bible translations use the phrase "the flesh is weak." However, the NIV translated the phrase "the flesh is weak" as "the body is weak." Jesus was referring to the principle of sin operating in Peter's heart, not his fatigue because it was late at night.

C.   What is God thinking and feeling about us when we discover the weakness of our own flesh? This is essential in understanding the grace of God. This is where the crisis of our faith begins.

## IV.   PETER'S DESPAIR BECAUSE OF HIS FAILURE WHEN HE DENIED THE LORD

A.   Why did Peter go fishing? He was not fishing because the apostolic team ran out of money so soon after Jesus' death (this is only 8 days after the crucifixion). They had enough money that Judas stole from the fund without being caught. They fished all night, thus we know Peter was not fishing for recreation.

*³ Peter said, "<u>I am going fishing</u>." They said to him, "We are going with you also." They went out and immediately got into the boat, and that night they caught nothing. (Jn. 21:3)*

B.     Peter was resigning from his God given leadership role as an apostle to return to the family fishing business. He was changing back to his former occupation. An occupation that he had been successful at before Jesus called him to apostolic leadership. Why? If he could not stay faithful to Jesus before the pressure of a young servant girl, then how would he stay faithful for a lifetime? He was saying, "I can be faithful to God as a fisherman without the added pressures of being faithful as an apostle."

C.     He didn't feel qualified to be an apostle. His heart was wounded by his failure in denying Jesus three times. Peter felt that he disappointed Jesus. He could not face the Lord because of this. When we feel this way, we run from God instead of to Him.

D.     In the crisis of discovering our sinful flesh, some determine that it is too painful to reach for the highest things in God if they believe they will constantly fail. As those who have a high vision to love God with all our heart, we face coming short many times. Some would rather resign once than face failing over and over. In other words, they lower their vision so they do not feel the pain of failing. It is easier to settle for living with a "second class relationship" with God rather than face the pain of failure that goes with having a high vision of loving God with all our heart.

E.     Such people become accustomed to a second rate relationship with the Lord. It is not because they do not love Him any longer. It is because they cannot face relating to God with so much shame. The truth is that we do not have to live with this shame in the grace of God.

F.     They imagine that God is angry, disappointed, grieved and even exasperated with them. They give up on walking in wholehearted obedience and devotion to Jesus and live in condemnation.

G.     Jesus asked Peter the same question, three times. He said, "Do you love Me?"

*15 Jesus said to Simon Peter, "Simon…do you love Me more than these?" He said to Him, "Yes, Lord; You know that I love You." He said to him, "Feed My lambs." 16 He said to him again a second time, "Simon…do you love Me?" He said to Him, "Yes, Lord; You know that I love You." He said to him, "Tend My sheep." 17 He said to him the third time, "Simon…do you love Me?" Peter was grieved because He said to him the third time, "Do you love Me?" And he said to Him, "Lord, You know all things; You know that I love You." (Jn. 21:15-17)*

H.     When God asks us a question, it is not because God needs information. Why was God asking Peter this question? He wanted Peter to discover information about himself. The Lord already knows that Peter loves Him. But He wants Peter to have confidence in his sincere love for Jesus. Jesus was calling Peter back into the same quality of relationship with Him that Peter had before he denied Jesus. The Lord was revealing to Peter how much Peter loved Jesus.

I.      The Lord was in essence saying, "Peter, You DO love Me. In the garden 8 days ago. I told you that you had weak flesh and a willing spirit. You didn't believe your flesh was weak. You need to understand that you DO have a willing spirit. You DO have a 'yes in your spirit' to Me. I saw it in you before you stumbled. When I see you, I don't only see your weak flesh, I also see your sincere love for Me. I saw your willing spirit when I first called you and I still see it in you."

J.      Jesus sees our willing spirit more than we do. The Lord was breaking shame from Peter s' heart for three denials of his faith. Jesus washed his spirit with these three questions. Jesus wanted Peter to say, "I love God." Shame is broken off of Peter as he is restored to confidence in God.

## V.    THREE STAGES OF VICTORY

A.      First, <u>our sincere intention to obey God</u>: The first step to spiritual victory is our sincere desire to obey God. Our sincere intentions must be distinguished from mature attainment of obedience. Our intentions are where our victory begins. The Spirit is the author of such sincere desires (not the devil, nor our flesh). Part of how God measures and defines our life is by these intentions. He rejoices in them. Some measure their life only by their attainments, resulting in condemnation.

B.      Second, <u>partial breakthrough yet with a continued struggle</u>: We are victorious on a regular basis yet still war with our flesh in a particular area of our life (Rom. 8:2-13; Gal. 5:16-17).

C.      Third, <u>substantial breakthrough with transformed desires</u>: Our desires are dramatically changed so that we rarely even struggle in a previous area of sin (Rom. 6:14-23).

## VI.   THE JOURNEY TO HOLY PASSION STARTS WITH THIS 2-FOLD REVELATION.

[5] *I am dark (in my heart),* **but lovely** *(to God),* **O daughters of Jerusalem, like the** <u>tents of Kedar</u>**, like the** <u>curtains of Solomon</u>**. Do not** <u>look</u> *(stare, NAS)* **upon me, because I am dark… (Song 1:5-6).**

A.      The crisis the young bride is facing in Song 1:5 is the same crisis that Peter walked through.

1.      Dark of heart (sinful desires): Our weak flesh is dark to God.

2.      Lovely to God (sincere intentions to obey Jesus): Our willing spirit is lovely to God.

B.      Throughout the Song, the Bride teaches the daughters of Jerusalem the spiritual principles of growing in passion for God. The daughters refer to those who are spiritually immature.

C.      The <u>dark tents of Kedar</u> speak of the darkness of the flesh. They were blackened tents that were made out of the dark skins of wild goats. This analogy was easily understood in that day.

D.      The <u>curtains of Solomon</u> were the white curtains in the holy place in the Temple. They speak of the inward work of grace in her life. The beauty of these curtains was not seen by all in the outer court but only by the priests who could go into the holy place.

E.      She is saying, "I am like dark tents on the outside, but inside I am beautiful like the curtains of Solomon in the holy place." Outwardly, people see her as the dark tents of Kedar. Inwardly, God sees that she is lovely like the white curtains of Solomon.

F.      She cries that "the sun has tanned me". In Solomon's book, Ecclesiastes, he often wrote of "living life under the sun." It means living life in the natural realm. She is speaking of the impact of being born under the sun or born in the natural weakness of sin. Natural life has impacted her and darkened her, as it has every other person born in Adam.

G.      She asks the people not to look at her and wag their head to shame her saying, "You are dark of heart." She says, "Yes, I am human and I have sinned greatly in my life this fallen world."

H.      She asks them to not stare at her (v. 6). She was overwhelmed with the darkness of her heart.

## VII.    HOW THEN SHALL WE LIVE?

A.      Many have sincerely repented yet lack confidence that they are beautiful to God because of what Jesus did for them and what the Holy Spirit has done in them by imparting a willing spirit.

B.      Others have seen the truth of our loveliness to God and sometimes live presumptuously by claiming God's beauty without seeking to live in sincere repentance and wholeheartedness.

C.      The issue is how is she going to relate to God when she discovers her own sinfulness? How are you going to relate to God when you discover you have weak flesh, a dark heart? What we do in this crisis is a very important part of our spiritual life.

D.      Many run from God instead of to Him in this spiritual crisis because they misunderstand how they look to God. They make the same mistake that Peter initially made. They resign, they give up and they get entrenched into a mindset of shame (stronghold of shame).

E.      A life of shame leads to a life of sin. If you feel dirty before God then you will live dirty. The Lord does not want us to resign ourselves to a second class status. There is nothing more powerful in the earth than a woman who feels loved along with feeling clean and full of dignity. Such a woman is tenacious in love. She is powerful. God is raising up a corporate Bride that will feel clean, desired, dignified, pursued and delighted in.

# Session 10 Her Journey Begins With Spiritual Crisis (Song 1:5-11)

## I. THE BRIDE'S JOURNEY BEGINS: THE PARADOX OF GRACE: "DARK, BUT LOVELY"

*⁵ I am <u>dark</u> (in my heart), but <u>lovely</u> (to God), O daughters of Jerusalem, like the tents of Kedar, like the curtains of Solomon. Do not look upon me, because I am dark… (Song 1:5-6).*

A.   The Bride's spiritual journey begins with a spiritual crisis common to every sincere believer as seen in her 2-fold confession of faith (Song 1:5). I refer to this as the "paradox of grace" because as she discovers her sin she also knows that she is lovely to God. The Holy Spirit allows her to see her sinfulness as well as her loveliness to God. This describes a sincere yet weak believer.

B.   We are beautiful to God even in our weakness for four reasons. First, our loveliness comes by receiving the gift of righteousness (2 Cor. 5:17-21). Second, at the new birth, the Holy Spirit put a "Yes, in our spirit" to God. Each movement of our heart to God is His work in us called a willing spirit. (Ps. 51:12 NAS; Mt. 26:41). Third, our beauty is related to God's emotional make up. The very affections and passions in God's heart determine how He feels towards us. <u>Beauty is in the eyes of the beholder</u>. God views things very differently than man does (1 Sam. 16:7; Isa. 55:7-9). Fourth, God sees us through the lens of our eternal destiny as the Bride of Christ.

C.   We must understand the three stages of our victory in Christ. First, <u>our sincere intention to obey God</u> is where our victory begins. Second, we have a <u>partial breakthrough yet with a continued struggle</u>. We are victorious on a regular basis yet still war with our flesh in particular areas (Gal. 5:16-17). Third, is a <u>substantial breakthrough with transformed desires</u> (Rom. 6:14-23).

## II. HER SPIRITUAL CRISIS: REJECTION AND SHAME

*⁶ Do not <u>look</u> (stare NAS)upon me, because I am dark…My mother's sons were <u>angry</u> with me; they <u>made </u>me the keeper of the vineyards, but my own vineyard (heart) I have <u>not kept</u>. 7 Tell me, O You (Jesus) whom I love, where you feed Your flock, where You make it rest at noon. For why should I be as one who veils herself by the flocks of <u>Your companions</u>? (Song 1:6-7)*

A.   She describes 5 different pressures related to her spiritual crisis in Song 1:6-7. She feels ashamed by those staring at her because of her failure; being rejected by her angry brothers; being overworked by being made to keep other vineyards; allowing her own vineyard (heart) to not be kept with fresh love for Jesus; and for serving Jesus at a distance.

B.   She describes her brothers as her "mother's sons". Throughout the Song (1; 6; 3:4, 11; 8:2, 5) the mother speaks of the Church since we are born of God through the agency of the Church by the Spirit. Paul and others wrote of the Church and its leaders and the New Jerusalem as a "mother" (Gal. 4:19, 26; 1 Thes. 2:6-7). Those who do God's will are His mother and brothers (Mt. 12:46-50). God is our father and the church is spoken of as our mother. Jesus, the foundation of the Church was born from the seed of a woman (Gen. 3:15). Redeemed Israel was represented as a "mother" that gave birth to Jesus the man-child (Rev 12:5).

C.       The sons were angry at her youthful zeal. They speak of older spiritually dull leaders who do not appreciate fervent young believers. Why? First, zealous believers bring conviction to spiritually dull believers (who often simply dismiss true spiritual zeal as legalism). Second, the untempered zeal and pride of zealous believers often make spiritually dull leaders angry. Our zeal must be seasoned with wisdom and humility. It is common for those with new fervency for Jesus to be self-absorbed and prideful in the way they call others to be wholehearted. Some exalt themselves and condemn others who do not express devotion to God in the same way they do.

D.       She was mistreated by the angry sons who overwork her by taking advantage of her fervency by giving her many responsibilities in different vineyards (plural). She burns out spiritually. Burn-out doesn't come from hard work as much as from a religious yoke, which speaks of working without connecting with the Holy Spirit in the work. Embracing too many responsibilities out of the fear of man and the desire to be noticed by others leads to burn out.

E.       She kept other vineyards, but did not keep her own vineyard (or heart). Our first responsibility before God is our own personal walk with Jesus. Originally, what she wanted most were the kisses of His Word. However, as time goes by her vineyard or the garden of her heart was choked by the weeds of spiritual coldness, sin, and shame. Taking care of her own vineyard means nurturing her personal communion with God and doing His will.

*⁶ They <u>made</u> me the keeper of the vineyards, but my own vineyard I have <u>not kept</u>. (Song 1:6)*

F.       She feels the pain of serving Jesus at a distance. This happens when we serve without connecting with the Holy Spirit. She feels like the veiled woman who served the Shepherd at a distance.

*⁷ Tell me, O You (Jesus) whom I love, where you feed Your flock…For why should I be as one who <u>veils herself</u> by the flocks of <u>Your companions</u>? (Song 1:7)*

1.       In the ancient world, women veiled themselves when working with strangers who they were unfamiliar with. Why should I serve down the road and not near to You like I used to? These two issues speak of living at a distance from the Shepherd that she so loves.

2.       She wants to be with Him wherever He is. She lost the sweetness in her communion with God. She longs for the kisses of His Word and the chamber experiences with the Lord.

## III.       HER DESPERATE CRY TO HAVE MORE OF JESUS

*⁷ Tell me, O You (Jesus) whom I love, where you <u>feed Your flock</u>, where You make it <u>rest at noon</u>. For why should I be as one who veils herself by the flocks of Your companions? (Song 1:7)*

A.       In the midst of this crisis, she cries out with a desperate prayer. She remembers the kisses of His Word and her chamber experiences. She asks the great Shepherd for counsel, "Tell me, where do you feed Your flock?" We can only offer this desperate cry if we have confidence that we are lovely to God even in our weakness.

1.  She still loves Him and cries out, ***"Tell me, O You whom I love"***. She knows that she failed in her weak love. Weak love is not false love. She is still a genuine lover of God. She is not a hopeless hypocrite as the enemy wants her to believe. She has confidence that her love is real even in her crisis and spiritual dullness.

2.  She did not say, "Tell me, since I am a helpless hypocrite." She cries out, "I know I am a lover of God." This is similar to when Peter cried out, "Lord, You know that I love You though I have just betrayed You."

B.  She is desperate to encounter Jesus. Ministry activity and even promotion is not enough. She wants to know where He feeds His flock. This is an expression of her prayer, "Draw me away."

C.  At noon, or in the heat of the day a sheep will lie down if its stomach is full. God wants us to rest in the midst of the heat of the day or the pressure of this life by connecting with Him, not just working for Him. Sheep will only lie down at noon when they are full.

> *² He makes me to <u>lie down</u> in green pastures... (Ps. 23:2)*

D.  She offers her prayer in the language of the shepherd. "Where will You satisfy me under the heat of the pressures of the day?" She longs to be satisfied again with Jesus or to rest at noon. She is saying: "I have been fed by others, but now I want You to feed me. Where will <u>You</u> satisfy the cry of my spirit?"

E.  Jesus longs that we would pray this prayer. He does not want us to give up and give in to a spiritually dull life in God. He does not want us to write ourselves off as a hopeless hypocrite. It pleases Him when we cry out, "Feed my heart like You used to? I am a veiled woman. I am serving at a distance. My own vineyard has weeds in it. Many things are going wrong. I am failing and the people are angry. I need to touch You whom I love." Regardless what it costs her, she wants the fire of intimacy with God to consume her again. She wants Him to feed her again. She cries out to recover her "first love".

## IV.   JESUS' GLORIOUS ANSWER: SEVEN ESSENTIAL STATEMENTS

> *⁸ If you do not know, O <u>fairest</u> (most beautiful) among women, follow in the footsteps of the flock, and feed your little goats beside the shepherds' tents. (Song 1:8)*

A.  Jesus hears her desperate prayer (Song 1:7) and personally answers her (Song 1:8-11). He gives her seven statements that answer where she can find Him. First, He affirms her as beautiful in His eyes, then gives a 3-fold answer (1:8b,c,d) and then a 3-fold affirmation (1:9-11). She responds with great gratitude (Song 1:12). A vital part of the theology of holy passion is found in Jesus' answer. This is the first revelation of Jesus to the Bride on her journey. He shows Himself as the "wonderful counselor" or the Shepherd who gives her practical counsel in how to go forward in her weakness.

B.     He addresses the Bride as, "O fairest of women." The word "fair" is translated in most other versions of the bible as "beautiful" (NAS/NIV). Jesus is saying, "O most beautiful of women." He is saying, "I know there are weeds in your garden and that you serve Me at a distance, but I see the cry in your heart to love Me." He woos her heart with the beauty she possesses in Him.

C.     Jesus starts by saying, "If you do not know." His answer shocks many people. We would expect a rebuke. He knows our garden isn't being kept and that we serve Him at a distance, however, we are most beautiful to Him. He calls us beautiful even in the midst of our disorientation and failure. We might be unlovely to the angry sons but we are most beautiful to Him. We may despise ourselves but we are most beautiful to Him. He speaks to her shame and rejection.

D.     Jesus calls her the most beautiful woman. This in light of the different women of the earth or the false religions who despise Jesus. He is not comparing her to a mature apostle. He looks at us in light of the 5-6 billion people on earth who have no interest in Jesus. We care intensely about Jesus and have the gift of righteousness. This is beautiful in God's eyes.

E.     In Song 1:4e, the Bride taught the virgins, "We will remember His love." Jesus is causing her to remember His love in answering her by telling how He views her in her weakness. Jesus first speaks to our heart in our crisis by calling us, "most beautiful." Then He gives us instructions.

F.     Jesus' 3-fold answer for where He feeds His flock and establishes us in intimacy with God emphasizes the importance of Body life. All three answers relate to life in the Body as well as answering the three most powerful temptations that are common to all.

*⁸ If you do not know, O fairest (most beautiful) among women, follow in the <u>footsteps of the flock</u>, and <u>feed your little goats</u> beside the <u>shepherds' tents</u>. (Song 1:8)*

1.     Commitment to Body life (v. 8c): refuse unsanctified isolation

2.     Commitment to servant ministry (v. 8d): refuse unsanctified idleness

3.     Commitment to spiritual authority (v. 8e): refuse unsanctified independence

G.     Drawing is singular because it is intimacy. Running is plural because it is ministry. God does not want us running in ministry in isolation, idleness or with an independent spirit.

H.     First, is commitment to Body life as we refuse unsanctified isolation (Song 1:8c). He tells her to follow in the footsteps of the flock, or get involved in the fellowship of the Body. The 'footsteps of the flock' is the place where all the sheep walk with God. The Lord says follow in the place where the Body walks. He is saying, "Get back into fellowship, do not over-react to the angry brothers who judge and mistreat you." Much isolation from the Body is not motivated by a desire to seek God but by rejection, bitterness and shame. The devil wants us in isolation to destroy us.

*²⁵ <u>Not forsaking</u> the assembling of ourselves together as is the manner of some… (Heb. 10:25)*

I.     Second, take care of your God given responsibilities as we refuse unsanctified idleness (Song 1:8d). We are to feed the little flock that God sets before us. Jesus will give us more of Himself as we take on the responsibility to feed the young ones or the little flock that God sends to us.

J.     Third, submit to spiritual authority by refusing unsanctified independence (Song 1:8e). She serves the Body beside the tents of the true shepherds. Jesus wants us to have an open spirit to the shepherds (leaders) that He places us under. The spirit of lawlessness is abounding (Mt. 24:12). God knows that every leader that He has ever placed over you or ever will is an imperfect leader. We find Jesus in deep ways as we relate to imperfect leaders. God uses imperfect shepherds to temper us and to reveal the unsettled things in our heart. When we see the faults of the imperfect leaders that God has put over us we are tempted to resist dwelling by their tents with a teachable spirit. Submission is about humility and having an open spirit to authority.

K.     **_Summary_**: Jesus' 3-fold answer touches 3 main temptations in the Body. First, is the temptation to isolation and bitterness when we feel rejected or mistreated by the angry sons and when we feel shame related to our sin. We are to stay in fellowship as God's way to heal us. Second, is the temptation to selfishness and fear. Jesus wants us to take care of the little ones. We find Jesus best in the context of serving others. Third, is the temptation to resist spiritual authority.

## V.     HER SINCERITY IS RE-AFFIRMED BY THE LORD

*⁹ I have compared you, <u>My love</u>, to My filly among Pharaoh's chariots. 10 Your cheeks are lovely with ornaments, your neck with chains of gold. 11 We will make you ornaments of gold with studs of silver. (Song 1:9-11)*

A.     In Song 1:9-10, He compares her to 3 things that reaffirm the loveliness of her sincerity and willing spirit before God. Then He gives her a promise in Song 1:11. The first thing He does is to speak to her heart to affirm her by calling her " My love." He speaks with love to her heart again.

B.     God sees her sincere and strong desire to follow Jesus in righteousness. She is as a filly among Pharaoh's chariots.

*⁹ I have compared you, <u>My love</u>, to My filly among Pharaoh's chariots.(Song 1:9)*

1.     A filly is a horse. The horse is a symbol of strength and power. The context speaks of her strength in righteousness. Pharaoh's chariots had the greatest and most trained, skilled horses in the earth. He likens her strength to them.

2.     "Among Pharaoh's chariots" speaks of the finest and strongest war horses in the world. The horses of Egypt were well known throughout the world in those days. Pharaoh had the most highly skilled and trained horses in the earth. Pharaoh chose the very best horses of all the horses of Egypt to pull his own chariot. Pharaoh's own chariot had the best of the best horses. Pharaoh had thousands of horses in his great stables and the one that pulls his personal chariot is the best one. Solomon as the wealthiest man in the world bought many of Pharaoh's horses. He was one of the few that could afford them.

C.      Our emotions are attractive to Him. He has touched our emotions with His Spirit. The emotional dimension of her life has been touched by God with her sincere devotion for Jesus.

*¹⁰ Your <u>cheeks</u> are lovely with ornaments, your neck with chains of gold. 11 We will make you ornaments of gold with studs of silver. (Song 1:10*

1.      The <u>cheeks</u> speak of emotion throughout the Song. They reveal anger and joy, etc. When we look at somebody's cheeks, we can tell if there is joy in their heart or if there is anger or sadness. The emotions of a person are expressed through the cheeks.

2.      The <u>ornaments</u> are created by the skillful work of an artist to beautify its object. Jesus is the artist that has worked to beautify us (Isa.61:3). Though God sees lust and anger in us, He also sees passion growing in us for Him. God is saying, "Your emotions are lovely, I have skillfully worked in you a "Yes!" for My Son. That moves the very heart of God.

D.      God sees her submission to divine authority and her resolute will to obey Jesus.

*¹⁰ Your cheeks are lovely with ornaments, <u>your neck with chains of gold</u>. We will make you ornaments of gold with studs of silver. (Song 1:10-11)*

1.      The neck speaks symbolically of the will. The Bible speaks of people that are stiff-necked, which means a stubborn or rebellious person. The neck also speaks of godly submission. The neck is what turns the head as it chooses which way to go, right or left. When a King triumphed over another nation, the conquering general put his foot over that defeated king's neck which spoke of submission.

2.      The chains of gold speak of royal authority. Only a king had chains of gold. In those days, few people could afford a chain of gold besides a King. A chain of gold was rare and expensive because it was only worn by royalty. A chain of gold with the king's emblem on it was worn by the prince as he walked through the town.

## VI.     THE LORD'S PROMISE TO FINISH THAT WHICH HE BEGAN IN US

*¹¹ We will make you ornaments of gold with studs of silver. (Song 1:11)*

A.      Ornaments of gold speak of divine character. She will be Christ-like in her golden character. This speaks of believers purified with fire (Mal. 3:1-4). Studs of silver speak of redemption. She will be used to bring redemption to other people. She will be equipped to deliver others.

B.      "We will make you" is a Divine promise to complete His work in her. He is still answering her question from v.7, "Where will You feed me?" God promises to work something special in her. He will <u>make</u> us into a person who fully chooses divine character (gold) and is equipped with silver to deliver others (silver). He promises us victory in the areas we have stumbled and we will be an agent of redemption to others.

## Session 11 The Bridal Paradigm: Foundational Truths (Song 1:12–17)

### I. REVIEW AND OVERVIEW OF SONG 1:5-17

A. The Bride asked Jesus, "Where will You feed me?" (1:7). He gave her a 7-fold answer declaring her beauty (1:8a) then gives her a 3-fold instruction (1:8b,c,d) and a 3-fold affirmation (1:9-11).

B. She gives a 3-fold response as she is fed by Jesus at His table (1:12-14). She is confident in Jesus' love even in her weakness as her heart was dark and like a vineyard not kept (1:5-7).

> *12 While the King is at <u>His table</u>, my spikenard sends forth its fragrance. 13 A bundle of myrrh is my Beloved to me…14 My Beloved is to me a cluster of henna blooms… (Song 1:12-14)*

C. Then she receives increased revelation of God's love for her and her beauty to God (1:15). The Bride gives a 5-fold response. She sees Jesus as handsome (beautiful God), the one she loves (my Beloved) and pleasant as He leads her life to rest now and then to eternal glory (v. 16-17).

### II. MEDITATION ON THE CROSS: GOD'S LOVE AND OUR BENEFITS (SONG 1:13)

> *13 A <u>bundle of myrrh</u> is my Beloved to me, that lies all night between my breasts. (Song 1:13)*

A. She receives revelation of Jesus' love and provision for us in going to the cross (Rom. 3-8).

B. Myrrh is an aromatic gum resin produced by various trees and shrubs in India, Arabia, and East Africa. It was very expensive and used in making perfume (Prov. 7:17), the holy anointing oil to burn incense (Ex 30:23) and in preparing a body for a funeral (Jn. 19:39-40). It has a bitter taste. The three wise kings brought myrrh to Jesus' birth as a prophetic symbol of His death (Mt. 2:11). On the cross, Jesus was offered myrrh (Mk. 15:23). It speaks of Jesus' death (Ps 45:8).

C. Myrrh speaks of the fragrant yet bitter reality of embracing death to our fleshly ways.

D. Esther's beauty preparations included bathing in myrrh and other perfumes (Esth. 2:12). Myrrh is referred to 8 times throughout the Song. (Song 1:13; 3:6; 4:6, 14; 5:1, 5, 13).

E. Some wealthy women in the ancient world went to bed with a bundle or large necklace of myrrh to provide fragrance through the night. Solomon gave her this extravagantly expensive gift.

F. The Bride proclaimed that Jesus was like a bundle of myrrh that lay on her heart through the night. The cross was King Jesus' extravagantly expensive gift to His Bride. Jesus' death was an "abundant offering." It speaks of what He endured because of us love for us. It reveals how valuable we are to Him. Our value is seen in what Jesus endured for us. The fact that we exist is statement of our value. Add to that, the fact that the God of Genesis 1 became human and was crushed by the wrath of God to make the way to have an eternal relationship with us.

G.     The myrrh lay all night on her heart. The night speaks of the nighttime of her temptation and/or trials as well as carrying the idea of consistency. It rests on her heart all the time.

H.     We will forever marvel at the Lamb slain for our sins (Rev. 5:8-12). When we really see who He is and what He did, for all of eternity our hearts will be awed and overwhelmed with gratitude. For endless ages, we will see Jesus as a "bundle of myrrh" that will lie on our hearts.

I.     We are to carry it in our heart all through the day and night. We are to continually remember His love as we meditate on the cross (Song 1:4d). The most obedient and worshipful saints think the most on the cross. It is their constant meditation and confession. We will never grow weary of meditating on it. If it becomes boring to us, it is only because we have not understood it.

## III.    REVELATION OF JESUS' BEAUTY AND DELIGHTFULNESS (SONG 1:14)

A.     Jesus was to her as a cluster of beautiful and fragrant henna flowers in full bloom. A henna is a shrub or a small tree with fragrant flowers. Jesus is as a cluster of henna flowers to those with revelation of His heart. He is not the burdensome and boring God that religion falsely proclaims.

*14 My Beloved is to me a cluster of henna blooms in the vineyards of En Gedi. (Song 1:14).*

B.     Jesus' commandments are not burdensome and His yoke is easy as we understand Him in truth.

*3 And His commandments are not burdensome. (1 Jn. 5:3)*

*30 For My yoke is easy and My burden is light. (Mt. 11:30)*

C.     Jesus' personality is as a "cluster" of blooms. He is more than one flower but a cluster. This emphasizes the diversity and abundance of the beauty He possesses. The vineyards of En Gedi were well known for their abundant fragrance. Jesus has fragrance that is beyond all others.

*16 Yes, He is altogether lovely. This is my Beloved, and this is my friend! (Song 5:16)*

D.     We must tell the whole earth the truth of Jesus, who is as a "cluster of henna blooms." They will repent much easier if they understand the truth. We must preach about the beautiful God who is filled with kindness. He is a fragrant and sweet God who intoxicates us with Good News.

*4 Or do you despise (minimize) the riches of His goodness, forbearance, and longsuffering, not knowing that the goodness of God leads you to repentance? (Rom. 2:4)*

## IV.    THE BRIDE FEASTS AT THE KING'S TABLE: HER WORSHIP ARISES (SONG 1:12)

A.     God has provided a table for us (1 Cor. 10:21) in which we feed on the cross and its benefits that come because we receive the gift of righteousness (2 Cor. 5:21). The Bride sits with Jesus at His table to feed on the truths related to her salvation. These truths cause her worship to ascend as fragrance. This parallels the truths that the prodigal son discovered when he returned home to sit at the Father's table (Lk. 15:20-28). The second revelation of Jesus expresses the Father's heart.

*12 While the King is at His table, my spikenard sends forth its fragrance (perfume). (Song 1:12)*

B.      Her worship ascends to God as the fragrance of spikenard (perfume). Spikenard is literally a "spike of nard". Nard was an eastern plant from India used to make expensive perfumes.

C.      What Jesus feeds us produces a worship that spontaneously ascends from our spirit like perfume.

D.      The Lord enjoys the fragrance arising from our spirit as we focus on the provision of His table. We are the fragrance of Christ to God. This is manifest in those filled with gratitude and love.

*14 Thanks be to God who…through us diffuses the fragrance of His knowledge in every place. 15 For we are to God the fragrance of Christ among those who are being saved and among those who are perishing. 16 To the one we are the aroma of death leading to death, and to the other the aroma of life leading to life. And who is sufficient for these things? (2 Cor. 2:14-16)*

E.      In Luke 7, a prostitute ran into the house of Simon the Pharisee. She broke the vial of perfume upon Jesus' feet. The perfume that filled the room speaks of the fragrance Jesus saw in her love.

F.      In the presence of the enemies of our soul, we can feed on the Lord's table. If we neglect to feed our spirit at the King's table, then our spirit starves as shame and guilt weigh us down.

*5 You prepare a table before me in the presence of my enemies…my cup runs over. 6 Surely goodness and mercy shall follow me all the days of my life. (Ps. 23:5-6)*

G.      We are to reckon or to see ourselves as those who stand before God in the same righteousness that Jesus possess (2 Cor. 5:21). We offer ourselves to God as those alive and free from the judgment of our sin. We present ourselves alive to God by saying, "Thank you for making me alive by giving me Your righteousness." Do not come as beggars filled with condemnation.

*11 Likewise…reckon yourselves (see yourself) to be dead indeed to sin, but alive to God in Christ…13 present yourselves to God as being alive from the dead…. (Rom. 6:11-13)*

*1 There is therefore now no condemnation to those who are in Christ Jesus… (Rom. 8:1)*

H.      What kind of fragrance is coming forth from your spirit before God? Does God smell the fragrance of confidence and gratitude? Many can say, "I am dark in my heart" but lack the understanding to say, "I am lovely to God." Our perfumed worship arises though the day, as we say, "I love You." We say, "Thank you that You love me. I love so You, Jesus."

I.      Jesus is a great King who has victory over all His enemies. The King speaks to us with affection. We trust that His plan will prevail because He is a King. The One that says, "I love you," is the same One who reigns as King over all created order. He has the authority to establish that which His love has determined. His plan will prevail because He is the great King.

J.      ***Summary of her three responses (Song 1:12-14)***: First, her life is filled with spontaneous worship and adoration that arises as spikenard as she feeds at the King's table (1:12). Second, she constantly meditates or feeds on the love Jesus has for her and what He accomplished for her as He endured the myrrh of the cross (1:13). Third, she sees His beauty and delightfulness (1:13).

**V.    REVELATION OF GOD'S LOVE FOR HER AND HER BEAUTY TO GOD (SONG 1:15)**

*[15] Behold, you are __fair__ (beautiful), **My love!** Behold, you are __fair__ (beautiful)! (Song 1:15)*

*[15] Behold, you are beautiful…My love… (Song 1:15, NAS/NIV)*

A.    In this passage, we see two foundational truths in the bridal paradigm. First, her beauty to Him in the grace of God and the revelation of His affection for her as the one He calls, "My love". She has presented herself with confidence in Jesus' love even in her immaturity (Song 1:12-14). This foundational truth equips us to receive more truth about our beauty to God.

B.    We are beautiful to God even in our weakness for __four reasons__. First, our loveliness comes by receiving the gift of righteousness (2 Cor. 5:17-21). Second, at the new birth, the Spirit put a "Yes, in our spirit" to God. Each movement of our heart to God is His work in us called a willing spirit. (Ps. 51:12; Mt. 26:41). Third, our beauty is related to God's emotional make up. The tender affections and passions in God's heart determine how He feels towards us. __Beauty is in the eyes of the beholder__. God views things very differently than man does (1 Sam. 16:7; Isa. 55:7-9). Fourth, God sees us through the lens of our eternal destiny as the Bride of Christ.

C.    Each believer is one that Jesus calls, "My love." He chose to love and pursue each one of us. Every believer can confess, "I am the disciple the Lord loves and His favorite one."

*[9] __As the Father loved Me, I also__ have loved you. (Jn. 15:9)*

*[20] Peter…saw __the disciple whom Jesus loved__, who had __leaned on His breast__… (Jn. 21:20)*

D.    When we feel loved and beautiful in the grace of a beautiful God, then our heart is exhilarated. We will spiritually grow the fastest and deepest as we confidently confess, "Because of Jesus, I am beautiful to God, even in my weakness." The Bride taught the virgins to remember His love.

*[4] We will __remember Your love__ more than wine. (Song 1:4)*

E.    The Bride's spiritual journey begins with her 2-fold confession of faith (Song 1:5). I refer to this as the "paradox of grace" because as she discovers her sin she also knows she is lovely to God. Without revelation, when we see our sin we only feel dirty and ashamed. As long as we feel ashamed we will continue to do shameful things. A person that feels dirty will live dirty. An immature believer that feels beautiful and loved by Jesus will run to Him not from Him.

F.    The more we see God's heart for ourselves, the more we see His ravished heart for others. God wants us to also see the beauty of the corporate Church. In relational difficulty, we must remember God's love (Song 1:4d) in knowing that He is ravished for all Christians (Song 4:9).

G.    *Review*: in an introductory way, she confessed, "I am dark in my heart but lovely to God" (1:5). Then Jesus said, "You are beautiful, You are My love and your cheeks are lovely" (1:8a, 1:9b, 10). Then she sees Jesus as beautiful (1:12-14). Now He emphasizes, "You are beautiful" (1:15).

## VI.    THE BRIDE HAS EYES LIKE A DOVE

*15 Behold, you are fair (beautiful), My love! Behold, you are fair! You have dove's eyes. (Song 1:15)*

A.    In the Scripture, a dove is a picture of the Holy Spirit. There are several implications to this.

B.    Single-minded: a dove has no peripheral vision. It only sees straight ahead. It is not distracted by what is happening at its right or left. To have dove's eyes is to have a good eye (single-minded).

*22 The lamp of the body is the eye. If your eye is good, your body will be full of light. (Mt. 6:22)*

C.    Loyalty: a dove will mate once in their life. If their mate dies, they never mate again. This speaks symbolically of loyalty. (**Note**: it is NOT disloyal for one to marry if their spouse dies).

D.    The impact of seeing herself as beautiful to God in v. 15, is having greater singleness of vision.

E.    The Holy Spirit is the ultimate One with "dove's eyes." He is single minded and loyal to Jesus. We ask the Spirit to give us "dove's eyes."

F.    Perspective: we want the Spirit's perspective of Jesus and of our life. We to see Jesus as henna blooms or as fragrant and beautiful and to be single-minded in our obedience and in our faith in God's grace that we would be confident by refusing all condemnation.

## VII.    HER WORSHIP AND FAITH: HER 5-FOLD RESPONSE

*16 Behold, You are handsome, my Beloved! Yes, pleasant! Also our bed is green. 17 The beams of our houses are cedar, and our rafters of fir. (Song 1:16-17)*

A.    The Bride's 5-fold response to the revelation of being loved and beautiful to God (1:15) is to see with dove's eyes. She sees Jesus as handsome (the beautiful God), as the one she loves (Beloved) and pleasant as He leads her life to rest and security now and eternal glory in the age-to-come.

B.    She proclaims to Jesus, "You are handsome, my Beloved." In other words, You are the beautiful God and I love you. The more she sees of Jesus' beauty and the more she loves Him, the more spiritual pleasure she has in her walk with God (v. 16). This is described more in Song 2:3-5. When we see Jesus as beautiful and pleasant, then full obedience seems much more reasonable.

C.    Jesus promised us that we would have fullness of joy or that it would be pleasant and enjoyable to walk with God as we obey Him and abide in His love. We do this as we continue in an on-going dialogue (1:12-17). Our spirit can know this joy even when circumstances are difficult.

*9 As the Father loved Me, I also have loved you; abide in My love. 10 If you keep My commandments, you will abide in My love, just as I have kept My Father's commandments and abide in His love. 11 These things I have spoken to you, that My joy may remain in you, and that your joy may be full. (Jn. 15:9-11)*

## VIII.   ABIDING IN JESUS' LOVE: REST, CONFIDENCE AND GLORY (SONG 1:16-17)

*<sup>16</sup> You are handsome, my Beloved! Yes, pleasant! Our <u>bed is green</u> (couch is luxuriant, NAS). 17 The beams of <u>our houses</u> are cedar, and our rafters of fir. (Song 1:16-17)*

A.      Abiding in Jesus' love brings her abundant rest and confidence in her life (1:16). The Bride is resting on a "luxuriant couch" or a bed that is green. Green fields were sometimes referred to as luxuriant fields or those with profuse growth. The couch of the Lord is plush, green and filled with life. It is not a desert (parched land). Our confidence is to be abundant as a luxuriant couch.

B.      The couch of the Lord speaks of our rest and confidence in the grace of God in two ways.

   1.      *The rest of forgiveness*: we experience this with the assurance that we are forgiven as a free gift in Jesus. We rest in receiving forgiveness because of the cross (2 Cor. 5:17).

   2.      *The rest of intimacy*: we experience this as we pursue intimacy with God. There is no rest until we conclude the highest purpose of our life is intimacy with God. Our intimacy with God includes the wisdom of obeying Jesus' leadership. Augustine wrote, "Man does not rest until he finds his rest in God." We only find our ultimate purpose for life in being wholehearted in our love for God. Many with the assurance of forgiveness still strive to find purpose and a life of greatness that has no regrets at the Judgment Seat of Christ.

C.      There is no fear of condemnation now nor fear of regret as we stand before the Lord on the last day. Living in the Bridal paradigm leads us to confidence in our love for God and in the wisdom of our choices to obey even as the Church calls us religious and the world calls us foolish.

D.      We will live forever in relationship with God and in a house filled with beauty and strength. She refers to "our bed/couch" because it comes only in deep union of salvation (1 Cor. 6:17).

E.      She said that the beams of their <u>houses</u> were of cedar, and their rafters were of fir (1:17). Beams and rafters provide the structure for a house. The structures of a house are hidden. Cedar and fir were the most permanent, expensive, beautiful and fragrant building material made of wood in Solomon's day. Cedar and fir trees were used in building the Temple, so that its structures would not decay. Wood in the Temple is a picture of humanity.

F.      God is building an enduring house. Our dwelling with the Lord is strong, permanent and durable. Jesus became a man so that He could provide a permanent house for His Bride. Our house in God is strong. It will last forever. It is beautiful. We will dwell together with Jesus in beauty and strength forever. She sees the house as "our house" or their dwelling place together forever.

   *<sup>19</sup> You are…members of the <u>household of God</u>…22 in whom you also are being built together for a dwelling place of God in the Spirit. (Eph. 2:19-22)*

   *<sup>5</sup> You…are being built up a <u>spiritual house</u>... (1 Pet. 2:5)*

## Session 12 The Bride's Identity and Life Purpose (Song 2:1-7)

### I. THE BRIDE'S IDENTITY AND LIFE PURPOSE: BEING JESUS' INHERITANCE

A. A foundational premise of God's Kingdom is the Father's promise to give Jesus an inheritance that He knew Jesus would greatly desire. An aspect of His inheritance involves the mandatory obedience of all creation. Jesus wants more than this. He longs for an eternal companion or a Bride who voluntarily chooses to be equally yoked to Him in love (Eph. 5:31-32; Rev. 19:7-9).

B. The Bride of Christ is the great prize of all the ages that Jesus awaits. The affections of the human heart are the most precious possession to God. Jesus died to redeem and thus, possess human affections. The reason we were created and redeemed is to love Jesus with all our heart. Satan attacks our hearts that we would not fully love God and thus, live as Jesus' inheritance.

> *²³ Keep your <u>heart</u> with all diligence, for out of it spring the <u>issues of life</u>. (Prov. 4:23)*

C. The Spirit is restoring the First Commandment to first place in the Body of Christ. It is the first commandment because it is the first priority to God. It is not called the "first option". Loving God is an ***end in itself*** and is the highest lifestyle possible. It is the ***great commandment*** because it always is great in the impact it has on God's heart and our heart (eventually others).

> *³⁷ Jesus said to him, "'You shall <u>love the LORD</u> your God with all your heart, with all your soul, and with all your mind.' 38 This is the <u>first</u> and <u>great</u> commandment." (Mt. 22:37-38)*

D. The Church as His Bride will be prepared in this age before the Second Coming. The power of the End-Time Church will be found in walking in the anointing to love God (Rev. 15:2-4). This includes the supernatural ability to feel God's love and then to feel love back to God.

> *⁷ For the marriage of the Lamb has come, and <u>His wife has made herself ready</u>. (Rev. 19:7)*

E. The Bride is pictured as a ***beautiful rose*** and a ***pure lily*** whose primary life purpose and identity is found in seeking to fully love (rose) and obey (lily) Jesus. The rose is chosen for its beauty and fragrance as the chief of flowers. A lily speaks of purity. The valley speaks of the low and dark places in this fallen world. She lives in purity in the midst of the dark valley of this fallen world.

> *¹ I am the <u>rose</u> of Sharon, and the <u>lily</u> of the valleys. (Song 2:1)*

F. In poetic language, the Bride declares her primary life purpose and identity as being Jesus' inheritance. The rose and the lily are the same people identified as the Bride in Song 2:2. The king sees her as a lily among the thorns which like the valley speaks of sin. Thorns came forth as the result of the curse of Adam's sin (Gen. 3:17-18; Heb. 6:8).

> *² Like a <u>lily among thorns</u>, so is My love among the daughters. (Song 2:2)*

G. We are the rose and lily whose love and obedience arises as fragrance that intoxicates Jesus' heart. We are the only prize Jesus longs for. The reason we were created and redeemed is to fully love (rose) and obey (lily) Jesus as His inheritance and thus, to bring joy and pleasure to God.

H.     The Bride's first confession was that she was dark in her heart but lovely to God through Jesus (Song 1:5). She sees much more in seeing her purpose for her life in confessing, "I am Jesus' desired inheritance." This revelation only comes after seeing the truths in Song 1:12-17.

I.     We must pray to receive revelation that we are the inheritance the Father promised the Son.

*<sup>17</sup> That the Father of glory, may give to you the <u>spirit of wisdom and revelation</u>… that you may <u>know</u>…what are the riches of the glory of <u>His inheritance in the saints</u>… (Eph. 1:17-18)*

J.     We cannot separate love and obedience. Jesus' inheritance is a people who walk out their purity. Our life choices are a real part of the Father's plan to reward and honor His Son. God has made a great investment in us by choosing us as the rose and lily that He is cultivating for Jesus. We are the reward of His sufferings. Many believers mock the call to purity by dismissing it as legalism.

*<sup>21</sup> He who has My commandments and keeps them, it is he who loves Me… (Jn. 14:21)*

K.     Our identity is determined by the way we define value or measure success. "Who am I? How do I become successful?" The issue of our function (ministry) is important but secondary to this.

L.     Our primary identity (value/success) is found in who we are in our <u>intimacy</u> with God which <u>consists of being loved by God and in being a lover of God</u>. I confess, *"I am loved (by God) and I am a lover (to God/others) therefore, I am successful."*

M.     We find our identity or success in being desired by God and in loving Him instead of seeking our primary value in how much we accomplish or the impact we make. We are most successful because we are desired by God and love Him. We no longer need to fear being a failure.

N.     Our primary identity is not what we do with our hands but what we pursue with our hearts. Seeing that we are *His rose and lily* breaks a sense of purposelessness, failure and inferiority. We measure our success in context to how much we grow in our intimacy with God by loving and obeying Him. It takes revelation to see the nobility of loving God and how it matters to Him.

O.     We must agree with God's definition of success. Many agree with lies about what success is and thus, feel like a failure and live aimlessly. They focus mostly on <u>externals</u> (what they do and possess) instead of <u>internals</u> (who they are to be in their hearts). They view their life in context to their struggle and lack of impact. Jesus corrected those who put their ministry before loving God.

*<sup>3</sup> You have labored for My name…4 I have this against you, you have <u>left your first love</u>. 5 Remember from where you have fallen; <u>repent</u> or I will…remove your lampstand. (Rev. 2:3-5)*

P.     Paul taught the truths of Song 2:1 in teaching that we are betrothed (engaged) to Jesus and live in devotion to Him. Our ultimate destiny in this age is to walk out a lifestyle as His inheritance.

*<sup>2</sup> For I <u>betrothed</u> you to one husband, that to Christ I might present you as a <u>pure virgin</u>. 3 I am afraid, lest as the serpent deceived Eve by his craftiness, your <u>minds should be led astray from the simplicity and purity of devotion to Christ</u> (2 Cor 11:2-3, NAS)*

## II. THE BRIDE'S REVELATION: JESUS ALONE CAN SATISFY HER HEART (SONG 2:3A)

A. The Bride declares that Jesus alone is the apple tree who refreshes (fully satisfies) the heart.

*³ Like an __apple tree__ among the trees of the woods, so is __my Beloved__ among the sons. (Song 2:3a)*

B. The apple tree speaks of that which refreshes.

*⁵ __Refresh me with apples__, for I am lovesick. (Song 2:5)*

C. There is only One who refreshes the human spirit at the highest level. When we receive the revelation of Jesus as an apple tree or as the primary source that satisfies our heart then we seek Him with all our heart. This is a foundational truth in marriage, business and ministry. Jesus is more than the savior who forgives or the healer and provider. He is the apple tree that satisfies. In vain, some transfer the primary source of their joy to their ministry, money and relationships.

D. Jesus is like an apple tree among all the great men of the earth. The trees of the woods speak symbolically of the great men of the earth who tower over others as lofty trees (Dan. 4:10-14).

*¹² The day of the LORD of hosts shall come upon everything proud and lofty…13 on all the __cedars__ of Lebanon that are high and lifted up, and on all the __oaks__ of Bashan… (Isa. 2:12-13)*

## III. THE BRIDE ENJOYS GOD'S PRESENCE: SITTING BEFORE THE KING (SONG 2:3B-4)

A. Jesus declared the wisdom of Mary's life as she sat at His feet. Mary is described three times in Scripture. Each time she is sitting at Jesus' feet (Lk. 10:39; Jn. 11:32; 12:3). Jesus forever settled the debate about the importance of sitting at His feet by calling it the "one thing needed" and choosing the "good" way to live (v. 42). She took seriously the call to live with extravagant devotion. We must choose this part. No one can choose it for us. That good part will not be taken away from Mary. Her decisions had eternal implications in being remembered by Jesus forever.

*³⁹ __Mary…sat at Jesus' feet__ and heard His Word. 41 Jesus answered, "__One thing__ is needed, and Mary has __chosen__ that __good part__, which __will not be taken away from her__." (Lk. 10:39-42)*

B. Like Mary of Bethany who sat at Jesus' feet, we must sit before Jesus and experience His refreshing shade that protects us from the scorching heat of this fallen age. One of the greatest pleasures available to the human spirit comes as we feed on His Word and feel His presence. The Word brings delight and is sweet to all who will continually feast on Jesus in spirit and truth.

*³ I __sat down__ in __His shade__ with __great delight__, and His fruit was __sweet__ to my taste. (Song 2:3b)*

C. She asked, "Where will You feed your flock?" (Song 1:7). She had been feasting at the King's table on God's love as seen in Song 1:12-17. The cross is the only tree that can shade from the scorching heat of our sin. We only enjoy the shade of God's Word by resting in the shade of Jesus' cross. We cannot rest in our achievements by relating to God based on our maturity.

D.   We must have a vision to be regularly exhilarated by the Word by pray-reading (meditating) it. Our inheritance is to experience the sweetness of the Word of God. This is for all believers not just a few. There is a sweetness that is within reach of every believer. We will never experience the delight and refreshing of Jesus as the apple tree without sitting long hours in the shade of the apple tree by feeding on His Word by the help of the Holy Spirit.

E.   We put our cold heart before the bonfire of God's presence by seeking Him in the Word. We can feed on the Word even in the presence of our enemies (sin, disappointment, difficulty, etc.).

*⁵ You __prepare a table__ before me in the presence of my enemies... (Ps. 23:5)*

F.   We must enjoy our relationship with God if we are to mature consistently. We can persevere through great difficulties if we find delight in His presence. A lover will always outwork a worker. When a worker becomes a lover, their paradigm about the work changes greatly. I have not seen anyone seek God diligently for decades without enjoying Him in the Word.

## IV.   JESUS' BANNER OVER HER LIFE: HIS LOVING LEADERSHIP (SONG 2:4)

*⁴ He brought me to the banqueting house, and __His banner over me was love__. (Song 2:4)*

A.   In the ancient world, an army would march in battalions under a specific flag or banner. Each unit had their own banner that was meant to clearly identify them. The banner or flag over our life that identifies who we are and where we are going in our life is Jesus' good leadership (wise, loving and powerful) that leads us to grow in love and in our identity as His inheritance (Bride).

B.   We are called to feast at God's banqueting table. The fulfillment of this ultimately occurs at the Marriage Supper of the Lamb (Rev.19:7). Jesus wants us to enjoy tokens of that "Wedding Table" in this age by the power of the Word and the Spirit. This is translated by some as the "house of wine" because it refers to the celebration of God's love.

C.   Jesus has a good and specific plan for each believer. It is to bring us to His banqueting house or to where we celebrate His love. His primary goal in His leadership over our life is to bring us to the banqueting house to celebrate His love for us and our love for Him. We may not know the details as to where Jesus is leading our ministries. Make no mistake about it, He is first leading us so that we feed at the "Wedding Table" or on truths about our identity as the Bride of Christ.

D.   Jesus' goal in His leadership over us is to lead us in a way that reveals His love to us as well as imparting it in us. He is determined that we grow in love, meekness and revelation. God's plan and first priority for our life is much bigger than our comfort or our function in ministry. There is great confusion in many because they think His banner over their life is comfort in this age.

E.  Jesus wants us to be strengthened in the revelation that we are His inheritance with our primary identity in being a lover of God. This occurs as He feeds us on His Word related to the "Wedding Table". He may "bring to us to the table" by giving us a dream or a vision that excites our heart about His love. He may give us the joy of a new friendship that ministers God's life to our heart.

F.  Jesus manifests His banner of leadership over us in various ways. First, His banner over us is His lovingkindness (mercy). When we fail, the banner over our life is confidence in His mercy not the fear of being rejected by God. We confess, "His banner over me is love even when I fail." Second, His banner over us speaks of His ability to overrule the negative circumstances in our life by causing everything for our good (Rom. 8:28). The banner over us is His goodness in not being neglected by God. Third, the banner over us is to be exhilarated in God's love instead of being deceived with the false comfort of sin.

G.  He brings us to the table using both positive and negative ways because He is jealous to remove everything that hinders love in us. First, the positive way in *voluntarily following His leadership* to the banqueting house by feeding on and obeying His Word. Second, the negative way is seen in *resisting His leadership* as He seeks to take us to the banqueting house. Thus, He is forced to discipline us by exposing our sin, taking things from us and shutting doors that frustrate us.

## V.  THE LOVESICK BRIDE CRIES OUT FOR GREATER ENCOUNTER WITH GOD (SONG 2:5)

A.  The Bride's experiences at the "Wedding Table" awaken a greater desire in her to go deeper in God. They cause her to be lovesick as she cries out to God to be sustained and refreshed by giving her more of His presence and Word.

> <sup>5</sup> *Sustain me with cakes of raisins, refresh me with apples, for I am lovesick. (Song 2:5)*

B.  As the apples speak of the refreshing of Jesus (Song 2:3), so the raisins speak of the ministry of the Spirit since they are dried grapes. Grapes symbolically point to the wine of the Spirit. In other words, she cries, "Sustain me with more of the Spirit and refresh me with more of Jesus."

C.  We are called to live lovesick for God. This caused us to have deep and even painful feeling of love and longing for more of Jesus. When we touch this, we can never go back to "business as usual" in our walk with God. She is ruined. I will mention two aspects of spiritual lovesickness.

1.  First, "*feelings of love*" that are very strong. We love to feel love for God.

2.  Second, "*spiritual hunger pains*" that come because of her life vision to walk in all that God has for the human heart in this age. God does not immediately satisfy this in us. Thus, we have a painful even agonizing hunger. Lovesickness will not be satisfied with anything less than persevering. These desperate hunger pains are proof that we have been touched by God.

> <sup>4</sup> *Blessed are those who mourn, for they shall be comforted. (Mt. 5:4)*

## VI.    EXPERIENCING GOD'S 2-FOLD EMBRACE (SONG 2:6)

*⁶ His <u>left hand</u> is under my head, and His <u>right hand</u> embraces me. (Song 2:6)*

A.    The Bride understands God's 2-fold activity in her life, the right and left hand of God. The *left hand of God* speaks of the activity of God that we cannot see. It is under the head therefore, it is out of view. The Lord does many things for us that we do not see. He withholds and releases many things to bless, provide and protect us. He spares us from troubles that we are not ever aware of in this age. For example, we have been delivered from accidents we did not discern.

B.    The *right hand of God* speaks of the visible or discernable activity of God. The idea is that Solomon stood in front of the Bride to embrace her. She can see and feel it. This speaks of the "sweet" manifest presence of God that can be felt and discerned. At times, we feel our heart tenderized by the working of God's right hand.

## VII.    THE HOLY SPIRIT GUARDS US IN STRATEGIC SPIRITUAL SEASONS (SONG 2:7)

*⁷ I <u>charge you</u>, O daughters of Jerusalem, by the <u>gazelles</u> or by the does of the field, do not <u>stir up</u> (disturb) nor awaken love until <u>it</u> pleases. (Song 2:7)*

A.    The Holy Spirit speaks here. He has ordained strategic seasons in each person's spiritual life. There are seasons, where He desires to establish our heart in new and deep revelations of His heart. The Spirit's agenda for the Bride in this season was to awaken lovesickness in her as she went deep in the Word as she fed on apples and grapes at the banqueting house (Song 2:3-5). Many do not see the necessity of dedicating seasons of their life to go deep in God and His Word. John was told to eat the scroll or to understand God's Word in a deep way (Rev. 10:9-11).

B.    The daughters of Jerusalem represent believers who lack discernment of the various operations of the Spirit and the different seasons in God. The Spirit solemnly charges other believers to not disrupt or disturb the devoted ones with the Bride's heart in this season by their opinions and judgments. We can trust Jesus to disturb us when the seasons change as seen clearly in Song 2:8. The Spirit tells those who were insensitive to the ways of the Spirit to not disturb the Bride from this particular season of sitting at the table to be sustained and refreshed by the Word and the Spirit. Many only have one counsel; that is to seek God less and increase in ministry activity.

C.    Solomon charged them by the gazelles or by the does of the field (Song 2:7). By the gazelles or the does" speaks of the importance of gentleness and sensitivity in relating to the young Bride in this season. A gazelle or doe has a sensitive nature and can be easily startled. Many are easily distracted from the Word. We must have sensitivity in relating to others in different seasons.

D.    In the phrase, "Until <u>it</u> pleases", the Hebrew can be translated as <u>it</u>, <u>he</u> or <u>she.</u> The NAS accurately translates the phrase as "Don't awaken love until <u>she</u> pleases" instead of "until <u>it</u> pleases." If the Hebrew was translated "<u>He</u>" it would refer to the Lord being stirred to action by the daughters of Jerusalem. The Lord has no need for this nor does He need to be protected by the gentleness pictured by the gazelles. It is the Bride that must be protected from distraction. Three times Jesus speaks this phrase, "Don't arouse or awaken my love until it pleases." (2:7; 3:5; 8:4). In 8:4, He uses the same phrase "don't disturb her". He embraces her like the other 2 times. However in this third reference, He omits the phrase "by the gazelles of the field" because she is no longer immature and easily tossed to and fro (Eph. 4:14).

## VIII.    SUMMARY: SEVEN CONFESSIONS OF FAITH IN SONG 2:1-7

A.    When we worship or when we are tempted we proclaim the *7 different confessions of the Bride* in (Song 2:1-7): I am the rose of Sharon (2:1); I am the lily of the valleys (2:1); like an apple tree so is Jesus among men (2:3a); I sat down in His shade with great delight, and His fruit was sweet to my taste (2:3b); Jesus brought me to the banqueting house, and His banner over me was love (2:4); I am lovesick (2:5); His left hand is under my head, and his right hand embraces me (2:6).

1.    I am the rose of Sharon (Song 2:1)

2.    I am the lily of the valleys (Song 2:1)

3.    Like an apple tree among the trees of the woods, so is my Beloved among the sons (Song 2:3a)

4.    I sat down in his shade with great delight, and His fruit was sweet to my taste (Song 2:3b)

5.    He brought me to the banqueting house, and His banner over me was love (Song 2:4)

6.    I am lovesick (Song 2:5)

7.    His left hand is under my head, and his right hand embraces me. (Song 2:6)

# Session 13 Challenging the Comfort Zone (Song 2:8-17)

## I.  THE BRIDE'S IDENTITY AND LIFE PURPOSE: BEING JESUS' INHERITANCE

A.  The Bride has just understood her spiritual identity and life purpose as being Jesus' inheritance that the Father promised Him. Jesus wants more than mandatory obedience. He longs for an eternal companion (Bride) who voluntarily chooses to love Him with adoring obedience.

B.  The affections of the human heart are the most precious possession to God. There is nothing that He wants more. Jesus died to redeem and thus possess human affections.

C.  Jesus has a specific plan or purpose for each believer. Its to bring each of us to the place of feasting at God's banqueting table. In other words, to celebrate His love for us and ours for Him. Jesus' primary goal in His leadership over our lives (His banner over us) is to lead us in a way that reveals and imparts His love to us. We are first called to remember His love (Song 1:2, 4).

*⁴ He __brought__ me to the banqueting house, and __His banner over me was love__. (Song 2:4)*

D.  She is lovesick, thus, Jesus' leadership in her life was effective. She cries out for more of Jesus.

*⁵ __Sustain__ me with cakes of raisins, __refresh__ me with apples, __for I am lovesick__. (Song 2:5)*

E.  The Spirit solemnly charged others to not disturb her as she sat at the wedding table under the apple tree. However, the Lord is now disturbing her as the season in her life suddenly changes.

*⁷ I __charge you__…do not __stir up__ (disturb) nor awaken love until __it__ pleases. (Song 2:7)*

## II.  OVERVIEW OF SONG 2:8-17

A.  This passage marks the beginning of a significant turning in the maiden's life. The depth her commitment as seen throughout Song 4-8 flows out of this new revelation of Jesus. He reveals Himself to her as the sovereign King over the nations (the third revelation of Jesus in the Song). She only knew Jesus as the counseling shepherd (Song 1:7-11) and the affectionate Father (Song 1:12) sitting at the table feeding her grapes and apples with love. Now she sees a different aspect of His personality as she sees Him as one who can easily leap over all mountains (obstacles).

B.  In Song 1:4 the maiden prayed, "Draw me and we will run after You." A spiritual crisis in her life begins as Jesus now introduces the "Let us run" phase of her life. This is her second crisis as she discovers her fear. In Song 1:5-7 she faced her first spiritual crisis as she discovered her sin.

C.  Jesus called her out of the comfort zone that she might experience deep partnership with Him. She refuses to obey because of fear as she tells Him to turn and go without her (Song 2:17).

D.  The Lord is testing her confession that the Lord's banner (purpose) over her life is to reveal love to her then to impart it in her. The issue before her is whether she believes that Jesus' leadership is good. In other words, is it safe to obey Jesus 100% even when it is costly and painful?

*Studies in the Song of Solomon: Progression of Holy Passion (2007) – MIKE BICKLE*
Session 13 Challenging the Comfort Zone (Song 2:8-17)

PAGE 70

## III.   JESUS REVEALS HIMSELF TO HER AS THE SOVEREIGN KING

*⁸ The voice of my Beloved! Behold, He comes <u>leaping upon the mountains</u>, skipping upon the hills. 9 My Beloved is like a gazelle or a young stag (adult male deer). (Song 2:8-9a)*

A.      The maiden receives a new revelation of Jesus as the sovereign King. She sees Him as the "Lord of all the nations" who effortlessly conquers all the difficult mountains or high places. She sees Jesus as a gazelle or a young stag who may easily leap in victory on the mountains. A gazelle or young stag (deer) has the ability to easily and quickly ascend a mountain with boundless energy.

B.      King Jesus triumphed over all demonic powers and principalities (Eph. 1:22). He has overcome all obstacles (human and demonic). We command the "mountains of adversity" to move. The hills being smaller than mountains speak of the smaller difficulties that we face.

*²³ For assuredly, I say to you, <u>whoever says to this mountain</u>, 'Be removed and be cast into the sea,' and does not doubt in his heart…those things he says will come to pass… (Mk. 11:23)*

C.      Zerubbabel was to speak grace to the mountains of adversity that stood before him.

*⁷ Who are you, O <u>great mountain</u>? Before Zerubbabel you shall become a plain! And he shall bring forth the capstone with shouts of "Grace, grace to it!" (Zech. 4:7)*

D.      She recognizes the voice of her Beloved or the One that she loves. Jesus speaks tenderly to us in love when He calls us out of the comfort zone to join Him on the dangerous mountains of risk. Each time the Bride speaks to Jesus she calls Him "my Beloved". When she speaks about Jesus to others she refers to Him as the One she loves. Each time Jesus speaks to the Bride in the Song, He calls her, "My love", referencing His affection or "fair one", referencing her beauty. The name "My love" is used 22 times in the Song. The name "Beloved" is used 22 times in the Song.

## IV.   THE WALL OF SECURITY AND PROTECTION

*⁹ Behold, He <u>stands</u> behind <u>our wall</u>; He is looking through the windows, gazing through the lattice. (Song 2:9b)*

A.      Jesus is pictured as standing or as ready for action. He is usually pictured in Scripture as sitting in rest and victory with His feet upon His enemies (Ps. 110:1). When Stephen died the Lord stood up to receive him (Acts 7:55). When He stands, then powerful things are about to happen.

B.      Jesus stands behind a wall looking into the house in which the maiden sits undisturbed. Jesus is described as standing outside the door of the Laodicean church as He knocked (Rev. 3:20).

C.      She rightly describes it as "<u>our</u>" wall. It is not <u>her</u> wall but <u>their</u> wall because she had been led by the Spirit's commission to remain undisturbed at the table until He awakened her (Song 2:7).

D.      Jesus looks at her through the windows with the intention of wooing her with His gaze to draw her forth into a deeper relationship with Himself.

## V.  CALLED OUT OF THE COMFORT ZONE TO DEEP PARTNERSHIP WITH JESUS

*[10] My Beloved spoke, and said to me: "Rise up, My love, My fair one, and come away." (Song 2:10)*

A.  Jesus is ready for action and deep partnership with the maiden. Therefore, He calls her to arise from her comfort and security to come away with Him to conquer the mountains of this fallen world. Jesus commissioned His Bride to work with Him as He brings the nations to obedience.

*[19] Go therefore and make disciples of all the nations… (Mt. 28:19)*

B.  Jesus challenges us to the mountains of total faith and obedience. These high places involve embracing difficult assignments and relationships that challenge our sense of security and comfort. She does not like the risk and heights of the mountains but wants to only sit under the shade tree eating apples with Jesus (Song 2:3).

C.  She doesn't like the risks of walking by faith and the struggles of spiritual warfare. John Wimber said that faith is spelled, "R I S K". Faith (confidence in God) is the way of the Kingdom.

D.  The question is, is it safe to go with Jesus out of the comfort zone? Will we miss out if we obey Him 100%? In the flesh, it seems safer to be in the boat without Jesus instead of being on the water with Him. This is one of the most practical foundational truths that all of us must live in.

E.  She must rise if she is to experience mature partnership with Jesus. We can still go to heaven with "comfort zone Christianity", but we will not of deep in partnership with Him. There are 7 verbs used in Song 2:8-10 to describe the process Jesus uses to awaken us to mature partnership. They include Jesus coming, leaping, skipping, standing, looking, gazing and speaking.

## VI.  THE PROPHETIC SIGNS OF FRUITFULNESS

A.  Jesus encouraged the maiden by revealing that it was the time for the harvest (fruitfulness).

*[11] For lo, the winter is past, the rain is over and gone. 12 The flowers appear on the earth; the time of singing has come, and the voice of the turtledove is heard in our land. 13 The fig tree puts forth her green figs, and the vines with the tender grapes give a good smell. Rise up, My love, My fair one, and come away! (Song 2:11-13)*

B.  He appeals to the signs of the times revealing that the season of harvest is not far away. Therefore, she must quickly learn to fully trust and obey Him now.

C.  The Lord reminds us of His faithfulness to us in the past in the winter season. The winter season is dark with cold rains. It is a difficult time when few things grow outwardly. When we are not sure if we are going to make it, the Lord proves that His banner over us is love. Jesus reminds us of His past interventions and past faithfulness in previous days in our journey. Jesus could say, "The winter is past and the cold rains are over and gone and your heart is still alive in Me." Jesus helps her to remember His love (Song 1:4). This is one of the main things in the Song.

D.      If Jesus was faithfully with us in the past difficulties, He will also be with us in the future ones. There is no reason to believe that Jesus will forget us as we go up the mountain with Him. We have no need to hide behind the wall.

E.      Jesus also points to the future as He highlights the prophetic signs of a soon coming harvest. We are encouraged by seeing the early stages of the Harvest. They guarantee that the full harvest is coming soon. Seeing this gives us urgency to be prepared. We don't have years to waste.

F.      Jesus encouraged the apostles by pointing out that the harvest was ready. Peter had recently given up his fishing business. Within three years, the Jerusalem revival was to begin followed by the revivals in the Book of Acts. It was essential that they learn to fully trust and obey Jesus.

*³⁵ Lift up your eyes and look at the fields, <u>for they are already white for harvest</u>! (Jn. 4:35)*

G.      Jesus points to the signs of the harvest. Flowers appear on the vine to signify that the harvest of grapes will soon follow. It is clear that the "flowers of revival" are budding across the nations.

H.      The voice of the turtledove is heard in Israel at the harvest time. The fig tree puts forth the green figs just before the mature figs. The fragrance of the young tender grapes indicates the harvest.

I.      The time of singing associated with the harvest has begun. The greatest revival in history is around the corner. The singing has begun as houses of prayer are raising up worldwide and as days of worship (Global Day of Prayer, The Call, etc.) gather multitudes to stadiums to sing.

J.      Jesus speaks tenderly to the maiden by calling her "My love and My fair (beautiful) one". Jesus knows that she will refuse Him but she is still as beautiful to Him as when her vineyard was not kept (Song 1:7-8). We are much more motivated to obey Him when we feel loved and beautiful in His eyes. He is not speaking in a harsh judgmental tone.

*¹³ Rise up, My <u>love</u>, My <u>fair</u> one (beautiful), and come away! (Song 2:13)*

## VII.    WE ARE SECURE BEFORE A TENDER GOD THROUGH THE CROSS OF JESUS

*¹⁴ O My dove, in the <u>clefts</u> of the rock, in the secret places of the <u>cliff</u>, let Me see your face, let Me hear your voice; for your voice is <u>sweet</u>, and your face is <u>lovely</u>. (Song 2:14)*

A.      The Lord reveals His tender affection for us even as we struggle through our fears. Jesus affirms her sincerity by calling her, "My dove." A dove speaks of purity and loyalty. The Holy Spirit is pictured as a pure dove. Jesus knew that it was in her heart to obey Him. Jesus knows that she will compromise in Song 2:17, yet He calls her, "My dove." He didn't call her a deceitful snake.

B.      We find our safety in God's grace in two places, the cleft and the cliff. The cleft of the rock speaks of the finished work of the cross. We are to stand with confidence before God in our weakness as we present ourselves to God as we trust in Jesus' death and resurrection.

C.      Jesus was the spiritual Rock in Moses' day and is the rock on which the Church is built.

> *[4] They drank of that spiritual Rock…and that <u>Rock was Christ</u>… (1 Cor. 10:4)*

> *[18] On this <u>rock</u> I will build My Church, and the gates of Hades shall not prevail… (Mt. 16:18)*

D.      God hid Moses in the cleft of the rock (open space in the mountain) to protect him from seeing God's face and being struck dead by the glory of God.

> *[20] You (Moses) cannot see My face; for no man shall see Me, and live… 21 Here is a place by Me, and you shall stand on the rock. 22 So it shall be, while My glory passes by, that I will put you in the cleft of the rock, and will cover you with My hand while I pass by. (Ex. 33:20-22)*

E.      This hiding in the cleft of the rock was a type of salvation through the cross. The cleft of the rock speaks of the "wounds" in Jesus' side that He received on the cross. We hide from the judgment of God in the cleft of the rock or in the atoning death of Jesus.

F.      The "secret places of the cliff" speaks of the mystery of Jesus' resurrection. It is the ultimate secret place in which a Man ascended to God. The cliff ascends upward as the stairway up to heaven as Jacob's ladder (Gen. 28:12-17). "The secret place of the cliff" is translated as "the secret place <u>of the stairs</u>" (KJV) or "the secret place <u>of the steep pathway</u>" (NAS).

G.      Jesus wants us to worship Him and not draw back from Him in times of weakness as we stand in the cleft of the rock and in the secret place of the cliff, or in the mysterious place of the resurrection. We are to stand confident in the grace of God as we ask Him for help.

H.      Jesus wants to see our face and hear our voice in worship and prayer as we cry for help in our weakness. We tell Jesus that we love Him without fearing that we are hypocrites in the process. Some think that when they struggle with sin that their voice is repulsive to God and their face is ugly to Him. God wants us to run <u>to Him</u> in confidence, instead of <u>from Him</u> in condemnation.

> *[14] Let Me see your <u>face</u>, let Me hear your <u>voice</u>; for your voice is <u>sweet</u>, and your face is <u>lovely</u>. (Song 2:14)*

I.      In the garden of Gethsemane, Jesus told Peter to pray in the time of temptation. Jesus prophesied that Peter would deny Jesus three times. This was due to Peter's fear and weak flesh.

> *[34] Before the rooster crows, you will deny Me three times… 41 <u>Watch and pray</u>, lest you enter into temptation. <u>The spirit indeed is willing</u>, but the flesh is weak. (Mt. 26:34, 41)*

J.      Jesus saw Peter's willing spirit even knowing that Peter would stumble that night. Jesus in essence was saying, "Pray to Me Peter. I want to hear your voice. I want to help you."

K.      The Lord enjoys a responsive heart. He enjoys us before we mature. She is still under the tree and behind the wall when He calls her fair (beautiful). Jesus knows our heart and sees our sincere desire to obey. He knows that our immature love will mature in time as hers does (Song 4:7).

## VIII.   PRAYING FOR DELIVERANCE FROM COMPROMISE

A.   The maiden responds to Jesus' exhortation to see her face and hear her voice as she prays for deliverance. She cries out for Jesus' help to catch the little foxes of compromise in her life.

*15 Catch us the foxes, the little foxes that spoil the vines, for our vines have tender grapes. (Song 2:15)*

B.   Foxes are cunning animals that will destroy a vineyard under cover of the night. They are not bold strong lions that attack during the day. They are small, fast and crafty and are hard to catch.

C.   The "little foxes" in the vineyard of our heart speak of our small compromises that include fear, sinful thoughts, attitudes, words and the small yet continual misuse of time and money. This is not referring to a defiance to the Word but to her fear to "to arise" (Song 2:13).

D.   Our vine refers to our fellowship with God. The tender grapes speak of her immaturity in life. She is keeping her vineyard in contrast to Song 1:6. The foxes keep destroying her fruitfulness.

E.   The maiden longs to go deep in God. She cried out that the Lord would sustain and refresh her because she was lovesick (Song 2:5). It is the little areas that hold us back from walking in the Spirit. She sees the seriousness of small areas that prevent her from going deep in God.

F.   We want more in God than just avoiding scandalous sin. We want our vineyard to be full of mature fruit. The issues of unwholesome speech, unclean thoughts and attitudes that resist servanthood and humility are the little foxes that destroy our intimacy with the Lord. Jesus is calling her out of the comfort zone, but the little foxes are destroying her vineyard.

G.   She prayed, "Catch us the foxes". In other words, we cannot catch them by ourselves but we cry for God's help. She acknowledges the presence of the little foxes (her compromise) in her life and then offers continual prayer for help. The Lord is so willing to help us.

## IX.   SHE EXPRESSES HER SINCERE LOVE FOR JESUS

*16 My Beloved is mine, and I am His. He feeds his flock among the lilies. (Song 2:16)*

A.   She states her spiritual identity. She knows who she is as a lover of God. When we struggle we do not cease to be a genuine lover of God nor do we cease to be loved by God. Our face does not cease to be beautiful to God and our voice in worship does not become offensive to Him.

B.   She sees Jesus as her Beloved or the One she loves. She declares, "I am His." Jesus' ownership over her heart will eventually be seen in her life. Her heart is His or it belongs to Him. Her love for God is expressed in the midst of her stumbling. She does not feel cast aside by the Lord because of her struggle. She is not a hopeless hypocrite. Her confidence is steadfast. She cries, "I know You are mine and that am Yours. I am not drawing back." She is sincere yet not mature.

C.    She asks Jesus to feed her several times (Song 1:7, 12; 2:4-5). Now, Jesus wants to feed her in a costly place among the lilies or in the place of her obedience and purity. Lilies speak of purity (Song 2:1-2; 5:3, 13; 6:2-3). She knows that her life purpose is to live in the purity of the lily in every area of her life and to catch all the little foxes (Song 2:1-2).

D.    In Song 2:1, "I am the lily of the valley," the lily is in the singular as she discovers her personal identity in the Lord. However, here the lilies are in the plural as they speak of the corporate people of God who love Jesus like she does.

      *³³ Do not be deceived: "Evil company corrupts good habits." ³⁴ Awake to righteousness, and do not sin; for some (in the congregation) do not have the knowledge of God. (1 Cor. 15:33-34)*

## X.    HER PAINFUL COMPROMISE

A.    She now gives her answer to Jesus' command to arise to join Him on the mountains (Song 2:13). She refuses to rise up. Instead, she tells Him to, "Turn to leap on the mountains as a gazelle without her." She refuses to obey Him because of fear due to her immaturity not rebellion.

      *¹⁷ Until the day breaks and the shadows flee away, <u>turn</u>, my Beloved, and be like a gazelle or a young stag upon the mountains of Bether. (Song 2:17)*

B.    With deep sadness she acknowledges that Jesus must go and be like the gazelle of Song 2:8. At the end of the Song, she calls out for Jesus again to be like a gazelle or a young stag (Song 8:14).

C.    She acknowledges the dark shadows in her heart. These are areas of her life that are not fully in the light. The day break comes in the morning when new light is present. It is the time when the dark shadows or the gray areas in her life are gone.

D.    She says to turn and go until the light of day breaks so as to provide her new light in a new day.

E.    In Song 4:6 goes eventually obeys as she arises to go with Jesus to the mountain. In this verse, Jesus answers her prayer by catching this "fox of fear" in her life. We are created to live in the high places with Jesus in the extravagant devotion of bridal partnership.

F.    She understands that her compromise will lead to fruit in her vineyard being destroyed or in separation in her intimacy with God. Jesus turns and goes for a season. Jesus honors our voluntary decision to draw back. Our relationship with Jesus is based on voluntary love.

G.    The word Bether in the Hebrew means "separation." Some Bible translations use the word "separation" instead of Bether. The mountains are the obstacles that bring separation. She acknowledges that there will be a separation as Jesus goes to "the mountains of separation." In Song 3:1, He separates from her until she repents and cries out in obedience (Song 3:2).

H.    She knows that her weakness does not mean that her love for Jesus is false. She continues to call Him "my Beloved Jesus".

## XI.    FOUR KEY STATEMENTS OF PROGRESSION

A.    There are four times in the Song where you are going to see a phrase repeated. The Lord is causing a progression of maturity to take place in her life and it is important to look over these verses in order to become familiar with it.

B.    The SONG describes her progression from being self-centered to being God-centered in 4 key statements. Four times through the book she changes and redefines her experience. She starts from being only self-conscious and ends up with a mature God-centeredness. We can follow her maturity throughout the SONG through these four statements which are in strategic places. They are statements of the progression of her maturity. Notice the transition from a self-centered to a God-centered focus in the 4 inheritance statements (1:14; 2:16; 6:3; 7:10). In the beginning stages, her <u>own</u> enjoyment of Jesus is her only focus. She talks about what He is <u>to her</u> without much awareness of what she is <u>to Him</u>. In 2:16 and 6:3 and then finally 7:10, she uses this same language but changes the order to express her concern about what she is <u>to Jesus</u>. Jesus is her inheritance.

C.    Her initial focus is **only** upon her spiritual pleasure. This is acceptable to Jesus as a beginning place in the grace of God. Her only focus is that she is loved and has an inheritance in Him. She has little regard at this stage for His inheritance in her.

*¹³ My Beloved <u>is to me</u>… (1:13-14)*

D.    In her second focus she is saying, "He is mine, He belongs to me. However, I now realize that I also belong to Him." She now adds a new dimension of His ownership of her life. She now sees the necessity of loving Him because she is His inheritance. However, it is her secondary concern at this stage of maturity.

*¹⁶ My beloved <u>is mine</u> and I <u>am His</u>. (2:16)*

E.    In her third focus she is saying the same words as in 2:16, however, she changes the order. She says, "I belong to Him and I continue to acknowledge that He is still mine. He belongs to me. My beloved is mine." The third progression says the same 2 truths but the order changes. She says, "It is His agenda first and my agenda second." She reverses the priority of her concern. His inheritance in her is now first in her heart. Her inheritance in Him is vital, yet secondary.

*³ I am <u>my Beloved's</u> and He <u>is mine</u>. (6:3)*

F.    In her fourth and final focus she is saying, "I belong to Him and what He desires is all I focus on. The fact that His desire is for me makes me want to make sure that I am 100% His. He owns me entirely. His concerns are what I care about most."

*¹⁰ I am <u>My Beloved's</u> and <u>His</u> desire is toward me. (7:10)*

---

## Session 14 God's Loving Discipline (Song 3:1-5)

### I. REVIEW OF SONG 2:8-17

A. The maiden received a new revelation of Jesus as the King or "Lord of all" who conquered the mountains. Jesus was like a gazelle who leapt victoriously over all the mountains (obstacles).

> *⁸ The voice of my Beloved! Behold, He comes <u>leaping upon the mountains</u>, skipping upon the hills. 9 My Beloved is like a gazelle or a young stag (adult male deer). (Song 2:8-9a)*

B. Jesus called her to rise up and come away with Him to the mountains (high places). This would involve embracing new assignments that required a new measure of faith and obedience. This challenged her security and comfort. In the maiden's original prayer she cried to Jesus, *"Draw me away! We will run after you"* (Song 1:4). Jesus now called her out of the comfort zone to a new place in the Spirit so that she might experience a deeper partnership with Him.

> *¹⁰ My Beloved…said to me: "<u>Rise up</u>, My love, My fair one, and <u>come away</u>." (Song 2:10)*

C. The maiden does not obey the call to rise up but rather tells Jesus to turn and go to the mountains without her. She does this because of her fear (spiritual immaturity not rebellion). The day break comes in the morning when new light is present and the dark areas in her life are gone.

> *¹⁷ Until the day breaks and the shadows flee away, <u>turn</u>, my Beloved, and be like a gazelle or a young stag upon the mountains of Bether. (Song 2:17)*

### II. OVERVIEW OF SONG 3:1-5

A. The Lord's response to the maiden's refusal to obey is to lovingly discipline her by causing His manifest presence to be lifted off her heart. He is not angry at her but jealously wants her to share His values as a mature Bride that she might walk in deeper partnership with Him.

B. The Father loves us too much to allow us to come up short of being the glorious mature Bride of Christ. He did this for her spiritual well-being. The Lord pries our fingers off the things that hold us in bondage. The cost of obedience is high. However, the cost of disobedience is higher. To neglect to obey the Holy Spirit's leadership is costly.

C. The Lord lifts the sense of His presence from the hearts of His beloved for several reasons. First, to alert us to the seriousness of our compromise that refuses to more deeply embrace the Holy Spirit's leadership. Second, to humble us so as to cause us to be aware of our need for Him. Third, to awaken deep hunger in us for Jesus.

D. We must be confident that God in His love for us will manifest His zeal or jealousy over us. God jealously requires that we live in wholehearted obedience. He zealously insists on that which deepens our relationship with Him and results in our greatness.

> *⁵ Do you think the Scripture says in vain, "The Spirit…in us <u>yearns jealously</u>"? (Jas 4:5)*

---

## III.    GOD'S DISCIPLINE IS NOT THE SAME AS HIS REJECTION OF US

A.    The message of the Song is that God enjoys us even in our weakness. However, this does not mean that He <u>approves</u> all that we do. He corrects the areas of our life that He disapproves of so that He might remove all that hinders love (holiness) in us.

*¹⁰ He (disciplines us) for our profit, that we may be <u>partakers of His holiness</u>. (Heb. 12:10)*

B.    When the Lord disciplines us He reveals His displeasure with an area in our life. This is not the same thing as God's displeasure with us as a person. God can be displeased with a certain behavior without despising us as a person. Some mistake divine correction for divine rejection, but it is proof of His love. God hates the sin yet delights in the one He disciplines (Heb. 12:6).

*¹² Whom the LORD <u>loves</u> He corrects, <u>just as</u> a father the son in whom he <u>delights</u>. (Prov. 3:12)*

C.    Jesus rebukes yet loves believers that are in need of repentance. Jesus rebukes them and calls them to repent because He loves them. Then He invites these very people to sit on His Throne.

*¹⁹ As many as I <u>love</u>, I <u>rebuke</u> and <u>chasten</u>. Therefore be zealous and <u>repent</u>…21 To him who overcomes I will grant to sit with Me on My Throne… (Rev. 3:19, 21)*

D.    To be disciplined means God cares and has not given up on us. It is a terrible thing to "get away with" sin long term because that means God is giving that person over to their sin. God's discipline is proof that He has not given up on us (Rom. 1:24-28).

*²⁴ <u>God gave them up</u> to uncleanness, in the lusts of their hearts… (Rom. 1:24)*

*³² When we are <u>judged</u>, we are <u>chastened</u> by the Lord, <u>that we may not be condemned</u> with the world. (1 Cor. 11:32)*

E.    God feels the pain of those He disciplines and continues to consider them as His dearly beloved.

*⁹ In <u>all</u> their affliction <u>He was afflicted</u>…in His love…He redeemed them… (Isa 63:9)*

*⁷ I have given the <u>dearly beloved</u> of My soul into the hand of her enemies. (Jer. 12:7)*

F.    When we neglect to honestly and thoroughly confront sin in our heart <u>we are not loved less by God</u> but we do suffer loss in several ways. We minimize our ability to experience the joy of our salvation, the spirit of revelation, godly fellowship and to receive eternal rewards.

G.    God has <u>tender patience</u> for a season with believers who do not repent. They must not confuse His patience with His <u>approval</u>. Jesus gave Jezebel and her disciples in Thyatira time to repent.

*²¹ I gave her (Jezebel) <u>time to repent</u> of her immorality…22 I will cast her into a sickbed, and <u>those</u> who commit adultery with her into great tribulation, unless they repent… (Rev. 2:21-22)*

H.    God patiently suffers long with us in His love as He works to lead us to repentance.

*⁴ Do you despise the riches of His goodness, <u>forbearance</u>, and <u>longsuffering</u>, not knowing that the goodness of God <u>leads you to repentance</u>? (Rom. 2:4)*

## IV.    GOD'S MANIFEST PRESENCE IS WITHDRAWN FROM THE MAIDEN

A.    The maiden sought God but did not find Him. This was a new experience for her. All through Song 1-2 when she sought Him she found Him in great sweetness.

*¹ By __night__ on my bed __I sought the One I love__; I sought Him, but __I did not find Him__. 2 "I will rise now," I said, "and go about the city; in the streets and in the squares I will seek the One I love." I sought Him, but I did not find Him. (Song 3:1-2)*

B.    There are four different "nights" in our spiritual life in which we must seek the Lord.

1.    **The night hours:** we sometimes seek God in the night hours because of our godly desperation to know Him through the inconvenience of these hours.

2.    **The night of pain:** in difficult circumstances as when David ran from Saul and Joseph was in the dungeon; they did not give up by concluding God's promises were false.

3.    **The night of temptation:** in times of failure and darkness we must continue to seek God.

4.    **The dark night of the soul:** in the Middle Ages some spoke of the dark night of the soul indicating God's presence being temporarily withdrawn in times of obedience (Song 5:6).

C.    The maiden was not supposed to be on her bed but on the mountains with the Lord. She was on "her bed" as contrasted to "their bed" or couch (Song 1:16; 3:7). Their partnership is disrupted.

D.    Her heart is set on loving Jesus in her struggles. She is not a hopeless hypocrite because of her fear to obey. We can continue to call Jesus "the One I love" even before we have victory in every area of our life. Sometimes we face a mountain of faith/obedience that seems out of reach. That is why it is a mountain. In between mountains are valleys. We're still lovers of God in the valley.

*¹ By night on my bed __I sought the One I love__; I sought Him, but I did not find Him. (Song 3:1)*

E.    She continues to seek God through the familiar spiritual disciplines of prayer and meditation on the Word as she did in the past (Song 2:3-5). Now she does not feel His presence because He requires a new measure of obedience. Prayer and fasting is no substitute for obedience.

*⁴ When Gideon came to the Jordan, he and the 300 men who were with him crossed over, __exhausted but still in pursuit__. (Judges 8:4)*

F.    When we feel nothing we must trust God's Word that He will draw near if we draw near Him.

*⁸ __Draw near to God__ and __He will draw near to you__. Cleanse your hands, you sinners; and purify your hearts, you double-minded. (Jas 4:8)*

*³ Who may ascend into the hill of the LORD? Or who may stand in His holy place? 4 He who has __clean hands__ and a __pure heart__… (Ps. 24:3-4)*

G.  God requires that we stir ourselves up to take hold of Him when He hides His face from us.

> *⁷ There is no one who calls on Your name, <u>who stirs himself up to take hold of You</u>; for You have hidden Your face from us, and have consumed us because of our iniquities. (Is. 64:7)*

H.  <u>*The Jer. 20:7 principle*</u>: in Jeremiah's youth, the Lord revealed His beauty to him and caused Him to love God. Jeremiah prophesied to the political and religious leaders of Israel. They did not receive him but put him in prison. Jeremiah then decided to quit prophesying. Then God's fire burned in him. You caused me to love You and now I am so connected to you I cannot walk away from You. In Song 1-2, the Lord connected the maiden's heart to God's love.

> *O LORD, You <u>induced</u> (deceived NAS/NIV) me, and I was <u>persuaded</u> (deceived NAS/NIV); You are stronger than I, and have prevailed….8 Because the word of the LORD was made to me a reproach and a derision daily. 9 Then I said, "<u>I will not…speak anymore in His name.</u>" But His word was in my heart like a <u>burning fire</u> shut up in my bones; I was weary of holding it back, and I could not. (Jer. 20:7-9)*

V.  **THE YOUNG BRIDE ADDS OBEDIENCE TO HER PRAYERS**

> *² "<u>I will rise now</u>," I said, "and go about the city; in the streets and in the squares <u>I will seek the One I love</u>." I sought Him, but I did not find Him. 3 The watchmen who go about the city found me; I said, "Have you seen the One I love?" (Song 3:2-3)*

A.  The maiden now arises as she was commanded to do in Song 2:10. Jesus withholds His presence to cause us to diligently seek His face and to draw us out of fear, unbelief and compromise. He holds out until we rise up and come to Him in new areas of obedience. The only safe place is in rising up in partnership with Him in faith and obedience.

B.  The pain of losing His presence motivates her to arise off her bed and leave the comfort zone. Jesus hides His face because He knows He can produce earnestness in our hearts by hiding His face. Jesus knows that she cannot live without His presence. Our soul becomes desperate for more of God as we remember former seasons of sweetness. She adds obedience to her prayer. She understands that prayer alone will not solve her problem. It requires active obedience.

C.  She arises to go about the city among the streets and squares which is where the people interact. This is the place of risk, conflict, danger and increased spiritual warfare outside of the comfortable bed and safety of the wall (Song 1:16; 2:9).

D.  Jacob wrestled with God through the night (Gen. 32:24-30). Jacob refused to give up until he touched God. He is a picture of prayer that wrestles with God until the breakthrough comes. Hosea described Jacob as seeking God earnestly with tears and supplication (Hos. 12:2-6).

E.  A friend of mind (Michael Sullivant) had a dream of wrestling with his son who he allowed to pin him. His son smiled and said, "I won dad." My friend felt pleasure in wrestling with his son. The Lord said to him, "I allow Myself to be pinned by you because it brings Me pleasure. God's heart is delighted when we wrestle Him so that our hearts may grow in love for Jesus.

## VI. JESUS' PRESENCE RETURNS IN RESPONSE TO HER OBEDIENCE

*⁴ Scarcely had I passed by them, when <u>I found the One I love</u>. <u>I held Him and would not let Him go</u>, until I had brought Him to the house of my mother, and into the chamber of her who conceived me. (Song 3:4)*

A. She found Jesus only as she rose up to seek Him in obedience. The Lord is bound by His own affection to respond to our earnestness. He will not long refuse us. He wants us to prevail!

B. ***Principle of spiritual hunger***: If there is something in the Word that we can't live without, we will receive it in due time. However, if we can live without it, then we will go without it. If you want something in God's will so much that you can't live without it, you'll have it in due time."

C. We do not have to live spiritually bored and in sin and unbelief. We can walk in the anointing to carefully obey Jesus in every area of our life even before the mountains (Ezek. 36:26).

D. She has a new resolution to hold on to Jesus with a determination that results from her painful season of spiritual struggle. She "never lets go of Him" throughout the remainder of the Song.

E. Times of spiritual turmoil sometimes birth "holy violence" in us to hold on to Jesus and to never again allow compromise to be tolerated in our lives (Mt. 11:12). She has an unquenchable resolution to do the will of God.

F. The maiden's resolve to obey extended to even the most difficult places.

*⁴ I held Him and would not let Him go, <u>until I had brought Him to the house of my mother</u>, and into the chamber of her who conceived me. (Song 3:4)*

G. She is an anointed ambassador of Jesus. She actually brings Jesus to places that He will not go without her obedience as a vehicle of the Father's choice. At the end of the SONG she brings Jesus to all people (Song 8:2).

H. The mother is a picture of the church. Those who do God's will are Jesus' mother and brother (Mt. 12:46-50). Mother Israel gave birth to the redeemed (Rev. 12:5, 17). Often the most difficult places to bring Jesus is among familiar family relationships.

I. Home represents the most difficult place to some because it is so familiar. A prophet has no honor in his own home. Bringing Jesus to her home is a significant manifestation of obedience to His command to arise.

J. Home also represents the place of smallness. We do not need to get on a plane before we do ministry. We can minister to the small number in our home and neighborhood.

## VII.  THE HOLY SPIRIT GUARDS US IN STRATEGIC SPIRITUAL SEASONS (SONG 2:7)

*⁷ I charge you, O daughters of Jerusalem, by the gazelles or by the does of the field, do not stir up (disturb) nor awaken love until it pleases. (Song 2:7)*

A.   The Holy Spirit speaks here. He has ordained strategic seasons in each person's spiritual life. There are seasons, where He desires to establish our heart in new and deep revelations of His heart. The Spirit's agenda for the Bride in this season was to awaken lovesickness in her as she went deep in the Word as she fed on apples and grapes at the banqueting house (Song 2:3-5). Many do not see the necessity of dedicating seasons of their life to go deep in God and His Word. John was told to eat the scroll or to understand God's Word in a deep way (Rev. 10:9-11).

B.   The daughters of Jerusalem represent believers who lack discernment of the various operations of the Spirit and the different seasons in God. The Spirit solemnly charges other believers to not disrupt or disturb the devoted ones with the Bride's heart in this season by their opinions and judgments. We can trust Jesus to disturb us when the seasons change as seen clearly in Song 2:8. The Spirit tells those who were insensitive to the ways of the Spirit to not disturb the Bride from this particular season of sitting at the table to be sustained and refreshed by the Word and the Spirit. Many only have one counsel; that is to seek God less and increase in ministry activity.

C.   Solomon charged them by the gazelles or by the does of the field (Song 2:7). By the gazelles or the does speaks of the importance of gentleness and sensitivity in relating to the young Bride in this season. A gazelle or doe has a sensitive nature and can be easily startled. Many are easily distracted from the Word. We must have sensitivity in relating to others in different seasons.

D.   In the phrase, "Until it pleases", the Hebrew can be translated as it, he or she. The NAS accurately translates the phrase as "Don't awaken love until she pleases" instead of "until it pleases." If the Hebrew was translated "He" it would refer to the Lord being stirred to action by the daughters of Jerusalem. The Lord has no need for this nor does He need to be protected by the gentleness pictured by the gazelles. It is the Bride that must be protected from distraction.

E.   Three times Jesus speaks this phrase, "Don't arouse or awaken my love until it pleases." (2:7; 3:5; 8:4). In 8:4, He uses the same phrase "don't disturb her". He embraces her like the other 2 times. However in this third reference, He omits the phrase "by the gazelles of the field" because she is no longer immature and easily tossed to and fro (Eph. 4:14).

F.   The Holy Spirit's charge is to not pressure the Bride to move on until she is prepared.

G.   The Lord has each of us on a tailor made journey made for who we are and where we are going. Jesus is telling other believers to not disrupt her. He does not want her disrupted from this particular season by unsanctified mercy and false comfort that undermines the Lord's discipline.

# Session 15 Revelation of Jesus' Safe Leadership (Song 3:6-11)

## I.  REVIEW OF SONG 2:8-3:5

A.  The maiden received a new revelation of Jesus as the King or "Lord of all" who conquered the mountains (obstacles). Jesus is like a gazelle who leaps victoriously over all the obstacles.

> *⁸ The voice of my Beloved! Behold, He comes <u>leaping upon the mountains</u>… (Song 2:8)*

B.  Jesus called her out of the comfort zone to a new place in the Spirit to experience more of Him.

> *¹⁰ My Beloved…said to me: "<u>Rise up</u>, My love, My fair one, and <u>come away</u>." (Song 2:10)*

C.  The maiden does not obey the call to rise up but rather tells Jesus to turn and go to the mountains without her. She does this because of her fear (spiritual immaturity not rebellion).

> *¹⁷ Until the day breaks and the shadows flee away, <u>turn</u>, my Beloved, and be like a gazelle or a young stag upon the mountains of Bether. (Song 2:17)*

D.  When Jesus called the maiden to arise it changed certain dynamics in her relationship with Jesus. Once Jesus raises the standard of what He wants in our faith and obedience in each season of our life then we must respond or go backwards in our relationship with Him. Yesterday's measure of obedience in not sufficient for today if we want to grow in the things of the Spirit. The Holy Spirit continually increases the light that He gives us and then makes us responsible to respond to it. He withdraws His presence if we neglect to respond so that He might get our attention.

E.  God's manifest presence is withdrawn from the maiden. She sought God but did not find Him. This was a new experience for her.

> *¹ By <u>night</u> on my bed <u>I sought the One I love</u>; I sought Him, but <u>I did not find Him</u>. 2 "I will rise now," I said, "and go about the city; in the streets and in the squares I will seek the One I love." I sought Him, but I did not find Him. (Song 3:1-2)*

F.  Jesus' response to our disobedience is to lovingly discipline us by lifting the sense of His manifest presence from our heart. He is not angry but jealously wants a deeper partnership.

G.  The Father loves us too much to allow us to come short of the fullness of what Jesus wants. He does this for our spiritual well-being. The Lord pries our fingers off the things that hold us in bondage. The cost of obedience is high. However, the cost of disobedience is higher. The Lord lifts the sense of His presence from our hearts to alert us to the seriousness of compromise that refuses to more deeply embrace the Holy Spirit's leadership and that we would resolve to never allow anything to get in the way of our relationship with the Holy Spirit.

H.  When the Lord disciplines us He reveals His displeasure with an area in our life. Some mistake divine correction for divine rejection, but it is proof of His love. God hates the sin yet delights in the one He disciplines (Heb. 12:6).

> *¹² Whom the LORD <u>loves</u> He corrects, <u>just as</u> a father the son in whom he <u>delights</u>. (Prov. 3:12)*

## II.    OVERVIEW OF SONG 3:6-11

A.    This is the fourth revelation of Jesus in the Song. Jesus is revealed to the Bride as a "safe Savior". She gains revelation of Jesus' safe leadership as He leads us out of the wilderness of this fallen world. This does not mean that we will not have difficulties. It means we are in a place where our heart will mature in obedient, grateful, trusting love for God. She received this revelation when she "held on" to Him (Song 3:4).

B.    The only safe place for our hearts is in the revelation of Jesus as the Bridegroom King who enables us to walk in 100-fold obedience and faith in facing the mountains. This will be an essential revelation during the Great Tribulation.

C.    The Holy Spirit asks a question (Song 3:6) then provides a 2-part answer along with an exhortation. First, He uses military language to reveal how safe we are under Jesus' leadership (Song 3:7-8). Second, He uses a royal wedding procession to reveal His safe leadership (Song 3:9-10). The pinnacle of our salvation is in knowing Jesus as our Bridegroom King (Song 3:11).

D.    The devil lies to us about Jesus not being a safe leader. This foundational revelation prepares the Bride for the fearless and deep commitment that she walks in throughout Song 4-8.

## III.   THE HOLY SPIRIT ASKS A SEARCHING QUESTION (SONG 3:6)

*⁶ **Who is this** coming out of the wilderness (of this fallen world) like pillars of smoke, perfumed with myrrh and frankincense, with all the merchant's fragrant powders? (Song 3:6)*

A.    We cannot be dogmatic about who is asking this searching question. In the spiritual interpretation, I believe it is the Holy Spirit as the unnamed person who represents Jesus. On three occasions, a question is asked using the same language "who is this?" (Song 3:6; 6:10; 8:5). It is clear that the Holy Spirit is the one asking the question on two occasions (Song 6:10; 8:5). Therefore, it seems reasonable that it is also the Holy Spirit speaking here.

B.    It is probably not the Bride asking the question, because in Song 3:11, the speaker refers to the wedding as "His" wedding. If the Bride was speaking she would refer to it as "our" wedding. Possibly, the Spirit is communicating this message through the lips of the Bride to the daughters.

C.    The Holy Spirit asks a question that points to the entrance of Jesus the king (v. 9) into the Eternal City after His crucifixion, resurrection and ascension. It is a question that provokes awe and wonder not perplexity. This question points to the majesty and wonder of the ascending Christ. This language describes Jesus in context to the Old Testament sacrificial system.

D.    Jesus came up victorious out of the wilderness of this fallen age. Israel's 40 year journey through the wilderness is a picture of our struggle in this fallen world on our way to the promised land. In Song 8:5, the Bride comes up out of the wilderness leaning upon her Beloved.

E.      Jesus ascending to heaven in God's glory is referred to here as pillars of smoke (Exod. 19:18; Isa 6:4; Rev 8:4). In the language of the tabernacle, smoke referred to the manifestation of God's presence. As the smoke of the sacrifices ascended upward as a sweet savor to God, so Jesus' sacrifice in God's fire ascended upwards like a pillar of smoke.

*⁸ The Temple was filled with <u>smoke</u> from the glory of God… (Rev. 15:8)*

F.      The ascended Christ is described as being perfumed with myrrh and frankincense and all the merchant's fragrant powders. Myrrh speaks of Jesus' death. In the ancient world, it was a costly fragrant burial spice. Jesus was perfumed with myrrh as He died on the cross.

G.      Frankincense speaks of Jesus' fragrant intercession (Heb.7:25). As the High Priest went into the Holy of Holies with a censer of frankincense (incense), so Jesus entered the Holy of Holies in heaven with His censer filled with intercession. The golden bowls of incense at the altar in heaven speak of our prayers (Rev. 5:8; 8:3-5).

H.      The merchant's powders speak of Jesus' commitment to us. Jesus spoke of merchants who sold everything to purchase beautiful pearls (His Bride). A merchant was scented as a result of handling (buying and selling) the perfumed powders in the marketplace. Jesus is the perfumed merchant who sold everything in His deep commitment to us.

*⁴⁵ The Kingdom…is like a merchant seeking beautiful pearls, 46 who, when he found one pearl of great price, went and <u>sold all</u> that he had and bought it. (Mt. 13:45-46)*

I.      Jesus suffered for us, how much more will He care for and protect us? His incarnation and death (v. 6) prove that He has our good in mind. During our journey in this wilderness, He protects us from our sin and all that assaults us by His death (myrrh) and His intercession (frankincense). We can risk leaving the comfort zone because He is so committed to us (merchant powders).

*³¹ If God is for us, who can be against us? 32 He who did not spare His own Son, but delivered Him up for us all, <u>how shall He not…freely give us all things</u>? (Rom. 8:31-32)*

## IV.    THE HOLY SPIRIT'S MINISTRY OF PROTECTION (SONG 3:7-8)

*⁷ Behold, it is <u>Solomon's couch</u>, with sixty valiant men around it, of the valiant of Israel. 8 They all hold swords, being expert in war. Every man has his sword on his thigh because of fear in the night. (Song 3:7-8)*

A.      We see the protection and security that we have in God's grace as described in military terms.

B.      King Solomon is a type of King Jesus in the Song. Solomon's couch or palanquin (v. 9), was a chariot used in his royal wedding processions. It was carried on the shoulders of the royal guard. Solomon's couch is the place his bride sat near him in security through the wilderness journey. Solomon's couch came through the wilderness to Shunem (the bride's city) to take her to his Jerusalem palace. The town's people saw a cloud of dust as the royal procession approached. They had never seen such a procession with valiant soldiers with swords and battle equipment.

C.    Solomon's couch speaks of the *"gospel couch"* or the wedding chariot. It has been prepared for us because Jesus came up victoriously out of the wilderness of this fallen world. Jesus rests on His couch with final triumph over all His enemies (Ps. 110:1-3; Eph. 1:20-22).

*²⁰ He (the Father) **worked in Christ when He raised Him from the dead and <u>seated Him</u> at His right hand in the heavenly places, 21 far above all principality and power… (Eph. 1:20-21)***

D.    In this couch we are <u>seated with Christ</u> in heavenly places and will be enthroned (Rev. 3:21).

*⁶ **Raised us up together, and made us <u>sit together in the heavenly places</u> in Christ… (Eph. 2:6)***

E.    The "gospel couch" provides all that we need for our hearts to be safe in our journey through the wilderness. The gospel chariot escorts us as a Bride sitting next to the King as we travel through the wilderness of this age in the protection and safety that it provides for us from sin and Satan.

F.    Solomon had 60 valiant men surrounding his couch to defend his bride through the wilderness from the enemy. In a spiritual sense, it points to spiritual warfare. Only a king could afford the abundant security of 60 highly skilled soldiers who were experts in war.

G.    The guard around the couch speaks of the Spirit's keeping, and protecting ministry pictured in military language. Solomon's guard pictures the Holy Spirit's extravagant protection. These valiant warriors picture God's extravagant protection. Solomon continues to use "tabernacle language." There were 60 pillars of support in Moses' tabernacle.

H.    The soldiers were "men of Israel" (native born) in contrast to being mercenaries or foreign soldiers who would flee from danger because they only served for money. The men of Israel had loyal and courageous hearts in defending the king's chariot.

I.    The bride is not afraid of the enemy's ambush as she sits in this couch because she is surrounded by valiant expert soldiers. The enemy seeks to ambush us. Jesus watches over us as depicted by the 60 valiant men surrounding us. The Spirit surrounds us in our journey.

J.    These soldiers all "hold swords" or are skilled in the use of a sword. They are "experts in war." In other words, they are not novices but are seasoned warriors. Their sword was girded on their thigh to be drawn at a moments notice in contrast to a soldier who takes his sword off while sleeping. These were diligent vigilant soldiers who were ready for action because of the fear of the night which speaks of the power of darkness or the attack of the enemy (Eph. 6:12).

*⁸ **They all hold swords, being expert in war. Every man has his sword on his thigh Because of fear in the night. (Song 3:8)***

K.    The Holy Spirit is an expert in war knowing every scheme of Satan (Eph. 6:10-12). He uses many agencies in the grace of God. For example, He may give us a prophetic dream, open or shut a door, stir someone to intercede for us, send an angel, release the gifts of the Spirit through us, give us revelation of the Word to reveal the Father's affection or Jesus' cross to lead us to safety. His protection over us is passionate, skillful, and diligent.

L.    He is able to keep us from quitting or backsliding. There is no sin too difficult for Him, if we give our hearts to God and stay within the simple boundaries of scriptural principles.

*¹³ No temptation has overtaken you except such as is common to man; but God is faithful, who will not allow you to be tempted beyond what you are able, but with the temptation will also make the way of escape, that you may be able to bear it. (1 Cor. 10:13)*

*²⁴ Now to Him who is able to keep you from stumbling, and to present you faultless before the presence of His glory with exceeding joy, (Jude 24)*

## V.    JESUS' LOVING SALVATION PROVIDES US GREAT SAFETY (SONG 3:9-10)

*⁹ Of the wood of Lebanon Solomon the king made <u>himself</u> a palanquin: 10 He made its pillars of silver, its support of gold, its seat of purple, is interior paved with love by (for KJV) the daughters of Jerusalem. (Song 3:9-10)*

A.    Our safety is described in the language of a royal wedding procession in (Song 3:9-10). The gospel couch (v. 7) is now described as a palanquin. King Jesus provides an eternal palanquin for us. Solomon made a portable chair enclosed with curtains that was carried by royal attendants.

B.    Solomon specifically "made himself" a chariot to carry his queen. He designed it. Jesus Himself made the palanquin that we rest in. He had to become man to save us. He did not stay in heaven.

C.    The gospel couch is made from the wood of Lebanon. The wood in the tabernacle was covered with gold. The wood spoke of humanity and the gold referred to deity. The cedars of Lebanon were used in building Solomon's temple which housed God's glory. The wood of Lebanon was the most beautiful, fragrant, expensive and strongest wood in Israel. The gospel was made of the strongest yet most costly flesh that ever walked the earth. Jesus came forth in perfect humanity.

D.    The gospel couch was made of silver and gold. Silver speaks of redemption and gold speaks of divine character. The pillars of silver were railings around the royal seat. The support system to the couch was made of gold. The word "support" in the Hebrew is the word "the railing." Its support is of gold or our protection is established on God's infinite wisdom and great power. The Bride never need fall out of this glorious chair.

E.    The gospel seat is purple which speaks of royalty and God's authority. The gospel releases the authority of Jesus through our lives as the enemy seeks to harass us.

F.    The interior tapestry of this palanquin (gospel) is woven by God's love for us. The interior is paved with God's passionate love for the daughters of Jerusalem or for weak people. The interior of the Gospel or its inner workings are decorated by God's love. He is gentle in His dealings.

G.  The gospel was motivated by God's own eternal love for us. It was "paved with love." This speaks of Jesus' affections for us. The inner lining of the gospel chariot is paved with God's love. We feel the love of God for Jesus and for one another. God's plans are only carried out through His love for the saints. "His banner over me is love," is her confession. All that Jesus does is paved in love. This revelation causes us to grow in love in both feeling loved and having the power to love back. We are most safe when God's affections are understood.

H.  The KJV accurately translates, "FOR" the daughters of Jerusalem" instead of the NKJ which wrongly translates it "BY" the daughters. The gospel is paved with love "for" the daughters of Jerusalem, not "by" them. It is the love of Jesus for the daughters, not the love of the daughters for Jesus that is in view.

## VI.   THE HOLY SPIRIT EXHORTS THE WHOLE CHURCH TO THE BRIDAL PARADIGM

*[11] Go forth, O daughters of Zion, and see King Solomon with the crown with which His mother crowned Him on the day of His wedding, the day of the gladness of His heart (Song 3:11).*

A.  We are called to see or gaze on Jesus as the Bridegroom King (Heb 12:2; Phil. 3:8; Isa. 33:17). We are to meditate on Jesus as the King crowned with all authority on His wedding day. When we see Jesus with His crown then we are not afraid of the mountains (Song 2:8-13) .

B.  The mother is a picture of the Church and those who do God's will are Jesus' mother and brother (Mt. 12:46-50). The agency He uses for our spiritual birth is the witness of a member of the Church. God is our father and the Church is spoken of as our mother.

C.  Jesus has many crowns. The wedding crown is unique from the crown gained in conquering a nation. A wedding crown was a distinct crown. Jesus was sorrowful as He entered Gethsemane, but He knew there was coming another day of gladness. The crown is the accumulated response of the redeemed throughout history. There is no greater dignity than being among those who crown Him with our love and make His heart glad. Our greatness and dignity is found walking in the anointing to love Jesus by the power of the Holy Spirit so that we may crown Him with our love. On that day, we will cast our crowns before Him in voluntary love. This defines our life.

D.  The "mother crowned Him". In the earthly human sense, the Church crowns Jesus as King when we respond in voluntary love to His kingship. When we love Jesus with all our heart we crown Him as our personal Bridegroom King. That is the crown He desires more than any other crown. It is the crown that makes Him glad. When we see who He is then we see who we are in Him. When the daughters of Jerusalem see their destiny then they live as the daughters of Zion. The day of His wedding is described in Rev. 19:6-8. It is the day that we fully give Him everything.

E.  How does Jesus feel about the coming wedding? He is glad about it. This is not a political wedding to create a political alliance with another nation. It is not a shotgun wedding.

*[5] As the bridegroom rejoices over the bride, so shall your God rejoice over you. (Isa. 62:5)*

# Session 16 The Cherished Heart: Equipped to Love Jesus (Song 4:1-8)

## I. REVIEW OF SONG 2:8-3:11

A. Jesus called the Bride out of the comfort zone to the mountain tops to experience more of Him. However, she does not obey but tells Jesus to turn and go to the mountains without her.

*⁸ He comes leaping upon the <u>mountains</u>…10 My Beloved said: "Rise up, My love…and come away…17 <u>Turn</u>, my Beloved, and be like a gazelle…on the mountains. (Song 2:8-10, 17)*

B. She experiences God's loving discipline as He removes His manifest presence. She sought Him but did not find Him. The Lord is not angry but jealously wants a deeper partnership (Heb. 12:6)

*¹ By <u>night</u> on my bed <u>I sought the One I love</u>; I sought Him, but <u>I did not find Him</u>. (Song 3:1)*

C. In Song 3:6-11, the Bride gained revelation of Jesus' safe leadership as the Bridegroom King who could enable her to walk in 100-fold obedience in facing the mountains. She sees Jesus as the King who desires her love. We can crown Jesus with our love as King of our heart. The "wedding crown" of love makes Him glad. He desires that crown the most.

*¹¹ Go forth, O daughters…and see King Solomon with the crown with which His mother crowned Him on the day of His wedding, the day of the gladness of His heart (Song 3:11).*

## II. OVERVIEW OF SONG 4:1-8

*¹ Behold, you are fair, My love…you have dove's <u>eyes</u>…your <u>hair</u> is like a flock of goats…2 Your <u>teeth</u> are like shorn sheep...3 Your <u>lips</u> are like…scarlet, and your <u>mouth</u> is lovely. Your <u>temples</u>…are like a piece of pomegranate. 4 Your <u>neck</u> is like the tower of David…5 Your <u>breasts</u> are like fawns…6 <u>I will go my way to the mountain</u>…7 You are <u>all fair</u>, My love, there is no spot in you. 8 Come with Me…My spouse…look from the top of Amana…from the mountains of the leopards. (Song 4:1-8)*

A. After a season of divine discipline, Jesus calls the Bride fair or beautiful <u>while</u> she was yet maturing in her obedience and faith. In Song 4:1-5, Jesus prophetically affirms 8 "budding virtues" in the young Bride's life. Jesus equips us in our weakness by affirmations that overpower Satan's accusations against us (Rev. 12:10).

B. This passage outlines 8 character traits that God wants to come forth in His Bride. The symbolism used here is developed through out the Scripture.
*Dove's eyes:* eyes of single-minded devotion and revelation
*Hair like goats:* dedication to God
*Teeth like shorn sheep:* chewing the meat of the Word
*Lips like scarlet:* speech that is redemptive
*Kisses of the mouth:* intimacy with God
*Veiled temples (cheeks/countenance):* emotions impacted by the grace of God
*Neck like David's tower:* setting our will to obey God
*Breasts like fawns:* the power to edify and nurture others

## III.    SETTING OUR HEART ON JESUS

A.    In Song 4:1-5, we see the cherishing heart of Jesus our Bridegroom King. She responds by setting her heart to fully obey and believe His Word (Song 4:6-8).

B.    Jesus washes and releases His glory in the Church by cherishing us.

*²⁶ that He might sanctify and cleanse her with the <u>washing</u> of water by the Word, 27 that He might present her to Himself a <u>glorious church</u>...29 For no one ever hated his own flesh, but nourishes and <u>cherishes</u> it, just as the Lord does the church. (Eph. 5:26-29)*

C.    God's primary method to change weak believers is to cause us to feel how much He cherishes us. In this way, He removes the stain of our sin and shame from our heart. When we feel cherished, we become confident and bold in our love for Jesus. The power of King David's life was found in feeling loved by God. God's cherishing heart is one of the most prominent themes in the Song.

*³⁵ Your right hand has held me up, <u>Your gentleness has made me great</u>. (Ps. 18:35)*

D.    Jesus cherishes us by esteeming us as His Bride and by treating us with gentleness and affection as He affirms the budding virtues in our lives (even in our weakness when we stumble).

E.    Jesus does not define our life by our struggles. He sees more than our failure. He defines us by the seeds of virtue that are in our heart and what we set our heart on, not only by what we attain. He sees a willing spirit in us (Mt. 26:41). He defines us by our longings to love and obey Him.

F.    Seeing how Jesus defines us determines how we think and feel about ourselves. He sees the seeds of character in our life. He sees the end of our journey with clarity.

G.    When Israel was being attacked by the mighty Midianites, Gideon hid in fear in the winepress (Judges 6). An angel appeared to him and said, "O mighty man of valor." The Lord saw in Gideon what he could not see in himself. The Lord saw seeds of faith and courage that he was not yet operating in. The Lord named Gideon according to what he would become in the future. Gideon went on to become one of Israel's great military leaders.

H.    Jesus called Peter the rock (the unmovable one; Matt.16:18) knowing that he would deny Him in his fear. Peter outwardly looked like a compromiser. Peter's instability was manifest again. The Lord saw the seeds of courage, stability and faithfulness in Peter and named him the rock.

*¹¹ When Peter had come to Antioch, I withstood him to his face, because <u>he was to be blamed</u>; 12 for <u>before</u> certain men came from James, he would eat with the Gentiles; but when they came, he withdrew...<u>fearing</u> those of the circumcision. 13 The rest of the Jews also played the <u>hypocrite</u> with him...even Barnabas was carried away with their <u>hypocrisy</u>. (Gal. 2:11-13)*

I.    We see the Lord's "editing process" in Abraham's life saying that he never wavered in his faith.

*²⁰ He <u>did not waver</u> at the promise of God through unbelief... (Rom. 4:20)*

J.    God's testimony of David is that he did all of God's will and fulfilled God's purpose.

*²² He raised up David…concerning whom He testified and said, "I have found David…a man after My heart, who will do <u>all My will</u>…" 36 For David, after he had <u>served the purpose of God</u> in his own generation, fell asleep… (Acts 13:22, 36; NAS)*

K.    The Lord calls sincere believers the disciples whom God loves (Jn. 13:23; 19:26; 20:2; 21:7, 20).

*²³ There was leaning on Jesus' bosom one of His disciples, whom Jesus loved. (Jn. 13:23)*

L.    The Devil calls us hopeless hypocrites. The enemy wears down many with accusation and condemnation. He wants us to feel like hopeless hypocrites so that we give up. He wants us to confuse immaturity with rebellion so that we give up.

M.    Many spend excessive emotional energy fighting the fires of condemnation and worthlessness. The baggage of condemnation and rejection takes a lot of energy to manage. This prevents us from effectively walking with the Lord because we are preoccupied with failure and shame.

N.    Many focus on measuring their attainment of maturity instead of being focused on setting the intentions of their heart to obey and believe. When we measure our attainment of maturity, we become vulnerable to two spiritual problems.

    1.    If we measure up good, we can feel proud and thus, criticize others who fail.

    2.    If we fail, then we feel condemned and thus, feel like quitting.

O.    Our primary focus is to be on God's emotions (beauty) and in setting the intention of our heart to fully love Him (obey and believe His Word). He will work mature victory in us in His timing.

*¹³ It is God who works in you both to will and to do for His good pleasure. (Phil. 2:13)*

P.    Cherishing is the way a man changes his wife or children. All of God's discipline occurs as He cherishes us. Parents often do not rightly interpret the budding virtues in their children. They see failure instead of the budding seeds of dedication and greatness.

## IV.    WE ARE BEAUTIFUL TO GOD EVEN IN OUR WEAKNESS

A.    Immediately after the maiden's season of discipline (Song 3:1-2), the Lord declares that she is beautiful to Him. Jesus emphasizes the importance of this revelation of her beauty by repeating it two times. The Holy Spirit blasts this divine trumpet before us, "Behold! You are beautiful and I love you. We are changed by the revelation that we are beautiful and loved with affection.

*¹ Behold, you are <u>fair</u> (beautiful), <u>My love</u>! Behold, you are fair! (Song 4:1)*

B.    The revelation that a sincere believer is beautiful to God even in their weakness is foundational to growing in God's grace. The word *fair* is translated in most Bibles as **beautiful**. This is one of the primary themes in the Song (Song 1:8, 15, 16; 2:10, 13, 14; 4:1 , 7, 10; 6:4, 10; 7:1).

C.     The progression of the theme of our beauty through the Song of Solomon is important.

D.     When we see Jesus as a King who is filled with gladness in loving us (Song 3:11) and who sees us as beautiful then we will arise to embrace every sacrifice. This empowers us to ascend any mountain or to face any obstacle.

E.     Next, Jesus affirms 8 "budding virtues" in her life (Song 4:1-5). Each characteristic starts out only in seed form and then they need to be called forth with affirmation. Jesus equips us against Satan's accusations by affirming the seeds of our love and obedience that He sees in our heart.

F.     Jesus speaks blessing on 8 different aspects of her life. He gives us a new name so that we might grow up into it. Every phrase is God's poetic divine romance that aims at the heart in a specific way. These 8 virtues are reflections of the Lord's beauty imparted to us and they make Jesus glad as we love Him in these ways (Song 3:11). These eight virtues will also make our heart glad.

G.     The king spoke to her in agricultural language that she is familiar with since she tended goats and kept vineyards. Each symbol is interpreted by the Scripture.

H.     The King tells her to go to the mountain. Up to this point, she only said yes to arise to go to the city not the mountain (Song 3:2). The Bride does not fully walk it out until Song 5-8. She has only said yes. The Lord values the yes, knowing that she will mature in time.

I.     Three things work together to cause us to come to 100% commitment to obey (Song 4:6). First, she receives divine discipline (Song 3:1-2). Second, she receives fresh revelation of Jesus (Song 3:6-11). Third, she receives fresh revelation of herself in Jesus' eyes (Song 4:1-5).

## V.     EYES: SPIRITUAL UNDERSTANDING AND REVELATION (SONG 4:1)

*¹ You have dove's <u>eyes</u> behind your veil. (Song 4:1)*

A.     Eyes speak of spiritual insight. Paul spoke of the eyes of our understanding (Eph. 1:18). Seeing was Paul's first priority because seeing is the doorway to growing spiritually (Phil 3:8-10; 2 Cor. 3:18). Obedience flows out of perceiving. When we see differently then we feel differently.

B.     Dove's eyes speak of purity and loyalty. The Holy Spirit is pictured as a dove. A dove never mates again when their partner dies. They are known for their loyalty. Dove's eyes can not focus on two things and has no peripheral vision. This speaks of singleness of mind. Instead of being dedicated and secure in God's love one moment then compromising or feeling condemned the next, she was single-minded. Her eyes are fixed upon Him instead of on lusts, failure or success.

C.     She has humility in her revelation. She "hides" behind her veil or holds back some aspects of what God tells. Her secret life in God or her life behind her veil is private. Abundant revelation tempted Paul to pride (2 Cor.12:7-9). Paul taught that knowledge often led to pride (1 Cor. 8:1).

## VI.     HAIR: DEDICATION TO JESUS (SONG 4:1)

A.      The Bride's hair spoke of her dedication to God. The hair of the Nazirite was an outward sign of their consecration or dedication (Num. 6). Anyone who took a Nazirite vow was not permitted to cut their hair. Samson cut his hair and thus broke his vow of dedication and therefore lost his power. Hair also speaks of the beauty of submission to God. Paul spoke of a woman's hair as showing forth her glory and dedication to God's authority (1 Cor. 11:5, 6, 15).

> *¹ Your <u>hair</u> is like a flock of goats, going down from Mount Gilead. (Song 4:1)*

B.      The maiden has a majestic and stately walk as represented by a flock of goats.

> *²⁹ There are three things which are <u>majestic in pace</u>, yes, four which are <u>stately in walk</u>…31 a <u>male goat</u> also, and a king whose troops are with him. (Prov. 30:29-31)*

C.      We walk out our dedication with stateliness or as coming from godly wisdom with dignity. It is common for our dedication to be tainted with fleshly zeal that draws attention to self.

D.      Her stately hair or dedication is the result of being well fed (on Scripture). The goats on Mount Gilead were abundantly fed. It was a fertile area with bountiful places where goats were known to eat in abundance. She was well fed on the love of God and the Word of God.

## VII.    TEETH: HER LIFE IN THE WORD (SONG 4:2)

> *² Your <u>teeth</u> are like a flock of shorn sheep, which have come up from the washing, every one of which bears twins, and none is barren among them. (Song 4:2)*

A.      Teeth speak of the ability to chew meat and thus to receive nourishment. Infants have no teeth to chew meat. Babes in Christ can not receive the meat of the Word (1 Cor. 3:1-2; Heb. 5:12-14). This virtue refers to her ability to receive the meat of God's Word. This 4-part description of her teeth is from an agricultural perspective. Her teeth are strong, abundant and effective.

B.      The wool of an unshaven sheep grows unevenly (unbalanced). Uneven wool speaks of fleshly zeal. The priests of Zadok had to wear linen garments and were forbidden to wear wool because it made them sweat (Ezek. 44:15-18). Our fleshly zeal must be under control of the Holy Spirit.

C.      To come up from the washing speaks of being cleansed from the dirt. As we eat the Word of God our teeth are like sheep that came up from the washing. The word washes us (Eph. 5:26).

D.      Diligence in the Word results in an abundant impact on others. Her teeth were like a flock of shorn sheep in which every one bore twins and none is barren. Her ministry impact is fruitful without spiritual barrenness. To bear twins speaks of abundant fruitfulness. By meditating on the Word, we can keep our lives as clean as sheep who just emerged from the washing. This cleanliness of teeth speaks of her commitment to meditate on God's Word (1 Tim. 4:6-16). Song 4:1-2 describes her eyes, hair, teeth and temple as does Song 6:5-6.

## VIII.   LIPS: GODLY AND ANOINTED SPEECH (SONG 4:3)

*³ Your lips are like a strand of scarlet… (Song 4:3a)*

A.   Her lips speak of her speech. Her words being like scarlet speak of words that bring redemption to others. The scarlet strand pictures God's redemption from the blood of Jesus. When the spies came to Jericho, Rahab placed the scarlet ribbon in her window to receive redemption (Josh. 2:21). Moses took the blood of calves with scarlet wool to sprinkle the people (Heb. 9:19).

B.   The scarlet strand must impact our lips as we speak in an edifying way (Col. 4:6). Wholesome speech is an indication of the grace of God on our lives (Eph. 4:29; Jas. 2:3).

## IX.   MOUTH: HER INTIMACY WITH GOD (SONG 4:3)

*³ Your mouth is lovely. (Song 4:3b)*

A.   In Song 1:2, the mouth was introduced in the Song in context to the kisses of His mouth which refers to intimacy with God. Our communion with Jesus is lovely to Him. In the Song of Solomon, the lips speak of speech as the mouth speaks of intimacy. The king is not being repetitive or redundant in this affirmation to the maiden.

B.   When we give our love to Jesus, it often seems weak. However, God declares that it is lovely to Him, even in our immaturity. The Lord delights in the communion He has with us.

## X.   TEMPLE: HER EMOTIONAL MAKE-UP (SONG 4:3)

*³ Your temples behind your veil are like a piece of pomegranate. (Song 4:3c, d)*

A.   The temples (cheeks or countenance) reveal one's emotions. The Hebrew word translated as temples can be translated as countenance or cheeks. Several translations use the cheeks instead of temples. Our emotions are expressed by our countenance or cheeks. We can see anger, joy, gladness, and sadness on the cheeks or countenance. They are windows into one's emotions.

B.   Her godly emotions were like a piece of sweet pomegranate. They were sweet to God. The pomegranate was a common fruit in Israel that was very sweet. They were represented on the gown of the high priest or on the ephod.

C.   When pomegranates are broken they are red. Red speaks of her modesty, her propensity for blushing in the presence of shameful things.

D.   A prostitute does not blush when acting immodestly. A red countenance speaks of one sensitive to shameful things (red from blushing). Behind her veil speaks of her hidden life in God as being modest. It is genuine and not just a show. There is a hidden life of modesty and tenderness.

## XI. NECK: HER RESOLUTE WILL (SONG 4:4)

*⁴ Your <u>neck</u> is like the tower of David, built for an armory, on which hang a thousand bucklers, all shields of mighty men. (Song 4:4)*

A.  In Scripture, the neck often speaks of the will that can be stiff necked (resistant) or submissive. When one put his foot on the neck of a conquered enemy it symbolized their submission.

B.  The Bride's will is like the heart of David who set his heart steadfastly before God (Ps. 57:6). This is in contrast to being double-minded.

C.  David's towers were strong and high to make them effective in defending the city of Jerusalem. Her choices were strong like the tower of David.

D.  An armory stored weapons for war (Neh. 3:19, 25). A resolute will to obey God is like a storehouse of weapons against Satan's kingdom. A buckler was a small, round shield often worn on the arm. 1,000 shields spoke of abundant protection against the enemy. Her will was like the shields of 1,000 skilled warriors which were proven in battle. They provided protection from the enemy. This refers to the shield of faith which is used to protect us (Eph. 6:16).

E.  Our unwavering resolution to obey Jesus is an essential aspect in our spiritual victory. There is no substitute for exercising our will to say yes to God. The Lord will not violate His own boundary lines of redemption by forcing us to say yes to Him.

## XII. BREASTS: ABILITY TO NURTURE OTHERS (SONG 4:5)

*⁵ Your two <u>breasts</u> are like two fawns, twins of a gazelle, which feed among the lilies. (Song 4:5)*

A.  Breasts speak of nurturing others as a mother nourishes her babies. Fawns are youthful animals. Her breasts are like two fawns which are twins. This speaks of a double portion, or a double ability to nurture others in giving them the milk of the Word. Breasts like fawns speak of the milk of a young mother that does not run dry. This is in contrast to an aging woman.

B.  The maiden's ministry is likened to fawns which feed among the lilies which speak of purity. He promised to make her an ornament of silver or to be equipped in ministry (Song 1:10).

## XIII. HER COMMITMENT IS FOUNDATIONAL FOR SPIRITUAL MATURITY (SONG 4:6)

*⁶ Until the day breaks and the shadows flee away, <u>I will go my way</u> to the <u>mountain of myrrh</u> and to the <u>hill of frankincense</u>. (Song 4:6)*

A.  She responds to these affirmations of her beauty by embracing the cross or committing to go to the mountain of myrrh. The mountain refers to obstacles that hinder her obedience (Song 2:8-9).

B.       Myrrh is a burial spice that is costly yet has a great fragrance. It speaks of Jesus' death. It is only a burial spice to our flesh but it as fragrance to our spirit. It is a mountain of myrrh (not comfort). It is mountain not a small hill. Jesus ascended the mountain of myrrh in His own life when He went to the cross. We take up our cross to deny ourselves (Lk. 9:26) to ascend the mountain.

C.       Frankincense or incense throughout Scripture speaks of prayer (Ps.141:2; Rev. 5:8). We ascend the hill of frankincense to receive strength to ascend the mountain of myrrh. Jesus exhorted Peter to pray to receive strength to face temptation (Mt. 26:40-41). The mountain of myrrh is too difficult to ascend without living on the hill of frankincense. Our prayer life empowers our heart to embrace the cross with self denial. We can only embrace the mountain of self denial to the measure that we go up the hill of prayer.

D.       The hill of frankincense is smaller than the mountain of myrrh. A small amount of prayer is sufficient to prepare us for a higher mountain. The impact of our prayer exceeds our efforts on the mountains. Short prayers go a long way. We get more than we deserve from our prayer life.

E.       The maiden makes a firm decision to leave the comfort zone to go up the mountain or to walk in all God's will without fear. *"I will go!"* How glorious these words are to God!

F.       She refers to it as *"my way"*. We must follow the unique path God has chosen for us. God calls each of us on our own tailor-made journey. Our unique way to the mountain of myrrh involves difficulties unique to God's purpose in our life.

G.       She commits to continue on the mountain of myrrh until all compromise is gone or until the day breaks and the shadows flee away. The shadows speak of the areas of weakness or compromise, like the little foxes (Song 2:15). The morning light brings a new day, or a new season of victory after struggling through the night. It speaks of both the day of eternity when we will live in the full presence of God and it speaks of a time of victory where we live in greater light on the earth.

## XIV.   JESUS' FRESH WORD OF AFFIRMATION (SONG 4:7)

*⁷ You are all fair (beautiful), My love, and there is <u>no spot</u> in you. (Song 4:7)*

A.       He calls her "beautiful" 13 times throughout the Song. He has called her "beautiful or fair" 8 times up to this point in the Song. "All fair" is translated "altogether beautiful" in the NAS. He adds the word "all" for the first time in the Song. This is because she set her heart to go to the mountain. She had only said yes. She had not yet gone to the mountain. He sees no spot in her or no area in which she consciously resists His leadership.

B.       She does not go up the mountain until she faces the 2-fold test (Song 5:2-8). He sees her willingness to embrace the Cross. The Lord defines her in terms of her willing spirit, not in terms of her weak flesh or her maturity.

## XV.    THE CALL TO SPIRITUAL WARFARE (SONG 4:8)

*⁸ Come with Me from Lebanon, <u>My spouse</u>, with Me from Lebanon. Look from the top of Amana, from the top of Senir and Hermon, from the lions' dens, from the mountains of the leopards. (Song 4:8)*

A.    The king calls her his spouse or bride for the first time in the Song. With her new commitment to go to the mountain, she is now living from her heart like the Bride. She now carries her heart as a loyal Bride. For the next 4 chapters in the Song, we see her development into mature love.

B.    Jesus' inheritance is an eternal companion that is an affection-filled Bride that will be equally yoked to Him in love. The Cross is not an end in itself. It provides Jesus with His Bride and the Father His family. The Church will live with a bridal identity in loving obedience (Rev. 22:17).

C.    Jesus invites her to come with Him from the mountains of Lebanon of spiritual warfare to follow Him wherever He was to go. He calls her to follow Him to Gethsemane (Song 5:2-7).

D.    She now obeys the original challenge given to go to the mountain (Song 2:10, 13). Solomon called his bride to his house in the forests in the mountain range of Lebanon in northern Israel. Lebanon is filled with fragrant flowers (4:11; Hos. 14:6). Its glory is mentioned in Is. 35:2.

E.    Lebanon is both a geographical area and a mountain range. Senir and Hermon are two different mountain peaks within the mountain range of Lebanon. Mt. Hermon is on the east side of the Jordan River. It was also called Mt. Senir by the Amorites (Deut. 3:8-9). Mt. Amana is not mentioned anywhere in the Bible, but is believed to be next to Mt. Senir and Hermon (Deut 3:9; 4:48; I Chron 5:23) which are both a part of the Hermon mountain range.

F.    She is to look from the top of Amana, Senir and Hermon" or from His point of view (heavenly perspective). If we see difficulties from only a natural point of view, then we lose heart. We must look from His point of view to prevail in spiritual warfare.

G.    After Israel conquered the Ammonites on the east side of the Jordan River, they climbed to the top of these eastern mountains to see the Promise Land on the west side of the Jordan River. Israel had to defeat two Amorite kings (Og and Sihon) before they could climb this mountain (Deut. 3:1-11). She is a warring Bride engaged in spiritual warfare and seated in heavenly places.

H.    There are lions and leopards on the mountaintops. She must war against lions and leopards, which are animals that devour humans. Satan is a roaring lion who seeks to devour us (1 Pet.5:8). This speaks of spiritual warfare (Eph. 6:10-12).

I.    The "mountains of prey" had wild animals that stalked the people of Israel (Ps. 76:4). Habakkuk wrote of plundering the beasts on the mountains of Lebanon that made Israel afraid (Hab. 2:17).

# Session 17 The Ravished Heart of God (Song 4:9-5:1)

## I.   REVIEW OF SONG 4:1-8

A.   After a season of divine discipline, Jesus surprised the Bride by calling her fair (beautiful) <u>while</u> she was in the process of maturing in her obedience and faith. He validated her desires to obey Him before they were manifest in her character. In Song 4:1-5, Solomon spoke of 8 aspects of the Shulamite using agricultural language. He affirmed 8 "budding virtues" in the maiden's life. They are identified by God as desires in her heart before they are formed in her character.

B.   Our obedience begins when we set our heart to obey not just after we gain victory in an area of our behavior. After we set our heart to obey God, we declare war on areas that we struggle in. Thus, we can confidently receive His affectionate mercy and feel His pleasure in each step of the growth process. We are not content with only setting our heart to obey, we want full victory.

C.   We are beautiful to God even in our weakness. Immediately after the maiden's season of discipline (Song 3:1-2), the Lord declares that she is beautiful to Him. The revelation that a sincere believer is beautiful to God even in their weakness is foundational to growing in God's grace. We are changed by this revelation.

*¹ Behold, you are <u>fair</u> (beautiful), <u>My love</u>! Behold, you are fair! (Song 4:1)*

D.   Her fearless wholehearted commitment (Song 4:6)

*⁶ Until the day breaks…<u>I will go my way</u> to the <u>mountain of myrrh</u>… (Song 4:6)*

E.   The Bride responds to Jesus' affirmations by setting her heart to obey His call to come with Him to the mountains (Song 2:8-13). She now embraces the cross by going to the mountain of myrrh. She makes a firm decision to leave the comfort zone to go up the mountain saying, ***"I will go!"***

F.   She had only said yes, she had not yet gone to the mountain. She does not go up the mountain until she faces the 2-fold test (Song 5:2-8). He sees her willingness to embrace the Cross. The Lord defines her in terms of her willing spirit, not in terms of her weak flesh or her maturity.

G.   Jesus pours out extravagant affirmation calling her all together beautiful (Song 4:7)

*⁷ You are <u>all fair</u> (altogether beautiful, NAS), <u>My love, and there is <u>no spot</u> in you</u>. (Song 4:7)*

H.   The Bride joins the King in spiritual warfare as He calls her His spouse for the first time in the Song. With her new commitment to go to the mountain, she now carries her heart as a loyal Bride. For the next 4 chapters in the Song, we see her development into mature love.

*⁸ Come with Me from Lebanon, <u>My spouse</u>…Look from the top of Amana, from the top of Senir and Hermon, from the lions' dens, from the mountains of the leopards. (Song 4:8)*

I.   Next, Jesus reveals His desire for His bride (4:9-10) and then affirms her godly life and fruitful ministry referred to as a flourishing garden (4:11-15). She prays for His full intervention (4:16).

## II.    JESUS' HEART IS RAVISHED FOR HIS PEOPLE

*⁹ You have ravished My heart, My sister, My spouse; You have ravished My heart with one look of your eyes, with one link of your necklace. (Song 4:9)*

A.    This verse summarizes the Song of Solomon. Many believers do not know that God is filled with desire for them. A working definition of the ravished heart of God is: ***To be filled with emotions of joy or delight because of one who is unusually attractive*** (Webster's Collegiate Dictionary).

B.    The revelation of Jesus' ravished heart equips us for 100-fold obedience. The Bride's decision for radical obedience (Song 4:6) is walked out in Song 5:2-8.

C.    Our salvation involves much more than receiving a legal position of righteousness before God (2 Cor. 5:21). We must understand God's affections for us. Why? Because we will never have more passion for God than what we understand about His passion for us. We love Him because we understand He first loved us (1 Jn. 4:19). God's heart is filled with delight for His people.

*¹⁰ I am my Beloved's, and <u>His desire is toward me</u>. (Song 7:10)*

## III.    THE CHRISTIAN PARADIGM OF GOD

A.    The Christian paradigm of God is founded on the revelation of God's deep emotions of love. The revelation of God as a tender Father and a passionate Bridegroom was a new idea in religious history (see William Barclay's commentary on Heb. 4).

B.    In Jewish tradition, what was most emphasized about God was that He is holy in the sense of being ***totally separate from sin***. They did not think of a holy God as sharing human experience. They thought of God as incapable of sharing it simply because He is God. In other words, they saw God as being "above" sharing the human dilemma by the very definition of being God.

C.    The Greek philosophers saw God as ***emotionally distant*** from humans. The most prominent Greek thinkers were the Stoics. They saw the main attribute of God as being apatheia, by which they meant God's <u>inability to feel anything</u>. They reasoned that if God felt something then He might be influenced or even controlled by what He felt. They argued that those who felt sorrow or joy were vulnerable to being hurt and thus controlled by those they had feelings for. They believed that anyone who affected God's emotions would be greater than God for that moment. The Epicureans (a school of Greek philosophy) believed that the gods ***lived detached*** in eternal bliss. They lived in the intermediate world and thus, were not aware of events occurring on earth. They were therefore, totally detached from human affairs as they lived in great happiness.

D.    The Jews understood God as a ***holy God*** separated from humans; the Stoics a ***feelingless*** god; the Epicureans a ***detached god***. In to this context of religious thought came the totally new idea of the Christian God who deliberately subjected Himself to human emotion, pain and weakness.

E.    Jesus came as the One who embraced human experience and was therefore, sympathetic.

> *15 For we do not have a High Priest who cannot sympathize with our weaknesses, but was in all points tempted as we are, yet without sin. (Heb. 4:15)*

> *8 Though He was a Son, yet He learned obedience by the things which He suffered. (Heb. 5:8)*

F.    It was inconceivable to the religious mindset of the first century that a holy God would have capacity for tenderness, sympathy and affection, who even wrapped Himself in the garments of humanity and then experienced God's wrath on a cross. It is difficult to realize how dramatic this Christian paradigm of God was at that time.

G.    The capacity to deeply love is unique to the human spirit. It distinguishes us from even the most exalted angels. Nothing in Scripture describes angels as having the capacity for affection. They have joy, but never are described as having affection. This capacity for affection brings us to unimaginable heights in God's glory, but it can also be dangerous by bringing us to agonizing depths of perversion, if we resist God's grace.

## IV.    JESUS' REVELATION OF HIS LOVE FOR US (REVIEW FROM SESSION 5)

A.    ***God loves us in the same way that God loves God***: The measure of the Father's love (affection) for Jesus is the measure of Jesus' love for us. This is the ultimate statement of our worth. It gives every believer the right to view themselves as "God's favorite."

> *9 As the Father loved Me, I also have loved you; abide (live) in My love. (Jn. 15:9)*

B.    I refer to "affection-based obedience" as the stronger type of obedience because it flows from experiencing Jesus' affection. It is the most consistent obedience because a lovesick person will endure anything for love. It is stronger than "duty-based obedience" (obedience when we do not feel God's presence) or "fear-based obedience" (motivated by fear of negative consequences).

C.    The gospel flourishes most when we understand the extravagant passions in God's personality. It is essential to know what He has done for us on the cross and what He will do for us in the coming revival or even eternity. We need to know how He feels, or why He does what He does.

D.    Experience of God's affection causes us to love Him more than our own lives.

> *11 They overcame him by the blood of the Lamb and...they did not love their lives to the death. (Rev. 12:11)*

E.    Paul reflected on his sacrifices for God and testified that what he gave up was rubbish when compared to the glory of knowing Jesus. There is no sacrifice too great for those in love.

F.    The great question is "Why is God's heart ravished for us?" His personality is filled with loving desire. He evaluates our lives with such kindness because of the type of personality that He has. Because of who Jesus is, how He feels and how He processes life, He sees loveliness in us.

## V.    JESUS' PASSIONATE AFFECTION FOR HIS BRIDE

*⁹ You have ravished My heart, My sister, My spouse (bride); You have ravished My heart with one look of your eyes, with one link of your necklace. 10 How fair is your love, My sister, My spouse! How much better than wine is your love… (Song 4:9-10c)*

A.    *My sister* – being called Jesus' sister refers to Him becoming human (Heb. 2:11-17). He endured indescribable humiliation and suffering to be like His brethren in all things (Heb. 2:17). He descended so far and we ascend so high to meet Him as His sister (Matt. 12:49-50).

B.    *My spouse* – being called Jesus' Bride speaks of His desire for affectionate partnership with us.

C.    Her 2-fold identity as His sister and bride is emphasized 7 times (4:8, 9, 10, 11, 12; 5:1, 2).

D.    *With one look of your eyes* – Jesus' heart moves with each look of devotion that we give Him. The very movement of our heart to love Him touches Him. Our obedience begins when we set our heart to obey Him, not just after we gain victory in a specific area. Thus, we can confidently receive His affectionate mercy and feel His pleasure in each step of the growth process. The glance that moves God's heart is the gaze of loving obedience. The obedient gaze is rooted in quality decisions. The bridal paradigm is rooted in the message of the true grace of God.

E.    *With one link of your necklace* – in Scripture, the neck often speaks of the will that can be resistant (stiff necked) or submissive. The king described her neck as being like David's towers which were effective in defeating the enemy (Song 4:4) and as a golden necklace that made her beautiful (Song 1:10). Each link of her necklace represented each individual response of obedience that she gave to him. Each decision for love that we make moves Jesus' heart. He remembers every movement of love that our heart makes towards Him.

*¹⁰ God is not <u>unjust to forget</u> your…love which you have shown to His name… (Heb. 6:10)*

*⁴² Whoever gives one of these little ones <u>only</u> a cup of cold water in the name of a disciple, assuredly, I say to you, he shall by no means lose his reward. (Mt. 10:42)*

F.    *How fair is your love* – Jesus considers our love as beautiful. Our obedience based in love beautifies us and brings great delight to Jesus.

*³ Do not let your <u>adornment</u> be merely outward--arranging the hair, wearing gold, or putting on fine apparel-- 4 rather let it be the <u>hidden person of the heart</u>, with the <u>incorruptible beauty</u> of a gentle and quiet spirit, which is <u>very precious</u> in the sight of God. (1 Pet. 3:3-4)*

G.    *How much better than wine is your love* – Jesus turns around her earlier statement when she cried out "For Your love is better than wine" (Song 1:2). The wine metaphor speaks of that which exhilarates the heart. Wine in the context of a marriage speaks of the drink of celebration. Scripture points to the "good wine" of God's blessing and the "bad wine" of sin. Experiencing God's love is better than other privileges and the best experiences we can have in this age.

H.     Jesus is saying, "Our love is more beautiful to Him than the splendor of His creation." He values our love more than everything under His authority. He would not have only to cleanse creation. Jesus' heart is filled with delight over her new decision for obedience (Song 4:6).

## VI.     JESUS' PLEASURE OVER HER HEART (HER THOUGHTS, WORDS AND DEEDS)

*¹⁰ How much better than wine is your love, and the <u>scent of your perfumes</u> than all spices! 11 <u>Your lips</u>, O My spouse, drip as the honeycomb; honey and milk are under your tongue; and the <u>fragrance of your garments</u> is like the fragrance of Lebanon. (Song 4:10-11)*

A.     *The scent of your perfumes* – refers to her mind being filled with God's Word. As the invisible fragrance of perfume expressed the inner quality of a plant, so our thoughts are the scent of our inner life. Our intentions to obey God and our meditation on the Word arise as fragrance to God.

*¹⁴ Thanks be to God who always leads us in triumph in Christ, and through us diffuses the <u>fragrance</u> of His knowledge…15 For we are to God the <u>fragrance</u> of Christ… (2 Cor. 2:14-15)*

B.     *Than all spices* – rare spices were used as expensive gifts. The queen of Sheba gave spices to King Solomon (2 Kings 10:2). The wise men brought spices to Jesus because they believed He was a king (Matt. 2:11). Spices were used in the priestly sacrifices and offerings (Ex. 30:23-24).

C.     *Your lips drip as the honeycomb* – speaks of her words as being sweet like honey when spoken to God in worship and prayer (Song 2:14) and when blessing others by feeding and sustaining them. Her redemptive lips or words were described as being like a strand of scarlet (Song 4:3). Honey is like that which delights the heart and is sweet to the taste. The production of honey requires much time and hard work from the bees.

1.     *O My spouse* – Jesus notices every word of love to Him that is spoken from His Bride.

2.     *Honey and milk are under your tongue* – two foods that described the prosperity of the Promise Land and that are used to feed babes (1 Peter 2:1). The recurring theme of speaking for the edification of others is prominent in Scripture (Eph. 4:29; Col. 4:6). The phrase "under his tongue" refers to the private thoughts. The mouth full of deceit has trouble "under its tongue" (or in his heart; Ps.10:7). The Bride has truth "under her tongue" (in her heart) as she speaks expressing agreement with what she really thinks. What she thinks and speaks are in unity and thus, sincere.

D.     *The fragrance of your garments is like the fragrance of Lebanon* – refers to the Bride's deeds as being fragrant before God. Garments speak of the Bride's acts of obedience (Rev. 19:7-8). Jesus warns us to "keep our garments" lest we end up with the shame of a life without service for God (Rev. 16:15). Jesus counseled the Laodicean church to buy from Him "white garments" so they would be clothed so that the shame of their nakedness would not be exposed (Rev.3:18). Mt. Lebanon was known for its fragrant cedar trees and flowers. This is in contrast to a life of spending our time and money mostly on ourselves. Paul spoke of receiving financial service from the Philippian church as a sweet smelling aroma well pleasing to God (Phil. 4:18).

## VII.   THE BRIDE'S EXTRAVAGANT DEVOTION TO JESUS

*¹² A garden enclosed is My sister, My spouse, a spring sealed up, a fountain sealed. (Song 4:12)*

A.   *A garden enclosed* – was a private garden (not open to the public). It was enclosed with a fence to keep animals from polluting it. The purpose of a king's garden was to provide pleasure and rest in contrast to most gardens used for growing food. It was costly and required much work from many servants to cultivate. The Church is God's garden (1Cor.3:6-9; Song 6:2, 3; 2:16).

B.   To live as an "enclosed garden" or "sealed spring or fountain" means to shut ourselves off from the defilement of sin and compromise. In locking our heart to compromise, we become a place of pleasure for our King. A water supply without a covering was considered defiled (Num. 19:15).

*15 Every open vessel, which has no cover fastened on it, is unclean. (Num. 19:15)*

C.   *A spring and fountain sealed up* – speaks of an undefiled water supply (not polluted by animals). In Israel, springs of water were rare and thus, provided a valuable water source to help a garden grow abundantly. It is rare and precious to God for us to live as a spring sealed up.

D.   Job made a covenant with his eyes to not gaze on anything unholy (Job 31:1). In doing this, he lived by carrying his heart as "an enclosed garden."

## VIII.  A DESCRIPTION OF THE YOUNG BRIDE'S FRUITFULNESS

*¹³ Your plants are an orchard of pomegranates with pleasant fruits, fragrant henna with spikenard,
14 spikenard and saffron, calamus and cinnamon, with all trees of frankincense, myrrh and aloes,
with all the chief spices. (Song 4:13-14)*

A.   She is described as an orchard filled with pleasant fruits, fragrant plants, many trees and chief spices. This speaks of her abundant fruitful life and ministry. Fruit refers both to godliness which is to have a vibrant heart in God (Rom. 6:22; 7:4-5; Gal. 5:22; Eph. 5:9; Heb. 12:11; 13:15; Jas. 3:18) and to our ministry to others (Jn. 4:36; Rom. 1:13; 15:28; Phil. 1:22; Col. 1:5-6).

B.   Pomegranates (v. 13a) and pleasant fruits (v. 13b) are sweet and speak of having a pleasant impact on others. Fragrant henna with spikenard (v. 13c) speaks of the precious and costly work of the Spirit in our life. Spikenard and saffron, calamus and cinnamon (v. 14a,b) speak of the diverse graces seen in her ministry. With all trees of frankincense (v. 14c) speaks of a ministry of prayer. Myrrh and aloes (v.14d) speak of the cross and death to self. With all chief spices (v. 14e) speaks of grace imparted to others through her ministry (2 Cor. 2:14-16).

## IX.    A 3-FOLD DESCRIPTION OF THE HOLY SPIRIT'S MINISTRY IN THE BRIDE'S LIFE

¹⁵ *A <u>fountain</u> of gardens, a <u>well</u> of living waters, and <u>streams</u> from Lebanon. (Song 4:15)*

A.    The Bride is described as having three sources of water which refer to the different ways in which we experience the Spirit in our lives. A believer is described as a tree planted by water (Ps. 1:3). A hardened heart is pictured as being dry (Is. 1:30). Jesus promised that we would be as a well of living water (Jn. 4:14; 7:38). The fountain is the indwelling Spirit. The well speaks of our history in God. The streams are like the Holy Spirit coming upon us from the high places.

B.    *A fountain* is a hidden source of water that is below the surface. This speaks an <u>inward source of supply</u> or the indwelling Christ (Col. 1:27). The gardens are plural (in contrast to the singular enclosed garden; v. 12) speaking of the anointing of God that brings blessing to others.

C.    *A well* speaks of the capacity to store water, so as to draw on when needed. Welled water is water that is stored up that provides a supply in dry times. This refers to our personal history in God that we draw on from our past experiences. This speaks of a past <u>stored up source of supply.</u>

D.    *Streams* speak of an outward flow of water. A stream is above the ground and a spring is below the ground. Streams speak of an energetic flow of water. These streams flow from the mountains or high places of Lebanon, thus, they speak of the Holy Spirit "water supply" coming from on High. This speaks of an <u>outward source of supply</u> (Acts 8:18).

## X.    HER CRY FOR INCREASED ANOINTING

¹⁵ *Awake, O north wind, and come, O south! blow upon <u>my garden</u>, that its spices may flow out.  Let My beloved come to <u>His garden</u> and eat its pleasant fruits... (Song 4:16).*

A.    She now has enough confidence in God's goodness to offer a 2-fold prayer. She prays for both the north winds of adversity and the south winds of blessing. She knew that both played a strategic role in her becoming a fragrant garden for God's pleasure.

B.    *Awake, O north wind* – this speaks of the bitter cold wind of testing and difficulty. This prayer is answered in Song 5:3-7 as she goes through what I call "the ultimate 2-fold test".

C.    *Come, O south wind* – her second prayer is that Jesus send the refreshing winds of blessing to mature her. Only God has the wisdom to know the right combination of the north and the south winds that are necessary in each season of our life. Only God knows our makeup and destiny.

D.    *Blow upon my garden* – she wants the garden of her heart and ministry to be deeply affected. Deep pockets of our unperceived pride, ambition, and anger, etc. are uncovered to us as we work under difficult circumstances. *That its spices may flow out* – she desires to be filled with God's fragrant Presence. In other words, she wants to grow in love.

E.      *Let my Beloved come to His garden* – is the transition from her garden to His garden. She desires to be totally God's. She wants an anointing of consecration. She sees her life and ministry as "His" garden instead of hers. Jesus has an inheritance in the church (Eph. 1:18). This is the turning point in the Song. For the first 4 chapters it was her inheritance, from now on it is His. *Let my Beloved eat its pleasant fruits* – that Jesus might enjoy what the Spirit has worked in her.

## XI.     JESUS ENJOYS HIS INHERITANCE WHICH IS A BRIDE

*¹ I have come to My garden, My sister, My spouse; I have gathered My myrrh with My spice; I have eaten My honeycomb with My honey; I have drunk My wine with My milk. Eat, O friends! Drink, yes, drink deeply, O beloved ones! (Song 5:1).*

A.      The bride now lives under Jesus' full ownership. Nine times He says "My," depicting His ownership of her life and ministry: My garden, My sister, My spouse, My myrrh, My spice, My honeycomb, My honey; My wine, My milk.

B.      *I have come to My garden* – Jesus answers her prayer from Song 4:16 where she asked Him to come and eat. Jesus comes to take full possession of her life as His inheritance in the 2-fold relationship of sister and spouse.

C.      *I have gathered My myrrh with My spices* – Jesus gathers what the Spirit has worked through the church. My myrrh speaks of the time in which we follow Jesus by embracing the cross. My spice speaks of the impartation of grace in her life.

D.      *I have eaten My honeycomb with My honey* – Jesus is feasting on the fruit of a mature church. She asked Him in 4:16 to come and eat. Jesus enjoys what the Spirit has released in the Church. Honey speaks of delightful food that Jesus may feast on from her life.

E.      *I have drunk My wine with My milk* – Jesus celebrates the love that the Bride has for Him. Wine is for celebration and milk is for strength. Jesus celebrates her love and is delighted by it.

F.      *Eat, O friends! Drink, yes, drink deeply, O beloved ones!* – Jesus wants the Church to enjoy the fruitfulness of mature believers. These beloved friends are other believers. Paul wrote of death working in him so that life would flow to others (2 Cor. 4:10-12). He embraced difficulties that God's spices would bless God and others. She is as a living sacrifice that the Lord Himself feasts on (Rom. 12:1) and feeds to the Church. We can strengthen and nourish others with the grace.

G.      *Summary:* of Jesus' 5 activities in Song 5:1. He gathers myrrh, eats honeycomb, drinks, and then He offers her as a feast for others to partake of. He <u>comes</u> into His garden (5:1a) or draws near to her. He <u>gathers</u> His myrrh with spice (5:1b) or uses what the Spirit has worked in her. He <u>eats</u> His honeycomb with honey (5:1c) or feasts on the fruit of her maturity. He <u>drinks</u> His wine with milk (5:1d) or celebrates her maturity and is delighted by it. He <u>invites</u> His friends to eat (5:1e) or wants the church to enjoy the fruitfulness of mature believers.

## Session 18 The Ultimate 2-Fold Test Of Maturity (Song 5:2-9)

I.  **REVIEW: THE BRIDE'S CRY FOR THE INCREASE OF GOD'S PRESENCE IN HER LIFE**

A.  The Bride prayed for both the north winds of adversity and the south winds of blessing to come to the garden of her heart that the spices of grace might flow in her life. She had the confidence to pray for the bitter **_north winds_** of testing which come in the 2-fold test of Song 5:3-7.

*¹⁵ Awake, O __north__ wind, and come, O __south__! blow upon __my garden__, that its spices may flow out. Let My Beloved come to __His garden__ and eat its pleasant fruits... (Song 4:16).*

B.  This is the time when the garden of her heart becomes His garden. She sees her life as "His" garden instead of hers. Jesus has an inheritance in His people (Eph. 1:18). This is the turning point in the Song. In the first 4 chapters, her focus is on her inheritance. In the last 4 chapters it is on being His inheritance. Jesus enjoys His inheritance in her as she lives under His ownership. Nine times He says "My" to depict His ownership in Song 5:1 and six times in Song 5:2.

*¹ I have come to __My__ garden, __My__ sister, __My__ spouse; I have gathered __My__ myrrh with __My__ spice; I have eaten __My__ honeycomb with __My__ honey; I have drunk __My__ wine with __My__ milk. (Song 5:1).*

II. **JESUS CALLS HER TO THE FELLOWSHIP OF SUFFERING (SONG 5:2)**

*² I sleep, but my heart is awake; it is the voice of my Beloved! He knocks, saying, "__Open for Me__, My sister, My love, My dove, My perfect one; for __My head is covered with dew__, __My locks with the drops of the night__." (Song 5:2)*

A.  Jesus reveals Himself as one who suffered in Gethsemane. He calls us to join Him in the fellowship of His sufferings (Phil. 3:10). She responds in obedience (Song 5:3-5) which is followed by a 2-fold test. First, Jesus tests her by withdrawing His presence from her (Song 5:6). Second, He allows the spiritual authorities to mistreat her (Song 5:7). She responds in love (5:8).

*¹⁰ That I may know Him…and the __fellowship of His sufferings__… (Phil. 3:10)*

B.  Jesus calls the Bride to intimacy by coming to her as the "Jesus of Gethsemane" with His hair covered with the dew (drops of the night) because of enduring the long night in Gethsemane.

C.  Jesus calls her to <u>open her heart</u> "for Him" in order to experience new depths in God. He is now taking full possession of her heart for Himself as He declared in Song 5:1. Jesus knocks on the door of her heart in answer to her prayer for the north winds in Song 4:16. The knock refers to God's initiative and desire to bring us forward in new dimensions of the Spirit. Opening the door speaks of entering a new measure of communion with God.

*²⁰ I stand at the door and knock. If anyone hears My voice and __opens the door__, I will __come in to him__ and __dine with him__, and he with Me. (Rev. 3:20)*

D.  She sleeps or rests with confidence in God as the north wind is about to come. Jesus knew the "rest of faith" as He slept in the storm (Mt. 8:23-27). Her heart is awake to spiritual things as she walks in obedience. We are to be spiritually awake (1 Thes. 5:6; Rom. 13:11; Eph. 5:14).

E. She hears His voice again as in Song 2:8. Jesus reveals Himself again to her as her Beloved. The voice of the Bridegroom is what John the Baptist heard as he became a voice

*²⁹ The friend of the Bridegroom…rejoices because of the Bridegroom's voice. (Jn. 3:29)*

F. Jesus empowers her to open to Him by calling her four names that describe different facets of her intimate relationship with Him and that gives her confidence in His love.

*² He knocks, saying, "Open for Me, My sister, My love, My dove, My perfect one…" (5:2).*

1. *My sister* – signifies His identification with her humanity. He endured indescribable suffering to be like His brethren in all things (Heb. 2:11-17).

2. *My love* – reminds her of His tender love for her. 'Grace motivation' is to be motivated by love and gratitude instead of fear and judgment. "Affection-based obedience" is the strongest type of obedience because it flows from experiencing Jesus' affection. It is the most consistent obedience because a lovesick person will endure anything for love.

3. *My dove* – speaks of her singleness of mind and loyalty. The Spirit is pictured as a dove. A dove never mates again when their partner dies. They are known for their loyalty. Dove's eyes can not focus on two things and has no peripheral vision. This speaks of singleness of mind without compromise. Her eyes are fixed on Him.

4. *My perfect one* – her intentions are to perfectly obey God. Perfect refers to being mature. She has mature obedience. Before this test (Song 5:2) and after it (Song 6:9), Jesus refers to her as His perfect one because she refuses all compromise.

## III. THE BRIDE RESPONDS TO JESUS IN FULL OBEDIENCE (SONG 5:3-5)

*³ I have taken off my robe; how can I put it on again? I have washed my feet; how can I defile them? 4 My Beloved put His hand by the latch of the door, and my heart yearned for Him. 5 I arose to open for my Beloved, and my hands dripped with myrrh…on the handles of the lock. (Song 5:3-5)*

A. The Bride arises in obedience to open her heart to Jesus. His first words to her after this time of testing make it clear that she responded in obedience (Song 6:4-5). We are covered with Jesus' robe of righteousness (Isa. 61:10; Zech. 3:1-5). Our righteousness or robe is as filthy rags (Isa. 64:6). She took off her defiled garments and put on His garments of righteousness. She refuses to wear her garments or to live in compromise. She declares, "How can I put on my robe again".
*¹⁰ He clothed me with the garments of salvation…with the robe of righteousness… (Isa. 61:10)*

*¹⁴ Put on the Lord Jesus Christ, and make no provision for the flesh… (Rom. 13:14)*

*⁶ All our righteousnesses are like filthy rags; We all fade as a leaf… (Isa. 64:6)*

B. She washed her feet. Jesus told Peter that he was clean, except that he needed his feet to be cleansed (Jn. 13:6-14). This spoke of his need for daily spiritual cleansing. She refuses to defile her feet through compromise (Song 5:3d). The NIV translates this as if she compromises by refusing to get out of bed. The context is clear that she is now relating to Jesus in obedience.

C.  The hand of God releases grace on the latch and lock of her heart (Acts. 11:21-23). She refers to Jesus as her Beloved or the One she loves. Her heart yearns with love for Jesus as she instantly arises to open the door to the Jesus of Gethsemane. Earlier she refused to arise (Song 2:13, 17).

*⁴ My Beloved put <u>His hand</u> by the <u>latch</u> of the door, and my <u>heart yearned</u> for Him. 5 I <u>arose</u> to open for my Beloved, and my hands dripped with myrrh, my fingers with liquid myrrh, on the handles of the <u>lock</u>. (Song 5:4-5)*

D.  Jesus putting His hands by the latch refers to helping her unlock the door of her heart. The lock on her heart speaks of her thoughts and emotions that affect her decisions.

E.  Her hands and fingers drip with myrrh the flowed like liquid on the lock of her heart. This speaks of the abundant grace to help her embrace the difficulty of the coming 2-fold test. Myrrh was a fragrant burial spice. It speaks of death to self and the commitment to embrace the cross. There is no such thing as liquid myrrh. Her fingers dripping with myrrh speak of the activity of working faith as she fulfills her commitment to go up the mountain of myrrh (Song 4:6).

## IV.  FIRST TEST: JESUS WITHDRAWS HIS PRESENCE FROM HER (SONG 5:6)

*⁶ I opened for my Beloved, but my Beloved had <u>turned away</u> and <u>was gone</u>. My heart leaped up when He spoke. I sought Him, but <u>I could not find Him</u>; I called Him, but <u>He gave me no answer</u>. (Song 5:6)*

A.  The Lord hides Himself from the Bride on two occasions in the Song (Song 3:1-2; 5:6). He withdraws His presence while she walks in full obedience in Song 5:6-7. Therefore, this season is different from the discipline she received in Song 3:1-2 because of her disobedience.

B.  In Song 5, Jesus calls her "My perfect one" (v. 2) because of her obedience to open her heart to Him as her heart yearns (v. 4) and leaps (v. 5) because she is lovesick (v. 8).

C.  Her greatest desire is to experience God's presence (Song 1:2-4; 2:3-6). Feeling loved by God and feeling love for God is the most powerful pleasure we can experience.

*¹ The LORD came to Abram…saying, "…I am your exceedingly great reward." (Gen. 15:1)*

D.  Jesus promised to never leave or forsake us (Heb. 13:5). However, He sometimes withdraws the discernable feelings of His manifest presence to test us and to bring our love to maturity as she prayed in Song 4:16. This is not because of sin, nor is it an attack of the devil. God sometimes hides His face from the obedient to draw out the yearning of their heart for Him in greater ways.

*⁵ For He Himself has said, "<u>I will never leave you nor forsake you.</u>" (Heb. 13:5)*

E.  Some Catholic contemplatives in the Middle Ages spoke of "the dark night of the soul" referring to seasons of divine testing for those walking in obedience to God. This is not a Biblical term but a term referring to times of when they could not sense His presence. This phrase was originated by St. John of the Cross in the 16th century. Most Protestants do not have any theology for this.

F.    Job was a righteousness man when he was afflicted then established an intimacy with God

*8 The LORD said to Satan, "Have you considered My servant Job, that there is <u>none like him on the earth</u>, a blameless and upright man, one who fears God and shuns evil?" (Job 1:8)*

*5 I have heard of You by the hearing of the ear, <u>but now my eye sees You</u>. (Job 42:5)*

G.    She seeks Him even more fervently by calling out to Him but she can not find Him. This season of divine silence is part of His training to cause our love for Him to mature. In the time of testing our confession of faith must remain constant, "His banner over me is love" (Song 2:4).

## V.    SECOND TEST: THE BRIDE IS PERSECUTED AND REJECTED (SONG 5:7)

*7 The watchmen who went about the city found me. They <u>struck me</u>, they <u>wounded me</u>; the keepers of the walls <u>took my veil away</u> from me. (Song 5:7)*

A.    The watchmen and the keepers of the walls speak of the leaders or spiritual authorities who guard the walls of God's city to protect His people. They strike and wound her. They wound her because she had a genuine relationship with them before they rejected and persecuted her. A stranger can publish accusation against you, but only a friend can wound you. Being wounded in the house of friends is part of God's pattern that even Jesus endured (Ps. 55:12-21).

B.    The leaders taking away her veil speaks of removing her spiritual covering therefore, her place of function in the body (1 Cor 11:10).

## VI.    HER RESPONSE OF HUMILITY AND LOVE (SONG 5:8)

A.    Her humility is seen in her teachable spirit to the immature Daughters of Jerusalem.

*8 O daughters of Jerusalem, if you find my Beloved…tell Him that <u>I am lovesick</u>! (Song 5:8)*

B.    She is lovesick for Jesus instead of offended at Him for allowing this 2-fold test.

*6 Blessed is he who is <u>not offended</u> because of Me (Jesus). (Mt. 11:6)*

C.    The Bride's 2-fold life vision was experiencing His presence and running with Him in ministry (Song 1:4). Many of her promises from God are based on this. Thus, all seems lost. The issue is whether she will obey Jesus without feeling His presence and when circumstances are difficult. Does she seek God primarily for her comfort or will she obey God for His sake? The Lord longs for a people who will obey Him regardless of what is happening in their lives. This is the primary issue in being Jesus' inheritance. He wants a Bride equally yoked in love.

D.    The Bride's 7 crisis in the Song include: the crisis of sin (1:5-6); the crisis of fear (2:8-9); the crisis of Divine discipline (3:1); the crisis of total obedience (4:6,16); the crisis of Divine withdrawing (5:6); the crisis of rejection in the church (5:7); and the crisis of persecution and division (6:13).

## Session 19 The Bride's Response To The 2-fold Test (Song 5:8-6:5)

I. **REVIEW: THE BRIDE'S CRY FOR THE INCREASE OF GOD'S PRESENCE IN HER LIFE**

    A.      The Bride prayed for both the north winds of adversity and the south winds of blessing to come to the garden of her heart that the spices of grace and God's presence might flow in her life.

         *[15] Awake, O <u>north</u> wind, and come, O <u>south</u>! blow upon <u>my garden</u>, that its <u>spices</u> may flow out. Let My Beloved come to <u>His garden</u> and eat its pleasant fruits... (Song 4:16).*

    B.      This is one of the greatest prayers for mature love and dedication in Scripture. The prayer is that God would do whatever it takes to cause our spices to come forth or for love for God and others to grow.

    C.      This is the turning point in the Song. The Song of Solomon has two main sections. First, Song 1-4 is focused on receiving ***our inheritance*** in God. Second, Song 5-8 is focused on God receiving ***His inheritance*** in us. The answer to the prayer for the ***north*** ***winds*** cones in Song 5:3-7.

    D.      The Lord calls the Bride to intimacy by coming to her as the "Jesus of Gethsemane" (Song 5:2) and asking her to <u>open her heart</u> "for Him" to experience new depths of intimacy with Him.

         1.      She responds in obedience (Song 5:3-5) which is followed by a 2-fold test. First, Jesus tests her by withdrawing His presence from her (Song 5:6). Second, He allows the spiritual authorities to mistreat her (Song 5:7).

         2.      She responds with deep love for Jesus (Song 5:8). We must go through the door of Song 5:2-9 to grow in love (Song 5:9-6:13) and fruitful ministry (Song 7:1-8:4).

    E.      Will we seek God if He withholds the things we deeply desire? Will we be His when we cannot feel His presence? Will we love and trust Him when we are disappointed by circumstances? We must work our "faith muscle" as the way to re-align our heart so as to grow in love in difficulty.

    F.      When we do not feel His presence or when circumstances are difficult, our first tendency is to be depressed or to complain. In the process of prayer we ask the question "why we feel this way". In this, we re-align our hearts with the truth that we are His inheritance and are in it for love.

II. **OVERVIEW OF SONG 5:8-6:5**

    A.      In difficulty, the Bride expresses her love for Jesus (Song 5:8-16). She is lovesick instead of offended at God. We confess, Jesus, <u>I am in it for love</u> because You are beautiful (Song 5:8-10).

         *[8] O daughters of Jerusalem, if you find my Beloved…tell Him <u>I am lovesick</u>! (Song 5:8)*

    B.      She responds to God in love and to others in humility by asking for help from the daughters of Jerusalem who are less spiritual. (She does not despise the church that wounded her).

C.      The immature daughters ask her two questions. First, "Why do you love Him so much?" (Song 5:9). He took His presence from you (v. 6) and let the leaders wound you (v. 7). Then after hearing her answer they ask the second question, "How can we know Him like you?" (Song 6:1).

D.      Jesus responds to the Bride with extravagant love by revealing what He thought about her during her struggle (Song 6:4-10).

## III.    FIRST QUESTION: WHAT IS IT ABOUT HIM THAT MAKES YOU LOVE HIM? (SONG 5:9)

[9] *What is your **Beloved** more than another beloved, O fairest (most beautiful) among women?*
*What is your **Beloved** more than another beloved, that you so charge us? (Song 5:9)*

A.      The spiritually immature daughters ask the Bride questions throughout the Song. They see that she is lovesick for Jesus in the midst of her difficulties instead of being filled with complaints and depression. Her deep love for Jesus provokes them more than her wisdom or giftedness. We are made beautiful to others by our love more than by our wisdom or power (1 Pet. 3:3-4).

B.      The "controversy" created by the watchman (Song 5:7) does not cause the daughters to draw back from the Bride. They call her the "fairest" or "most beautiful" (Song 5:9). They deeply respect her as they see her devotion and purity. This is in contrast to how the Saul-type leaders (watchmen) evaluated her. Saul could not see the spiritual beauty in David.

C.      "What is your beloved more than another?" They saw that Jesus has the power to awaken love in the Bride in the midst of severe trials or "Why are you so loyal to Him? What do you know about Him, that we don't know?" The daughters do not understand this kind of dedication.

D.      The daughters had "other beloveds" that were more important to them than Jesus. The other loves in the lives of believers include people, friends, ministry, money, leisure, pleasure, power, prominence, and comfort, etc. Many born again people love these things more than Jesus.

E.      The definition of spiritual maturity is when Jesus becomes the first Beloved of our soul. The Holy Spirit is restoring the First commandment to first place in the Body of Christ worldwide.

F.      The same question is repeated for emphasis. It expresses their earnest desire to know the answer. We see the sincerity of their question in Song 6:1, because they ask a follow up question.

G.      The most important question is the one Jesus asked, "Who do you say that I am?" (Mt. 16:15). Pharaoh asked Moses this question, "Who is the Lord that I should obey Him?" (Ex. 5:2).

H.      Passion for Jesus is the most powerful dimension of any ministry (2 Cor. 2:14-17). Do people seek you out to show them how to walk in the devotion that they see in you? This can be part of your life vision to so show forth devotion to Jesus in difficulty that people want to know what you know and how you carry your heart.

## IV.   THE BRIDE'S ANSWER: THE MAJESTIC SPLENDOR OF JESUS (SONG 5:10-16)

A.   The Bride answers the question by proclaiming Jesus' beauty. The Spirit uses metaphors of the human body to convey 10 attributes of God's personality. Each attribute has two descriptions.

B.   Song 5:10-16 is one of the most powerful revelations of Jesus in Scripture. She starts with a general statement of His beauty, develops ten attributes and then gives a summary statement.

*¹⁰ My beloved is <u>white</u> (dazzling, NAS)…and <u>chief among ten thousand</u>. 11 His <u>head</u> is like the finest gold; His <u>locks</u> are wavy…12 His <u>eyes</u> are like doves…13 His <u>cheeks</u> are like a bed of spices…His <u>lips</u> are lilies…14 His <u>hands</u> are rods of gold…His <u>body</u> is carved ivory…15 His <u>legs</u> are pillars of marble…His <u>countenance</u> is like Lebanon…16 His <u>mouth</u> is most sweet, Yes, <u>He is altogether lovely</u>. This is my Beloved, and this is my friend… (Song 5:10-16)*

1.   His head – His sovereign leadership over all

2.   His locks – His dedication to God and the Church

3.   His eyes – His infinite knowledge, wisdom, understanding, discernment

4.   His cheeks – His diverse emotional makeup

5.   His lips – His word

6.   His hands – His divine activity

7.   His body – His tender compassion

8.   His legs – His walk and administration of His purposes

9.   His countenance – His impartation to His people

10.  His mouth – Intimacy with Him

11.  He's altogether lovely – His comprehensive beauty

12.  He is my Beloved and my Friend

C.   She is lovesick because she focuses on Jesus instead of being preoccupied with her 2-fold test. She overcomes her self-focus by going deep in searching out Jesus' beauty. Revelation of these attributes will bring stability to our heart when we go through the storms of life.

D.   When I am in turmoil I read books on the attributes of God such as, The Existence & Attributes of God (Steven Charnock), Knowledge of the Holy (AW Tozer), Knowing God (JI Packer) and The Pleasures of God (John Piper). I wrote several books on the personality of God (Passion for Jesus, the Pleasures of Loving God, After God's Own Heart).

## V.    THE MAJESTIC BEAUTY OF JESUS (SONG 5:10-16)

A.    She starts by making a general statement about Jesus' beauty (Song 5:10). In her difficulty, she refers to Jesus as her Beloved or the one she loves. The NIV translates "is white" as "is radiant". He is ruddy or red. This is a reference to His humanity. Jesus is chief among ten thousand is a metaphor denoting that Jesus is incomparably superior to all others.

*10 My Beloved is white and ruddy, chief among ten thousand. (Song 5:10)*

B.    Jesus' head speaks of His sovereign headship over all creation (Eph.1:21). It is like finest gold to her. Gold speaks of divine nature. Finest speaks of the highest degree of quality and excellence.

*11 His head is like the finest gold… (Song 5:11)*

C.    Jesus' locks (hair, NIV) speaks of His dedication to God and His people. The Nazarite's vow forbid one to cut their hair because it was an outward sign of their dedication to God (Num. 6).

*11 His locks (hair) are wavy, and black as a raven. (Song 5:11)*

1.    His hair is "wavy and black as a raven" or his dedication is as vigorous as one with youthful energetic zeal. The wavy hair and black hair of a young man in the prime of life is in contrast to an old man whose thinning and graying hair has lost its vitality and fullness. In other words, Jesus' consecration to God and His people is eternally vigorous.

2.    Hair also speaks of the beauty of submission to God. Paul spoke of a woman's hair as showing forth her glory and dedication to God's authority (1 Cor. 11:5, 6, 15).

D.    Jesus' eyes speak of His ability to see or His omniscience (infinite knowledge, wisdom and discernment). His eyes being like doves speaks of singleness of vision (Song 1:15; 4:1).

*12 His eyes are like doves by the rivers of waters washed with milk, and fitly set. (Song 5:12)*

E.    Jesus' cheeks reveal His emotional make-up including His passions and pleasures. Our emotions are expressed in our cheeks. They are windows into one's emotions enabling us to discern if a person has joy, sadness or anger. Jesus' emotional life is like a bed of spices. Banks of scented herbs speaks of the extravagant amount and diversity of fragrance of His affections.

*13 His cheeks are like a bed of spices, like banks of scented herbs. (Song 5:13)*

F.    Jesus' lips speak of His words which are sweet and pure like lilies. They contain myrrh which refers to exhortations to embrace death to self.

*13 His lips are lilies, ripping with liquid myrrh. (Song 5:13)*

G.    Jesus' hands (or arms, NIV) refer to His works and activities. He has all power (omnipotent) so He can accomplish anything He pleases. Rods of gold speak of divine character.

*14 His hands are rods of gold set with beryl. (Song 5:14)*

H. Jesus' body (or belly, KJV) speaks of His tender compassion. In Song 5:4 she says "My heart yearned," and is translated here as body. It speaks of deep feelings or tender compassions. Jesus' compassion is rare like ivory (and requires skill like carved ivory).

*14 His **body** is carved ivory inlaid with sapphires. (Song 5:14)*

I. Jesus' legs refer to His walk or the administration of His purposes. The legs provide the forward motion of the body. The way Jesus fulfills His purposes and proceeds in His plans are like pillars of marble. Pillars speak of strength, orderliness, and beauty. Marble was a strong and permanent type of building material. Jesus' ways are strong, lovely, permanent, established and orderly.

*15 His **legs** are pillars of marble set on bases of fine gold. (Song 5:15)*

J. Jesus' countenance speaks of His impartation of glory to His people. David prayed, "Lord lift up the light of your countenance on us." This was a prayer for manifestations of God to come to His people. Lebanon is symbolic of that which is stately and honorable (Song 4:8, 11, 15).

*15 His **countenance** is like Lebanon, excellent as the cedars. (Song 5:15)*

K. Jesus' mouth is associated with intimacy with His people throughout the Song. In Song 1:2, the mouth was introduced in the Song in context to the kisses of His mouth which refers to intimacy with God. His mouth is distinct from His words as signified by His lips (Song 5:13). Intimacy with God is most sweet because nothing delights her heart more than this.

*16 His **mouth** is most sweet… (Song 5:16)*

L. Jesus is altogether lovely. This is a summary statement. The One she loves is the One she calls her friend. He is not only radiant in His majesty but He humbled Himself to be our friend.

*16 Yes, He is **altogether lovely**. This is my Beloved, and this is my **friend**, O daughters of Jerusalem! (Song 5:16)*

## VI. SECOND QUESTION: WHERE IS HE THAT WE MAY SEEK HIM WITH YOU? (SONG 6:1)

*1 **Where** has your Beloved gone, O fairest among women? **Where** has your Beloved turned aside, **that we may seek Him with you**? (Song 6:1)*

A. The conversation that began between the Bride and the daughters in Song 5:8 is continuing. Here the daughters see the Bride's intimacy with Jesus and conclude that she knows something about Jesus that they do not know. Therefore, they ask a second question, "Where is your Beloved that we may seek Him like you do?" We want to know Him like you do. We want what you have.

B. The Bride's answer in Song 5:10-16, cause the daughters to change the question from "What is He?" to "Where can we find Him?" They are no longer content to serve Jesus at a distance. They ask the same question the Bride asked in Song 1:7, "Where does Jesus feed His flock?"

C. The daughters refer to Jesus as "your Beloved" because He is not yet their Beloved. They continue to see her as a godly person filled with God's Presence. "O fairest among women?"

D.     The daughters of Jerusalem want to seek Jesus with the Bride (Song 6:1d). The Bride's proclamation of Jesus' beauty stirs them to seek after Jesus with passion. They are now willing to let go of their "other beloveds". We all have "other beloveds" until we see Jesus' splendor.

E.     The Bride's testing results in the lives of others being dramatically changed. We never know who is watching us as we love Jesus in our difficulties. The Holy Spirit is raising up lovesick messengers who know Jesus in a way that will change the expression of Christianity in the whole earth and prepare the Bride to be strong in love in the End-Time pressures (Rev. 15:2-4).

## VII.    THE BRIDE ANSWERS THE SECOND QUESTION (SONG 6:2-3)

*² My Beloved has gone to <u>His garden</u>, to the beds of spices, to feed His flock in the <u>gardens</u>, and to <u>gather</u> lilies. I am my Beloved's, and my Beloved is mine. He <u>feeds</u> His flock among the lilies. (Song 6:2-3)*

A.     Jesus is in His Church and is building it. The Bride teaches them where they can find Jesus in an intimate way. Jesus dwells in His garden to gather and feed His people. His garden (singular) speaks of the worldwide Church which is made up of local churches or the gardens (plural).

*¹⁸ I will build My church, and the gates of Hades shall not prevail against it. (Mt. 16:18)*

B.     The Bride declares, "My Beloved has gone to the beds of spices" (Song 6:2). The beds (plural) are within His one garden (The Church). There is one Church in the earth, but there are many diverse beds of spices. Spices speak of manifestations of grace. Each ministry is a unique spice. Each "spice bed" in the garden has a rich fragrance of Christ. Jesus loves the whole Church.

C.     Jesus' cheeks are like a bed of spices (Song 5:13). The different reflections of Jesus' personality in the Church will all meet together in the New Jerusalem or the mountain of spices (Song 8:14).

D.     When we compare Song 1:7-8 to Song 6:2-3, we see that the Bride gives the same answer that Jesus gave her (see session 10). She asked Jesus, "Tell me, where do you feed Your flock?" In Song 1:8, Jesus gave her a 3-fold instruction as to where He feeds His flock.

*⁷ Tell me, O You whom I love, where You <u>feed Your flock</u>...? 8 O fairest among women, follow in the <u>footsteps of the flock</u>, and <u>feed your little goats</u> beside the <u>shepherds' tents</u>. (Song 1:7-8)*

1. Commitment to Body life (v. 8c): refuse unsanctified isolation
2. Commitment to servant ministry (v. 8d): refuse unsanctified idleness
3. Commitment to spiritual authority (v. 8e): refuse unsanctified independence

E.     In our next session: Jesus <u>breaks the silence</u> as He lavishes affection on her. He proclaims that she is as awesome as a victorious army with banners. Jesus is "conquered" only by His Bride's extravagant love. Our eyes of devotion deeply touch His heart. All the armies in hell cannot conquer Jesus, but the eyes of His Bride "conquer" Him when they are true to Him in testing.

*⁴ O My love, you are as beautiful as <u>Tirzah</u>, lovely as <u>Jerusalem</u>, awesome as an <u>army</u> with banners! 5 Turn your eyes away from Me, for they have <u>overcome</u> Me. (Song 6:4-5)*

# Session 20 Jesus Praises Her After Her Season of Testing (Song 6:4–10)

## I. REVIEW: THE BRIDE'S CRY FOR THE INCREASE OF GOD'S PRESENCE IN HER LIFE

A. The Bride prayed for both the north winds of adversity and the south winds of blessing to come to the garden of her heart that the spices of grace or God's presence might flow in her to others.

*16 Awake, O __north__ wind, and come, O __south__! blow upon __my garden__, that its __spices__ may flow out. Let My Beloved come to __His garden__ and eat its pleasant fruits... (Song 4:16).*

B. This is the turning point in the Song. The Song of Solomon has two main sections. First, Song 1-4 is focused on receiving __our inheritance__ in God. Second, Song 5-8 is focused on God receiving __His inheritance__ in us. The answer to the prayer for the __north winds__ comes in Song 5:3-7.

C. The Lord calls the Bride to intimacy by coming to her as the "Jesus of Gethsemane" (Song 5:2) and asking her to open her heart "for Him" to experience new depths of intimacy with Him.

*2 It is the voice of my Beloved! He knocks, saying, "__Open for Me__...My love..." (Song 5:2)*

D. She responds in obedience (Song 5:3-5) which is followed by a 2-fold test. First, Jesus tests her by withdrawing His presence from her (Song 5:6). Second, He allows the spiritual authorities to mistreat her (Song 5:7). The Bride responds to God in love (Song 5:8).

E. The daughters then ask her two questions. First, "Why do you love Him so much?" (Song 5:9). The Bride answers by proclaiming ten facets of Jesus' beauty (Song 5:10-16). After hearing her answer they ask her the second, "How can we know Him like you?" (Song 6:1).

*10 My beloved is __white__ (dazzling, NAS)...and __chief among ten thousand__...16 His __mouth__ is most sweet, Yes, __He is altogether lovely__. This is my Beloved, and this is my friend... (Song 5:10-16)*

## II. OVERVIEW OF SONG 6:4-10

A. In Song 6:4-10, Jesus breaks the silence with the Bride that began in Song 5:6. He praises her beauty and reveals what He was feeling about her during her time of testing. (He does not rebuke her for disobedience in Song 5:3). He describes her beauty using three metaphors (v. 4) and His passion for her (v. 5) in terms as extravagant as her declarations about Him in Song 5:10-16.

B. Jesus describes the Bride's maturity (Song 6:5c-7) and her pre-eminence in His royal court with angelic attendants including seraphim, cherubim and angels without number (Song 6:8-9).

*8 There are __60 queens__ and __80 concubines__, and __virgins without number__. 9 My dove, my perfect one, is the...only one of her mother, the favorite of the one who bore her... (Song 6:8-9)*

C. The Holy Spirit describes the Bride's glory (Song 6:10).

*10 Who is she who __looks forth as the morning__, __fair as the moon__, __clear as the sun__, awesome as an army with banners? (Song 6:10)*

## III.   JESUS DESCRIBES THE BRIDE'S BEAUTY IN THE TIME OF TESTING (SONG 6:4)

*⁴ O My love, you are as <u>beautiful</u> as Tirzah, <u>lovely</u> as Jerusalem, <u>awesome</u> as an army with banners! (Song 6:4)*

A.   Jesus breaks His silence to praise her beauty using 3 metaphors, after she proclaimed, "I am lovesick because He is dazzling and altogether beautiful." (Song 5:8-16). The Bride is praised for her beauty which is found in her love for Jesus. Augustine said the only praise to be desired and the only praise that is true is the praise that comes from God. Jesus describes her beauty more fully in Song 7:6-9. He celebrates the beauty worked in her by the Spirit. In the Song, He affirms the Bride's beauty 9 times (Song 1:15 {2x}; 2:10, 13; 4:1 {2x}; 4:7; 6:4; 7:7).

B.   He first communicates how He feels about her by calling her, "O My love".

C.   Jesus declares that the Bride is as beautiful as the city of **Tirzah.** It was one of the most attractive cities in the ancient world. Tirzah means "beautiful". Before Israel captured the land of Israel under Joshua, it was a capital city of the Canaanites (Josh. 12:24; 1 Kings 15:33; 16:61). Thus, some commentators present this Canaanite city as symbolic of the unbelieving Gentile nations. In other words, the Bride is beautiful to unbelievers thus, she is effective in winning unbelievers.

D.   Soon after Solomon's death, a civil war divided the nation of Israel (931 BC). Jeroboam, the king of the Northern Kingdom chose Tirzah as his capital city (1 Kings 14:17; 15:21; 16:6) because it was the most beautiful city in the north. It was in the territory of Manasseh's tribe.

E.   Jesus declares that the Bride is as lovely as **Jerusalem.** It was the spiritual capital of Israel. It was the city chosen by God for the building of Solomon's Temple which was the only place on earth continually blessed with the manifest presence of God (Shekinah glory in the Holy of Holies). God ordained this city as His worship center for the whole world (Isa. 2:1-4; Zech. 14:16-19). Jerusalem's beauty speaks of the beauty of holiness found in worshipping God.

F.   Tirzah speaks of natural beauty that affects even unbelievers. Jerusalem refers to spiritual beauty that believers greatly value. The Bride being as beautiful as Tirzah and Jerusalem refers to her impacting both believers and unbelievers. Her beauty reaches both groups. Unbelievers see the Bride's self-sacrificing love and pure motives. They see her as one who gives everything for love.

G.   When an army in the ancient world returned victorious from battle, they displayed their banners in a military parade. A defeated army lost its banners. She defeated her greatest enemies which were those found in her heart. She finished her time of testing as a victorious army with banners because she did not give in to sin and unbelief. She gained the victory over her own heart. When we feel nothing, His heart feels so much when we gaze on Him with eyes of devotion. The shadows of her compromise and fear are gone (Song 2:17; 4:6). She conquered them by grace.

*⁴ O My love, you are…awesome as an army with banners! (Song 6:4-10)*

## IV.    JESUS DESCRIBES THE IMPACT THE BRIDE HAS ON HIS HEART (SONG 6:5)

⁵ *Turn your eyes away from Me, for they have <u>overcome</u> Me. (Song 6:5)*

A.    This is one of the great statements in the Scripture. By her eyes we understand her love for Him.

B.    Jesus is not asking her to literally look away from Him. He speaks poetically in the language of extravagant love. His heart is overcome or deeply moved by our steady love for Him as expressed in Song 5:10-16 in the midst of testing. When the daughters asked, "Why do you love Him?" She spoke of Him as being altogether lovely and dazzling".

C.    Our eyes of devotion move Jesus' heart. Our greatest glory is that we can move God's heart.

D.    What overcomes His heart? The greatness of the stars, oceans and mountains do not. The vast armies of men or demons are nothing before Him. The greatest warrior in history is "conquered" by our love, when we are true to Him in times of testing. Yes, our eyes of love move Him. This steady gaze of Song 6:5 is even more intense than her single glance (Song 4:9).

E.    ***Do you know the way you move Him?*** He is overcome by weak and broken people who truly love Him. While she felt nothing in her time of testing He felt so much. Our love for Him in the midst of the testing is more precious to Him than we understand. She did not know the impact her love was having on His heart because she did not feel His presence in the time of testing.

F.    In this age, we will never understand the fullness of the impact that we have on Jesus' heart. The woman did not know that Jesus marveled at her when He seemingly refused her (Mt. 15:21-28).

²⁸ *Jesus said to her, "O woman, <u>great is your faith</u>!" (Mt. 15:28).*

## V.    JESUS DESCRIBES THE BRIDE'S SPIRITUAL MATURITY (SONG 6:5C-7)

⁵ *Your <u>hair</u> is like a flock of goats going down from Gilead. Your <u>teeth</u> are like a flock of sheep which have come up from the washing; every one bears twins, and none is barren among them. Like a piece of pomegranate are your <u>temples</u> behind your veil. (Song 6:5c-7)*

A.    Jesus describes her maturity by highlighting 3 aspects of her character signified by her hair, teeth and temples. They refer to her dedication (hair), life in the Word (teeth) and godly emotions (temples). These are same qualities that He prophesied of when they were only budding virtues (Song 4:1-3). Now they have come to maturity in her life. Song 4:1-2 describes her eyes, hair, teeth and temple as does Song 6:5-6. Song 4:2 adds the word "shorn".

B.    He repeats these affirmations, using nearly the same words to prove that the test of Song 5:6-7 was necessary and fruitful. He causes everything to work together for good (Rom. 8:28).

C.    The Bride's hair speaks of her dedication to God. The hair of the Nazirite was an outward sign of their consecration or dedication (Num. 6).

*⁵ Your __hair__ is like a flock of goats going down from Gilead. (Song 6:5)*

D.    Her stately hair or dedication is the result of being well fed. Mount Gilead was a bountiful place in which the goats were abundantly fed. Her dedication is the result of being well fed on the Word of God. Song 4:1 adds the word "Mount" in referring to Gilead.

E.    Goats walk in a stately order (Prov. 30:29-31). The Bride's dedication is like a flock of goats in the sense that it is manifestation of godly order (wisdom) in contrast to fleshly zeal.

*²⁹ There are three things which are __majestic in pace__, Yes, four which are __stately in walk__: 30 A lion, which is mighty among beasts…31 a __male goat__ also… (Prov. 30:29-31)*

F.    Teeth speak of the ability to chew solid food thus, to receive the meat of the Word (Heb.5:12-14). Infants have no teeth and thus can only receive nourishment through milk (1 Cor. 3:1-3).

*⁶ Your __teeth__ are like a flock of sheep which have come up from the washing; every one bears twins, and none is barren among them. (Song 6:6)*

1.    We receive the meat of the Word and maintain cleanliness or healthy teeth by long and loving meditation on God's Word. In this way, we keep as clean as the sheep who come up from when the shepherd washes the mud off (Eph. 5:26-27; Jn. 13:10; 17:17).

2.    Her ministry fruitfulness comes from her life in the Word. To bear twins speaks of a double portion of fruitfulness. She is compared to the sheep in which none are barren. A diligent life in the Word guarantees fruitfulness (1 Tim. 4:6-16). The sheep in this passage are both clean and fruitful due to their life in the Word (Jn. 15:7-8).

G.    The Bride's temples being like pomegranates speaks of her godly emotions. The temples (cheeks) reveal one's emotions. The Hebrew word translated as temples can also be translated as cheeks. Our emotions are expressed by our cheeks. We can see anger, joy, gladness, and sadness on the cheeks. They are windows into one's emotions.

*⁷ Like a piece of pomegranate are your __temples__ behind your veil… (Song 6:7)*

1.    The pomegranate is a very sweet fruit. Her emotions are godly and sweet to God.

2.    When pomegranates are broken they are red. Red speaks of her modesty, her propensity for blushing in the presence of shameful things. Prostitutes do not blush with immodesty. A red countenance speaks of one sensitive to shameful things (red from blushing).

H.    Behind her veil speaks of her hidden life in God. Her emotions of love for God and her modesty is genuine when no one is watching. It is not just a show before people as in Song 4:3.

## VI.  THE ROYAL COURTS OF THE HEAVENLY BRIDEGROOM (SONG 6:8)

*8 There are sixty queens and eighty concubines, and virgins without number… (Song 6:8)*

A.    The Bride is preeminent in honor among the glorious hosts in Jesus' heavenly court. In the ancient world, a king's court included his harem which was comprised of women of various ranks. King Solomon's earthly royal court symbolized King Jesus' heavenly court. Three positions of honor in Solomon's court are used (queens, concubines and virgins).

B.    At the time this Song was written, Solomon had 60 wives who were each called a queen. He eventually had 700 wives (1Kings 11:3). These queens did not have the same of honor as the Shulamite which was his favorite. The king's bride was the most honored among his queens.

C.    The numbers 60, 80 and a group 'without number' represent the different degrees of glory in Solomon's court. The 60 queens had the highest ranks in Solomon's court. The number with "queenly glory" is the smallest number listed. The concubines were next in rank with 80. Concubines in a king's court had lesser honor than queens, yet still more than virgins because they were legally part of the King's family and owned property. The virgins were in the King's court as "staff members" but had no legal claim to the King's family or property.

D.    The primary point is to see that Jesus' Bride has more honor than all the hosts in His court. Jesus is surrounded by a host of glorious beings with different ranks. The Bride surpasses them all.

E.    Our purpose here is not to seek specific angelic groups that correspond to queens, concubines and virgins but to point out there are degrees of glory in a king's court. There are positions of varying rank in God's court including the seraphim, cherubim, archangels, the 24 elders, etc.

F.    We are not to think there are specifically 60 and 80 in various ranks around God's Throne. These merely convey different positions of honor in a king's court. We are not meant to categorize the heavenly court into the three groups in Song 6:8. For example, some compare the virgins without number in Solomon's court to the unnumbered multitudes of angels.

## VII.  THE BRIDE'S HONOR IN GOD'S FAMILY (SONG 6:9)

*9 My dove, My perfect one, is the only one, the <u>only one</u> of her mother, the <u>favorite</u> of the one who bore her. The daughters saw her and called her blessed, the queens and the concubines, and they praised her. (Song 6:9)*

A.    The Shulamite is referred to as His dove and His perfect one. Being His dove speaks of her singleness of heart and that she walks in the Spirit as God's dove walking in bridal identity.

B.    Being His perfect one means she has matured spiritually. Jesus' End-Time Church will become mature in love as she is filled with God's glory without any spot or wrinkle (Eph. 5:26-27).

C.    Of all the glorious hosts in Jesus' courts in the Eternal city, He has only one Bride. The only one" is translated "is unique" (NAS/NIV). She is unrivaled. She has no competition. Jesus is saying, "Of all the attendants in My court, she is the only one I want and the only one that I would die for." Jesus is saying to her what she said to Him (Song 5:10, 16), that she is unique or a one of a kind that has captured His heart. She is the chief among ten thousand in His heart as He is in her heart. He wants no other.

D.    The mother is a picture of the Church through history. God is our father and the Church is spoken of as our mother. Paul spoke allegorically of the New Jerusalem as "the mother of us all" (Gal. 4:26). The redeemed from history are represented as a "mother" that gave birth to Jesus (manchild) and as well as the believers that come after her (Rev. 12:5, 17). God is the author of our natural and spiritual birth. The agency He uses for our natural birth is our natural mother. The agency He uses for our spiritual birth is the witness of the Church, our spiritual mother. Those who do God's will are His mother (Mt. 12:46-50). The Lord uses the Church to win the lost that they may become a part of His Church. The mother crowns Jesus with her love on His wedding day (Song 3:11).

E.    I define the Bride as the Church becoming mature in love for God and people. This has never happened. The Church in the Book of Acts was not fully mature. It had moments of glory in several cities. Before the Lord returns the worldwide Church will be mature or spotless and blameless (Eph. 5:26-27). The End-Time Church that survives the Great Tribulation has a unique honor in history being the only generation to walk blameless before Jesus returns.

F.    The Bride is by definition made up of those who walk in mature in love. Living like the heavenly Bride while on earth is to walk in mature in love. The interesting thing to note is that the Bride is the <u>favorite</u> of the one who bore her, in other words, the favorite of her mother which speaks of the redeemed through history. The worldwide End-Time mature Bride is unique in history and is the favorite of the one who bore her.

G.    The Church from history is our mother. The favorite work of the historical Church is the great End-Time harvest of souls and its full maturity (Rev. 14:14-16; Eph. 5:27).

H.    The End-Time Church will enter into the measure of the stature of maturity that belongs to the fullness of Christ (Eph. 4:13). God will finish what He began and the gates of hell will not prevail in the Church (Mt. 16:18; Phil. 1:6). The Church throughout all history did not walk in maturity. They lived much more like the daughters of Jerusalem. The Church through history from heaven's point of view will see the End-Time Church and will call her blessed.

I.    The honor of the Bride in her maturity is seen in the phrase the daughters saw her and called her blessed (6:9). The daughters speak of the immature believers throughout history. They will call her blessed as they did in Song 6:1. The redeemed through history will praise God for the End-Time Church as it prevails in love while still on earth. The queens and the concubines will praise the End-Time Church. They may speak of the heavenly host rejoicing with gladness as the Bride comes into her honored position. God has brought to pass a people that are mature on the earth.

## VIII.   THE HOLY SPIRIT DESCRIBES THE BRIDE'S 4 FOLD CROWN OF GLORY

*<sup>10</sup> Who is she who looks forth as the __morning__, fair as the __moon__, clear as the __sun__, awesome as an __army__ with banners? (Song 6:10)*

A.   The Bride is described as possessing a 4-fold glory as co-heir with Jesus of the Eternal City. The Spirit here uses four metaphors to show the Bride's beauty by comparing her to heavenly objects in the way Jesus compared her to earthly cities (Jerusalem and Tirzah) in Song 6:4.

B.   The Spirit asks a rhetorical question, "Who is she?" Jesus just declared the Bride's preeminent place in His court. The Spirit is now affirming her place of preeminence. The Spirit speaks three times in the Song asking the same question, "Who is this...?" (Song 3:6, 6:10; 8:5).

C.   The Bride's ministry in the culture is as one "who looks forth or shines forth as the morning". After the long night, the sunlight of the morning shines forth with hope on the horizon. The Church in this age functions as salt (flavor, preservation) and light (direction, life) in Mt. 5:13-16. This emphasizes the impact that God's people will have on individuals and society (political, military, economic, educational, family, media, arts, technology, social institutions, etc).

D.   The Bride's ministry in this age is as one "who shines forth as beautiful as the moon". The mature Church is as beautiful as the moon. The moon was established by God to provide light in the nighttime (Gen. 1:14-19). It does not have its own light but receives the reflected light of the sun. The mature Church is a source of God's light in a dark and fallen world.

*<sup>16</sup> God made two great lights: the greater light (sun) to rule the day, and the lesser light (moon) to rule the night… (Gen. 1:16)*

E.   The Church in this age is to shine like the moon in the darkness as we work in evangelism and transformation of our culture (Mt. 5:16; Phil. 2:15). This age is in a time of darkness as the Millennial Kingdom is a worldwide time of day).

F.   The Bride's ministry in the age-to-come is as one "who shines forth as bright as the sun". Her full glory is in the brilliant light of Jesus' glory. The Church will reflect the glory of Jesus' light in the New Jerusalem. Jesus is the "sun" in the Eternal City (Rev. 21:23).

*<sup>23</sup> The city (New Jerusalem) had no need of the sun or of the moon to shine in it, for the glory of God illuminated it. __The Lamb is its light.__ (Rev. 21:23)*

G.   The Church will reflect God's light in the New Jerusalem as co-heir of the Eternal City.

*<sup>11</sup> Having the glory of God. __Her light__ (the Church's) was like a most precious stone, like a jasper stone, clear as crystal. (Rev. 21:11)*

*<sup>36</sup> The whole body will be __full of light__, as when the __bright shining of a lamp__… (Lk. 11:36)*

*<sup>3</sup> Those who are wise shall __shine like the brightness__ of the firmament… (Dan. 12:3)*

H.  The Church rules with Jesus and reflects God's light in time and eternity (Rev. 21:23-24, 11; 1:16; Isa. 60:1-3, 19-20; 24:23; 59:19; 62:1; Ezek. 43:2; Ps. 50:2; Mal. 4:2; 2 Cor. 4:6; Jn. 8:12; 1 Jn. 1:5; Mt. 5:14-16; Phil. 2:15; Dan. 12:3; 1 Cor. 15:41-42; Song 6:10).

I.  The Bride's government is as one "who is as awesome as a powerful army with banners".

*You are as awesome (majestic, NIV) as an army with banners (NAS). (Song 6:10)*

J.  The Bride will rule in the governmental administration of Jesus' Kingdom forever (Dan. 7:27).

*²⁷ Then the kingdom and dominion, and the greatness of the kingdoms under the whole heaven, shall be given to the people, the saints of the Most High. (Dan. 7:27)*

*²¹ To him who overcomes I will grant to sit with Me on My throne, as I also overcame and sat down with My Father on His throne. (Rev. 3:21)*

K.  In Song 6:4, Jesus emphasizes the victory over her heart in earthly difficulties. Here, the Spirit emphasizes her victory over all powers.

L.  *Summary*: the Bride's 4-fold glory is seen in three progressive stages in the glory of God. First, she experiences the dawning of God's light to bring salt and light to the culture (Mt. 5:13-16). Second, she shines forth as a beautiful moon in warfare and evangelism in this age. Third, she shines forth as the sun in the age-to-come. In all this, she rules as God's weapon in His government forever.

M.  It has not yet appeared what we will be like.

*² It has not yet been revealed what we shall be, but we know that when He is revealed, we shall be like Him, for we shall see Him as He is. (1 Jn. 3:2)*

N.  The 7-fold comparison of the triumphant Bride who walks in the Holy Spirit

1.  She is compared to Tirzah speaking of her beauty to unbelievers.

2.  She is compared to Jerusalem speaking of her beauty to believers.

3.  She is compared to an earthly army speaking of her triumph over her own heart.

4.  She is compared to the dawn speaking of persevering in God's order on earth in this age.

5.  She is like the moon speaking of her triumph in evangelism and transformation.

6.  She is like the sun speaking of her triumph in glory as a co-heir of the Eternal City.

7.  She is like God's army with government over all things.

## Session 21 Vindication of the Persecuted Bride (Song 6:11-7:9)

### I.  REVIEW OF SONG 6:4-10

A.  In Song 6:4-10, Jesus <u>breaks the silence</u> with the Bride that began in Song 5:6. He praises her beauty and reveals what He was feeling about her during her time of testing. He describes her beauty using 3 metaphors (v. 4). He describes the impact the Bride has on His heart (v. 5).

> *⁴ O My love, you are as <u>beautiful</u> as Tirzah, <u>lovely</u> as Jerusalem, <u>awesome</u> as an army with banners! 5 Turn your eyes away from me, for they have <u>overcome</u> me. (Song 6:4-5)*

B.  When an army in the ancient world returned victorious from battle, they displayed their banners in a military parade. A defeated army lost its banners. She defeated her greatest enemies which were those found in her heart. She finished her time of testing as a victorious army with banners because she did not give in to sin and unbelief. She gained the victory over her own heart. When we feel nothing, His heart feels so much when we gaze on Him with eyes of devotion. The shadows of her compromise and fear are gone (Song 2:17; 4:6). She conquered them by grace.

C.  Jesus describes the Bride's maturity (Song 6:5c-7) and her pre-eminence in His royal court with angelic attendants including seraphim, cherubim and angels without number (Song 6:8-9).

> *⁸ There are <u>60 queens</u> and <u>80 concubines</u>, and <u>virgins without number</u>. 9 My dove, my perfect one, is the…only one of her mother, the favorite of the one who bore her... (Song 6:8-9)*

D.  The Spirit describes her 4-fold glory as co-heir with Jesus of the Eternal City (Song 6:10).

> *¹⁰ Who is she who <u>looks forth as the morning</u>, <u>fair as the moon</u>, <u>clear as the sun</u>, awesome as an army with banners? (Song 6:10)*

E.  First, the Bride's ministry in the culture is as one who looks forth or shines forth as the morning. Second, the Bride's ministry in this age is as one who shines forth as beautiful as the moon in the darkness as we work in evangelism and transformation of our culture (Mt. 5:16; Phil. 2:15). Third, the Bride's ministry in the age-to-come as one who shines forth as bright as the sun will occur because we will reflect Jesus' light in the New Jerusalem (Rev. 21:11). Fourth, the Bride's government is one who is as awesome as a powerful army with banners.

### II.  OVERVIEW OF SONG 6:11-7:9A

A.  As the Bride walks in the Song 6:4-10 revelation, she is overcome by love for the whole Church. She commits to serve the weak and immature ones in God's garden (Song 6:11-12). A primary theme of the Song is that Jesus is equipping His Bride to walk in mature partnership with Him.

B.  After this season of service, the Bride is persecuted. She receives two different responses from the Church. First, she is supported from part of the Church (Song 6:13a). Second, another part of the Church gives her a sarcastic response (Song 6:13b). The Bride is vindicated by the daughters who express respect for ten areas of her life (Song 7:1-5). Next, the Bride is vindicated by Jesus who endorses her as His partner by releasing His grace on her in a great measure (Song 7:6-9a).

## III.   THE BRIDE'S COMMITMENT TO SERVE THE WHOLE CHURCH (SONG 6:11)

*¹¹ I went down to the <u>garden</u> of nuts (walnut grove) to see the verdure of the <u>valley</u>, to see whether the vine had <u>budded</u> and the pomegranates had <u>bloomed</u>. (Song 6:11)*

A.      The garden of God is mentioned 9 times in the Song. The first 3 references are to her garden (Song 4:12, 15, 16). The last 6 references are to His garden (Song 4:16; 5:1; 6:2, 11; 7:12; 8:13).

B.      The Bride goes down to God's garden to help the plants that were merely budding and blooming. She taught the daughters that Jesus is found in His garden feeding His people (Song 6:2-3). Thus, she goes down to His garden to partner with Him because she wants to be with Him where He is.

C.      The garden includes a walnut grove which gives a clear picture of spiritual truth. Walnut trees have dense shade thus they provide refuge from the summer heat as well as having economic value in producing food. Oil is also produced from walnuts that was used to making soap, which speaks of cleansing. Its leaves were used in medicinal ways to aid in physical healing.

D.      The life in a walnut seed is on the inside. However, the seed must die and be broken before it can provide food, oil or healing for others. We must die to ourselves to provide food, cleansing (soap) and healing for others. The life within is hidden and not immediately observable.

E.      She went to see the verdure or the vibrant greenness of God's garden. One dictionary defines verdure as the fresh vibrant greenness of flourishing vegetation.

F.      She "went down" to invest herself in God's vineyard in other places outside of her familiar sphere. She sees God's flourishing garden in the midst of the valley in this fallen world. She goes to see if the vine had budded or to gain insight into God's work in other places.

G.      In Scripture, the vine and vineyard speak of God's people and His work (Isa. 5; Jn.15). The budding vineyard speaks of the vine that did not yet have fruit. In other words, it speaks of the immature Church. She sees God's vineyard without much fruit but he sees buds and blooms. In Song 2:11-13, the budding vineyard was a prophetic sign of God's visitation coming soon.

H.      The blossoming pomegranates speak of individual believers. She goes down to invest into the budding vine that had not yet matured instead of being impatient with them.

*¹¹ To see whether the vine had <u>budded</u> and the pomegranates had <u>bloomed</u>. (Song 6:11)*

I.      The Bride sees the budding virtues in others as the Lord saw her virtues in seed form (Song 4:1-5). Her enthusiasm for them comes from His enthusiasm for her while she was immature.

J.      The Bride is saying "Yes!" to the Great Commission. We can "go down" to help immature ones in our own neighborhood. We do not have to get on a plane to serve in God's garden. In principle it speaks of leaving the comfort zone to embrace the difficulty of caring and helping others.

## IV.  LOVE FOR GOD'S CHURCH OVERCOMES HER (SONG 6:12)

*12 Before I was even aware, <u>my soul had made me as the chariots</u> of my noble people. (Song 6:12)*

A.    While she is down in the valley working with the budding vineyard, suddenly her soul becomes like the chariots of her noble people. This depicts the zeal she feels for others. The Bride's soul moved like a chariot. In the ancient world, a chariot was the fastest and easiest way to travel with luggage for a long distance. The best chariots belonged to the noble people or the royal family. (KJV translates "noble people," as "Ammi-Nadib" which is a prince's name).

B.    *My soul had made me (my desire set me among, NIV)*. Her soul was made like a king's chariot that moved swiftly. In other words, she suddenly found strong desires to serve God's people.

C.    As she went down to see how the work of God was progressing, she was suddenly overcome with desire to help others. She is "beside herself" or is compelled by love (2 Cor. 5:11, 14). Instead of being put off by the immaturity, pride, wrong applications of the Word and lack of discernment of these "budding vines" she is surprised by the tender compassion that she feels.

D.    Her heart moves forward in this burden without any resistance like a swiftly moving chariot. She is surprised by this new movement of her heart. Before she was even aware, she had new desires and burdens with great enthusiasm to help others. This is the work of the Spirit.

E.    God loves the whole Church, not just the part we are involved in. He wants us to have ownership of the whole Church not just the small part under our authority. Zeal for the whole Church is foundational to the unity in the End-Time Church (Jn. 17:21). Most only support what is theirs.

F.    The Lord is raising up shepherds who care about His larger purposes and who train the people to love the whole Church. She is filled with love for the Body like Joseph was for his brothers without any sense of bitterness over the way she was mistreated (Gen. 50:15-21).

G.    The Bride follows through on this burden by walking it out with diligence.

*12 Let us get up <u>early</u> to the vineyards; let us see if the vine has <u>budded</u>, whether the grape <u>blossoms are open</u>, and the pomegranates <u>are in bloom</u>. (Song 7:12)*

## V.   THE TWO RESPONSES OF THE CHURCH TO THE BRIDE (SONG 6:13)

*13 <u>Return, return</u>, O Shulamite; return, return, <u>that we may look upon you</u>! What would you see in the Shulamite-- As it were, the dance of the two camps? (Song 6:13)*

A.    The first response to the Bride is one of respect and admiration. The daughters of Jerusalem wanted to seek the Lord with the Bride in Song 6:1. Here, they urgently express this desire to learn from her by crying out to her four times "to return." They wanted her to return from her labors in the garden in the valley seen in Song 6:11-12.

B.     The Ephesian elders wept because Paul left them to go to other parts of the Lord's vineyard.

> *[37] They all <u>wept freely</u>, and fell on Paul's neck and kissed him, 38 sorrowing most of all for the words which he spoke, that they would see his face no more… (Acts 20:37-38)*

C.     The Bride is called the Shulamite because she grew up in the Israelite city of Shunem. This is the only place in the Song in which the Bride is called the Shulamite. Solomon and Shunem come from the same root word that means peace. Jesus and His Bride have the same name.

D.     The second response is one of sarcasm from the jealous watchman who had recently struck and wounded her in Song 5:7. Here they sarcastically challenge the daughters' respect for the Bride (who they recently censored) by saying, "What do you see in the Shulamite?" or "Why do you want her to return? They undermine their desire to look to the Bride for spiritual input.

E.     The dance of two camps speaks of the conflict between the daughters and the watchman over the Bride. The KJV translates this as "the dance of the two armies," NAS as the "dance of the two companies," and the NIV translates it as "the camp of Mahanaim." Mahanaim in Hebrew may be translated as "two camps, two armies" or as the name of the city. Since Mahanaim is the city in which Jacob and Esau had a great conflict, either translation brings us to the same conclusion.

> *[13] What would you see in the Shulamite-- as it were, the <u>dance of the two camps</u>? (Song 6:13)*

F.     Mahanaim is famous for the conflict between Jacob and Esau. In Gen. 32, Esau pursued Jacob with the intent of killing him because Jacob stole his birthright. At Mahanaim, Jacob divided his people into two camps so Esau could only destroy one if he caught them. Jacob saw angels at Mahanaim that intervened to help him in this great conflict.

> *[1] So Jacob went on his way, and the <u>angels</u> of God met him. 2 When Jacob saw them, he said, "This is God's camp." And he called the name of that place <u>Mahanaim</u>. (Gen. 32:1-2)*

G.     The dance is an interaction between two camps (companies) in the Body of Christ. This is a dance of spiritual warfare that also involves two realms in the spirit (angelic and demonic).

H.     There are always two extreme positions in the Body of Christ. Those who pursue Jesus with great fervency and those who do not. Wholeheartedness is the core issue of many divisions.

I.     Jesus brought division between the sincere and the insincere not between the mature and the immature (Mt. 10:34-36). The Lord will unify the Church after He purges it of compromise.

> *[34] Do not think that I came to bring peace on earth. <u>I did not come to bring peace but a sword.</u> 35 For I have come to set a man against his father, a daughter against her mother, and a daughter-in-law against her mother-in-law… (Mt. 10:34-35)*

J.     The two camps are represented by Saul attacking David. Paul's ministry resulted in division as he confronted disobedience to God as he turned the world upside down (Acts 17:6).

> *[6] These who have <u>turned the world upside down</u> have come here too. (Acts 17:6)*

## VI. THE BRIDE IS VINDICATED BY DISCERNING BELIEVERS (SONG 7:1-5)

*¹ How beautiful are your feet in sandals, O prince's daughter! The curves of your thighs are like jewels, the work of the hands of a skillful workman. 2 Your navel is a rounded goblet; it lacks no blended beverage. Your waist is a heap of wheat set about with lilies. 3 Your two breasts are like two fawns, twins of a gazelle. 4 Your neck is like an ivory tower, your eyes like the pools in Heshbon by the gate of Bath Rabbim. Your nose is like the tower of Lebanon which looks toward Damascus. 5 Your head crowns you like Mount Carmel, and the hair of your head is like purple; a King is held captive by your tresses (hair). (Song 7:1-5)*

A.  This passage answers the sarcastic question, "Who is the Shulamite?" The Bride is vindicated first by sincere believers (Song 7:1-5). Next the Lord Himself vindicates her and promises to release a greater measure of the Spirit on her (Song 7:6-9). The Holy Spirit always raises up sincere believers to vindicate those who radically pursue the Lord as His Bride.

B.  These sincere ones discern many of the same affirmations that Jesus gave the Bride (Song 4:1-5). They speak of 10 virtues in the Bride as she spoke of 10 virtues of Jesus (Song 5:10-16).

C.  It is good to compare the 10 affirmations of the Bride in Song 7:1-5 with 8 given to her in Song 4:1-5. There are 4 main differences. In Song 4:1-5, Jesus began by describing her head (giving 6 of the 8 affirmations about her head) and worked down her body. Whereas, in Song 7:1-5, the daughters start by describing her feet as they work up to the head (4 affirmations are related to her head). The qualities in Song 7 relate to her ministry. In Song 4 the focus is on her character.

D.  We also see what the Lord delights in when He sees these 10 characteristics and what He wants in bringing us to maturity. They are practical definitions of holiness and fruitfulness.

E.  It is clear that the daughters are speaking in Song 7:1-5 and that Jesus speaks in Song 7:6. For example, the daughters call the Bride the "Prince's daughter" (7:1), whereas Jesus calls the Bride "My love" or "My spouse" each time throughout the Song. In Song 7:5, Jesus is referred to as "a King" (instead of Him speaking in the first person to the Bride). In Song 7:8, Jesus speaks in the first person saying, "I will," indicating a change of speakers in v. 6-9 from v. 1-5.

F.  The daughters take a stand for the Bride declaring that "she is beautiful" and by calling her the prince's daughter which points to her royal character or character befitting of royalty. We all have a royal bloodline by our new birth.

    *¹ How beautiful are your feet in sandals, O prince's daughter! (Song 7:1)*

G.  The Bride's feet in sandals speak of evangelism. Her success in evangelism is a sign of her beauty. Our feet are to be shod by the preparation of the Gospel (Eph. 6:15). How beautiful are the feet of those who bring good news (Isa. 52:7). The place our feet walk speaks of our inheritance (Josh.1:3). Shoes speak of prosperity and honor (Lk. 15:22). The poor in the ancient world often did not have shoes. Bare feet speak symbolically of shame, poverty, and humiliation.

H.   The Bride's thighs or legs speak of the strength behind her walk in God. Jesus' legs are like pillars of marble (Song 5:15). The curves of her thighs speak of the muscular definition in her legs giving her strength. This athletic feature was developed through much discipline. Thus, her strong walk is costly and esteemed as rare like the jewels worked on by a skillful workman.

*¹ The curves of your <u>thighs</u> are like jewels, the work of the hands of a skillful workman. (Song 7:1)*

I.   The navel speaks of the nourishment a child receives in their mother's womb. This refers to our formative years in the Lord as the time in which our inner life in God is developed. A rounded goblet speaks of a healthy navel. This is opposite of being malnourished. A goblet which lacks no beverage speaks of a full range of nourishment. She is healthy with a balanced diet with all the necessary nutrients for a strong life. This speaks of a good spiritual foundation in our life.

*² Your <u>navel</u> is a rounded goblet; it lacks no blended beverage. (Song 7:2)*

J.   The daughters see the Bride as prepared for the coming harvest. A heap of wheat speaks of an abundance of wheat which only occurs during the harvest. She is pictured as pregnant (large waist) with an abundant harvest. She is pregnant with the harvest wheat that is set about with lilies. The harvest that comes forth from her will be established in purity and holiness.

*² Your <u>waist</u> is a heap of wheat set about with lilies. (Song 7:2)*

K.   Breasts speak of the ability to nurture others. Babes are nurtured through milk from the breast. She is ready to nurture the harvest that she gives birth to. Her breasts are like youthful fawns (young deer less than one year old) in contrast to being elderly and without the ability to nurture with milk. Twins of a gazelle speaks of a double portion in her ability to nurture. This is in contrast to the little sister (immature believer) who is not prepared to nurture others (Song 8:8).

*³ Your two <u>breasts</u> are like two fawns, twins of a gazelle. (Song 7:3)*

L.   In Scripture, the neck speaks of the will that can be stiff-necked (resistant) or submissive. The rebellious neck speaks of pride (Isa. 3:16). The Bride's will is like an ivory tower which is rare and costly. Her resolute choices are as costly as an ivory tower which provides her protection.

*⁴ Your neck is like an ivory tower… (Song 7:4)*

M.   Eyes speak of our ability to receive revelation (Eph. 1:18). She has keen spiritual insight (Song 1:15; 4:2, 9; 6:5). In Song 4:1, Jesus compared her eyes to dove' eyes speaking of her purity and loyalty. Here, her eyes are like the pools in Heshbon. These pools were not muddy but clean and easy to see through. To see clearly is our first priority because seeing is the doorway to growing spiritually (Phil 3:8-10). When we see differently we feel differently. The gate of Bath Rabbim was a resort area with clean water in the once royal city of Heshbon (Num. 21:25-26).

*⁴ Your <u>eyes</u> like the pools in Heshbon by the gate of Bath Rabbim. (Song 7:4)*

N.   The nose speaks of discernment. A tower provides protection. Her nose is like a protective tower that looked toward Damascus the capital of Syria (Israel's greatest enemy). Lebanon was on the north side of Judah facing Syria. She had discernment of her fiercest enemies.

*⁴ Your <u>nose</u> is like the tower of Lebanon which looks toward Damascus. (Song 7:4)*

O.     The Bride's thought life is powerful like the beautiful mountain tops of Carmel. Her thought life
       is filled with royal thoughts or crowned like Mount Carmel (Isa. 35:2). Our thoughts are
       significant in spiritual warfare, especially related to our image of God.

> *⁵ Your __head__ crowns you like Mount Carmel, and the __hair__ of your head is like purple; a King is
> __held captive__ by your tresses (hair). (Song 7:5)*

P.     In Scripture, hair spoke of one's dedication to God. The hair of the Nazirite was an outward sign
       of their dedication to God (Num. 6). A Nazirite did not cut their hair. Her hair is like purple
       which speaks of royalty. Her dedication is like the resolution of a king (NAS says "The King").

Q.     The Bride's dedication holds the heart of God. His love is so powerful that it binds Him to weak
       people who love Him. It is His glory (not His weakness) to be captivated by love for His people.
       His unique ability is to love those so much lower than He. His heart is "held" by us. He
       possesses all authority, but gives His heart without any reserve to His Bride.

R.     God's love binds Him to His people. For example, five intercessors captured His heart: Daniel,
       Noah, Job, Moses and Samuel (Ezek. 14:14; Jer.15:1; Ex. 32:7-14).

## VII.   THE BRIDE IS VINDICATED BY JESUS (SONG 7:6-9A)

> *⁶ How fair (beautiful) and how pleasant you are, O love, with your delights! 7 This __stature__ of yours is
> like a palm tree, and your breasts like its clusters. 8 I said, "I will go up to the palm tree, I will __take__
> __hold__ of its branches." Let now your __breasts__ be like clusters of the vine, the fragrance of your __breath__
> like apples, 9 and the roof of your __mouth__ like the best wine. (Song 7:6-9a)*

A.     Jesus vindicates His Bride (the speaker changed in Song 7:6). The watchmen asked, "Who is the
       Shulamite that anyone should pay attention to her?"

B.     Jesus' heart is truly held captive by the Bride (Song 7:5) as He says, "How beautiful and pleasant
       you are, O love, with your delights!" (v. 6). Jesus sees His people as beautiful and pleasant. His
       fruit is sweet and pleasant to her (Song 1:16; 2:3). Her fruit is pleasant to Him (Song 4:16-5:1).

C.     "O love" expresses the passion in God's heart for her. God loves us to the measure He loves
       Jesus (Jn.15:9; 17:23). It is beyond human comprehension (Eph. 3:18). Our love is greater than
       wine to Him (Song 4:10). There is nothing more delightful to Jesus than the love of His people.
       Our voice is sweet and our face is lovely to Him even in our weakness and struggle (Song 2:14).

D.     Jesus affirms the stature of the Bride's spiritual maturity as proclaimed by the daughters in Song
       7:1-5. A palm tree is a sign of victory and conquest (Rev. 7:4) and is a picture of maturity (Jer.
       10:5). It thrives even in a drought because it's roots go down deep finding water far below the
       surface. Thus, it grows exceptionally high and straight. Strong winds cannot break a palm tree.
       Her breasts or ability to nurture, are like the clusters of a palm tree that nourishes many.

> *⁷ This stature of yours is like a __palm tree__, and your __breasts__ like its clusters. (Song 7:7)*

E.    Jesus promises to "take hold" of His people or to release a great manifestation of His presence through them. Jesus said that He is the vine and we are the branches that He releases His power through (John 14:12). Jesus promises to "go up" to the palm tree to take hold of His servants.

*8 I said, "I will go up to the palm tree, I will take hold of its branches." (Song 7:8)*

*5 I am the vine, you are the branches. He who abides in Me…bears much fruit… (Jn. 15:5)*

G.    As the Lord "lays hold" of His people, He commissions her in three significant ways.

*8 Let now your breasts be like clusters of the vine, the fragrance of your breath like apples, 9 and the roof of your mouth like the best wine. (Song 7:8-9a)*

F.    His first commission is to nurture others in the power of the Spirit. Her breasts are to nurture people with the dimension of the Holy Spirit's activity operating in her in a new measure.

G.    His second commission is to let the fragrance of her breath refresh people like apples. Her breath speaks of her inner life. Apples speak of refreshing (Song 2:3). It is to refresh others in the Spirit.

*22 He breathed on them, and said, "Receive the Holy Spirit." (Jn. 20:22)*

H.    Her third commission is that her mouth or intimacy with God is to be like the best wine to God. The mouth throughout the Song speaks of the kisses of the mouth (Song 1:2, 4:3, 5:16). Our intimacy with Jesus is the best thing that the Spirit works in us for Jesus.

I.    We are to give Him the best we have in our relationship with Him. We must not neglect our intimacy with Him for any reason.

J.    Jesus said that the roof of her mouth was the best wine of the Holy Spirit. The roof of the mouth refers to the palate of the mouth or the taste of her mouth. The Hebrew word is roof or palate. It is simply that which comes from her mouth. It is to be the best wine or that which brings the greatest joy to Jesus (Song 4:10).

*10 How fair is your love…How much better than wine is your love (Song 4:10)*

K.    The wine speaks of the influences of the Holy Spirit (Eph. 5:18). The best wine to God is the wine of our intimacy. It is the most pleasurable thing to God outside of their fellowship within the Godhead.

L.    The best wine of all the works of His Kingdom or the best work of the Holy Spirit or the wine that Jesus enjoys most is when the Church walks in mature love (John 17:26).

*26 That the love with which You loved Me may be in them… (Jn. 17:26)*

*37 You shall love the LORD…with all your heart, with all your soul…and mind. (Mt. 22:37)*

# Session 22 The Bride's Mature Partnership With Jesus (Song 7:9b-8:4)

## I. REVIEW OF SONG 6:11-7:9

A.  In Song 6:11-12, the Bride committed herself to minister to those who were spiritually immature. Jesus equipping His Bride to walk in partnership with Him is a primary theme of the Song.

B.  In Song 7:8-9a, Jesus commissioned her in ministry in a 3-fold way: to nurture others, to release the presence of the Spirit and to maintain her intimacy with Jesus.

## II. OVERVIEW OF SONG 7:9B-8:4

A.  In Song 7:9b-8:4, she walks out the 3-fold commissioning of ministry from Song 7:8-9a. We see her enthusiasm for this as she says, "The wine goes down smoothly for my Beloved".

B.  In Song 7:9b-8:4, the Bride describes 4 aspects of walking out bridal partnership with Jesus. She walks it out in her instant obedience (7:9b-10), her intercession for more power (7:11-13), her boldness and humility in public ministry (8:1-2) and in her unbroken union with Him (8:3-4).

## III. BRIDAL PARTNERSHIP EXPRESSED IN INSTANT OBEDIENCE (SONG 7:9B-10)

*⁹ The wine <u>goes down smoothly</u> for my Beloved, moving gently the lips of sleepers. I am my Beloved's, and His desire is toward me. (7:9b-10)*

A.  The flow of thought changes significantly in the middle of Song 7:9. In response to the affirmation that the Bride receives from Jesus in Song 7:6-9a, she enthusiastically proclaims her agreement with the three things that Jesus commissioned her to do in Song 7:8-9a.

B.  In the poetic language of love the "wine going down smoothly" refers to her living in instantaneous agreement with the Holy Spirit's leadership. The wine of the Spirit will go down smoothly because she receives it without resistance or without choking on it. To be continually filled with the Spirit means to continually live under the Holy Spirit's leadership (Eph. 5:18).

C.  She delights in the Spirit's leadership and drinks the cup of God's will without hindrance.

*⁸ <u>I delight to do Your will</u>, O my God, and Your law is within my heart. (Ps. 40:8)*

*²² Are you able to <u>drink the cup</u> that I am to drink…? They said, "We are able." (Mt. 20:22)*

D.  When she refers to Jesus as "my Beloved" it indicates that she obeys the Spirit out of love for Jesus. As we live in more agreement with the Spirit, then He pours more love for Jesus into our heart (Rom. 5:5; Jn. 16:14). When obedience is difficult, we confess, "The wine goes down smoothly because You are my Beloved and because I love You, Jesus."

E.   The Spirit desires to awaken carnal believers who are spiritually asleep.

   *¹⁴ Awake, you who sleep, arise from the dead, and Christ will give you light. (Eph. 5:14)*

F.   The Spirit will minister through her to those who are asleep as she obeys Him in her own life.

   *⁹ The wine goes down smoothly for my Beloved, moving gently the lips of sleepers. (Song 7:9)*

   1.   The proof that the Spirit has awakened the sleepers is that their speech comes under His leadership. He will move the sleepers so that they speak in purity and righteousness.

   2.   The Spirit gently woos us to speak on His behalf with subtle impressions. He calls us to voluntary love, therefore, He will gently move us without violating our free will.

G.   The OT prophets spoke of wine to symbolize the blessing and presence of the Spirit (Joel 3:18; Amos 9:13; Hos. 2:22; Zech 9:17; Acts 2:15-16).

   *¹⁵ These are not drunk, as you suppose…16 This is what was spoken by…Joel… (Acts 2:15-16)*

H.   It would be easier to understand Song 7:9 if it were divided into two verses. The Lord speaks in the first line of v. 9 and the Bride speaks after that. Through the Song she addresses Jesus as "my Beloved" (Jesus never refers to her this way). He refers to her as "My love" or "My fair one".

## IV.   THE BRIDE'S 2-FOLD SPIRITUAL IDENTITY IN THE LOVE OF GOD (SONG 7:10)

*¹⁰ I am my Beloved's, and His desire is toward me. (7:10)*

A.   The Bride's obedience in Song 7:9 is rooted in this 2-fold spiritual identity. *Her spiritual identity #1:* She sees herself as one that Jesus desires. *Her Spiritual identity #2:* She sees herself as belonging totally to Jesus as her Beloved. Note that she is her Beloved's *because* His desire is for her. Understanding His desire comes first. We love Him because He first loves us.

   *¹⁹ We love Him because He first loved us. (1 Jn. 4:19)*

B.   *Spiritual identity #1:* She sees herself as one that Jesus desires. The most prominent theme in the Song is the revelation of God's desire for us. She has deep insight into Jesus' affection and enjoyment of her. This revelation will powerfully change us. This is her primary motivation for obedience and diligence (Song 4:9; 6:4-5; 7:6-10). Insight into God's desire gives us strength to refuse to live by the opinions of others. This gives us emotional security. We speak the Word to the enemy, saying, "It is written: "His desire is towards me, regardless if others reject me".

C.   *Spiritual identity #2:* She sees herself as a lover of God in saying, "I am my Beloved's" or "I belong to Jesus, I'm under His leadership, I want to please Him, His desires are what I care most about." She has revelation of Jesus' total ownership of her (1 Cor. 6:20). She exists for Him without other considerations (Rev. 14:4). She serves God without concern for what happens to her. Her focus is now entirely on Him, without self-interest. The question of what He desires is the most relevant issue in her life. This is what she values most.

D.  We are defined most by the fact that we are desired by God and that we desire (love) Him. We confess our identity, "I'm a lover of God. That is who I am. That is what I do.

E.  We live a life of sacrificial obedience because He already desires us (not to gain His love). The wine goes down smoothly <u>because</u> Jesus desires her and she belongs to Him (Song 7:9-10).

## V. JESUS HAS GREAT DESIRE FOR HIS PEOPLE (SONG 7:10)

A.  Our greatest glory is that we can move God's heart. His heart is deeply moved by our steady love for Him. The movements of our heart are so important to God that they are recorded in His books.

   *⁸ You number my wanderings; put my tears in Your bottle; <u>are they not in Your book?</u> (Ps. 56:8)*

B.  Do you know the way you move Him? He is overcome by weak people who truly love Him. Our responsive love for Him is more precious to Him than we understand. The Bride did not know the impact her love was having on Jesus' heart because she did not feel His presence in the time of testing. Jesus reveals how He feels about our faithful love when we are in times of testings.

   *⁵ Turn your eyes away from Me, for they have <u>overcome</u> Me. (Song 6:5)*

C.  Jesus' love for us is so powerful that it binds Him to weak people who love Him. It is His glory (not His weakness) to be captivated by love for His people. His ability to love those so much lower than Him is unique. Jesus' heart is truly held captive by the Bride (Song 7:5).

D.  God loves us to the measure He loves Jesus (Jn.15:9; 17:23). This is beyond our comprehension (Eph. 3:18). There is nothing more delightful to Jesus than the love of His people. Our voice is sweet and our face is lovely to Him even in our weakness and struggle (Song 2:14).

E.  We regularly pray, "Release this revelation to me and pour Your love into my heart.

   *⁵ Now may the Lord <u>direct your hearts</u> into the love of God… (2 Thes. 3:5)*

   *⁵ The love of God has been <u>poured out in our hearts</u> by the Holy Spirit. (Rom. 5:5)*

## VI. OUR PARTNERSHIP IS EXPRESSED IN INTERCESSION FOR POWER (SONG 7:11-12)

*¹¹ <u>Come</u>, my Beloved, <u>let us</u> go forth to the field; <u>let us</u> lodge in the villages. 12 <u>Let us</u> get up early to the vineyards; <u>let us</u> see if the vine has budded, whether the grape blossoms are open, and the pomegranates are in bloom. There I will give You my love. (Song 7:11-12).*

A.  Our partnership with Jesus is expressed in our intercession to see more of His power released. In Song 7:8 Jesus promised to release the Spirit in her life. She intercedes according to this promise. Here, we see the Bride following through on her commitment to go forth in ministry (Song 6:11).

B.  Earlier she went down to the garden to partner with Jesus in bringing the immature ones under His blessing and leadership. Now, she intercedes that He would <u>come with her</u> in the sense of releasing His presence through her labors. She changed her language in Song 6:11 from "<u>I went down</u>" to "<u>let us go</u>". She uses "let us" 4 times (Song 7:11-12) indicating that they work together.

> *<sup>11</sup> <u>I went down</u> to the garden…to see whether the vine had budded… (Song 6:11)*

> *<sup>20</sup> They went out and preached everywhere, the <u>Lord working with them</u> and confirming the word through the accompanying signs. (Mk. 16:20)*

C.  In Song 7:11, the Bride commits to go to the villages and fields of the harvest (Jn. 4:35).

> *<sup>11</sup> Come, my Beloved, let us go forth to the <u>field</u>; let us lodge in the <u>villages</u>. (Song 7:11).*

> *<sup>9</sup> For we are God's fellow workers; <u>you are God's field</u>… (1 Cor. 3:9)*

> *<sup>35</sup> Behold…<u>look at the fields</u>, for they are already white for harvest! (Jn. 4:35)*

D.  The field of service begins in our family, job, church and neighborhood. It is where God places you. It may be any where that people live. We do not have to get on a plane to serve in the field.

E.  The villages speak of the small out of the way areas where Jesus has an inheritance and desires to build His Church. She sees God's value for unknown people and places not just the big cities. She is willing to lodge or stay for a season even in a remote village (Song 7:11).

F.  Getting up early speaks of her diligence and urgency in the assignment that the Lord gave her.

G.  She goes down to invest into the budding vines that had not yet borne fruit. She goes to "to see" the budding vine because she sees them as Jesus' inheritance and "His garden" thus, she values them and is patient with them. The budding vines, the grape blossoms and the blooming pomegranates speak of different people and ministries that need maturity (Song 4:12, 13; 6:11).

H.  The Moravian missionaries lived in sacrifice that, "the Lamb might receive the reward of His sufferings". In this passage she's running with Him under the influence of the Spirit.

## VII.  THERE I WILL GIVE YOU MY LOVE (SONG 7:12)

*<sup>11</sup> Come, my Beloved, let us go forth to the <u>field</u>; let us lodge in the <u>villages</u>. 12 Let us get up early to the <u>vineyards</u>…<u>There</u> I will give You my love. (Song 7:11-12).*

A.  The Bride experiences undistracted intimacy with Jesus in the midst of ministry. "There" is the place of selfless labor, the risks of faith, disappointments and mistreatment. She embraces both being drawn along in intimacy and running together in ministry (Song 1:4). She learns to love Him while serving others instead of losing her intimacy in the rigors of ministry. She runs effectively with Jesus in the fields and villages that He might receive His inheritance from them.

B.    It is much easier to give Jesus our love at the banqueting table under the shade tree (Song 2:3-4). The immature maiden could love Jesus in private but could not sustain it while serving others.

C.    It requires maturity to walk in undistracted love for Jesus while in difficulty, persecution and disappointment. The Bride is walking in apostolic Christianity as outlined in Phil. 3:10 which calls us to walk in intimacy and ministry while embracing hardship. Paul loved Jesus in context to being mistreated in being sent to prison and while ministering to the jailer in Acts 16.

*10 That I may know Him (intimacy with God) and the power of His resurrection (ministry), and the fellowship of His sufferings (hardship), being conformed to His death… (Phil. 3:10)*

D.    Paul labored in ministry more than all the other apostles and suffered great difficulties.

*10 I labored more abundantly than they all, yet not I, but the grace of God which was with me. (1 Cor. 15:10)*

*23 In labors more abundant…27 in weariness and toil, in sleeplessness often, in hunger and thirst, in fastings often, in cold and nakedness-- 28 besides the other things, what comes upon me daily: my deep concern for all the churches. (2 Cor. 11:23-28)*

## VIII.    THE BRIDE WANTS JESUS TO ENJOY THE FRUIT OF HER LABOR (SONG 7:12-13)

*12 There I will give you my love. 13 The mandrakes give off a fragrance, and at our gates are pleasant fruits, all manner, new and old, which I have laid up for you, my Beloved. (Song 7:12-13)*

A.    The fragrance of the mandrake flows as they labor in love together in the harvest. The mandrake fruit has a purple flower with a beautiful fragrance. Mandrakes symbolize intimacy with God. Barren women in ancient times used to use the mandrake fruit to enhance their chances of bearing children. It became known as a fruit associated with love and fertility because of the story of Rachel who while struggling with barrenness was told by her sister Leah to use mandrakes. The unspoken idea was that she might gain a higher chance of fertility (Gen. 30:1, 14-16). This is the only time outside of the Song that the mandrake is mentioned in Scripture. Even to this day the mandrake fruit in Jewish traditions is known as a fruit associated with love.

B.    The impact of her ministry results in pleasant fruit. There is joy in knowing that the fruit of her ministry is pleasant to Jesus (Song 4:16). Having fruit at my gates speaks of it being before me.

C.    The Spirit anoints us to bear all manner of pleasant fruit both new and old. Jesus spoke of drawing out of our treasury that which is old and new. This includes the proven truths from her past along with her former victories and experiences as well as the new and fresh ones.

*52 Every scribe instructed…brings out of his treasure things new and old. (Mt. 13:52)*

D.    The Spirit gives us treasures from our life of loving obedience and faith that are laid up in heaven. We lay them up to give to Jesus. She laid up pleasant fruits for Jesus her Beloved.

*20 Lay up for yourselves treasures in heaven, where neither moth nor rust destroys… (Mt. 6:20)*

E.    We will cast our treasure at His feet when we stand before Him (Rev. 4:10). This stored up treasure will be our crown on the last day. Our life goal is to accumulate riches to offer at Jesus' feet on the last day. Our toil and sacrifice is motivated by love for Him. This is what compels us to go to the fields of service.

*¹⁰ The 24 elders fall down before Him...and cast their crowns before the Throne... (Rev. 4:10)*

## IX.    PARTNERSHIP EXPRESSED IN HER HUMILITY IN PUBLIC MINISTRY (SONG 8:1-2)

*¹ Oh, that You were like my brother, who nursed at my mother's breasts! If I should find You outside, I would kiss You; I would not be despised. 2 I would <u>lead You</u> and <u>bring You</u> into the house of my mother, she who used to instruct me. I would <u>cause You</u> to drink of spiced wine, of the juice of my pomegranate. (Song 8:1-2)*

A.    The mother throughout the Song is a picture of the Church through history. God is our father and the Church is spoken of as our mother. The redeemed from history are represented as a "mother" that gave birth to Jesus (manchild) and the believers that come after her (Rev. 12:5, 17).

B.    She longs to boldly show her loyalty and affection to Jesus in public. She prays, "O, that You, Jesus were like my brother." It was improper to express public affection to members of the opposite sex that were not in one's immediate family. She wishes that she could publicly relate to Jesus with the liberty that she had with a brother. A woman at that time in history could be more "familiar in public" with her brother than her fiancé.

C.    Like the apostles, she wants continual boldness in her life as expressed in the apostolic prayers (Acts 4:29; Eph. 6:19). Boldness is more than a personality trait but is an operation of the Spirit.

D.    A brother who nursed at her mother's breasts speaks of a full brother instead of a half brother. Children from the same mother is meant as a contrast to children with one father but different mothers. In ancient times, men had several wives. Therefore, many siblings had the same father but a different mother. They often were rivals as Absalom was with Amnon (2 Sam. 13).

E.    The Bride prays that if she should find Jesus outside in a public place that she would be able to kiss Him without being despised. To kiss Jesus in public without being despised speaks of expressing the fullness of her heart to Him in public without being misunderstood and despised.

F.    She recognizes the necessity to be restrained in public in certain aspects of her private life with Jesus. There are certain expressions of our life in God that are meant to be kept private. There are intimate expressions of prayer and worship that are not best suited for public settings.

*¹² Since you are <u>zealous</u> for spiritual gifts, let it be for the <u>edification</u> of the church that you seek to excel...19 In the church I would rather speak five words with my understanding...than 10,000 words in a tongue. 20 Do not be children in understanding...23 If the whole church comes together...and all speak with tongues, and there come in those who are uninformed or unbelievers, will they not say that you are <u>out of your mind</u>? (1 Cor. 14:12, 19-20, 23)*

G. She will be despised or label as "out of her mind' if she has an inappropriate boldness in public. It causes hindrances to the gospel. We don't express everything God gives us in every setting. We **walk in love** when we restrain our liberty on some occasions because of those who do not understand (Rom.14:14-15:2; 1Cor.14:20, 23-33, 6-19).

H. Bridal partnership is expressed in anointed ministry (Song 8:2).

*² I would <u>lead You</u> and <u>bring You</u> into the house of my mother, she who used to instruct me. I would <u>cause You</u> to drink of spiced wine, of the juice of my pomegranate. (Song 8:2)*

I. Jesus gives the Bride the dignity of leading and bringing Him into places that honor Him. She prays to be able to bring Jesus to places through anointed ministry. She longs to "bring Him" without seeking to establish her own name and ministry.

J. She prays, "I would lead You". Jesus allows us to make some of the decisions in His kingdom. He blesses some of what <u>we</u> decide in the outworking of His purposes. This reveals the dignity He has given us as co-heirs with Him (Rom.8:17). A mature believer only desires to lead Jesus in a way that honors Him.

K. She desires to bring Jesus to her mother's house or to those who instructed her. This speaks of those she has been in a long-term relationship with. It is to the very people that initially taught her the things of God. It is sometimes more difficult to minister to those to whom we are in a familiar relationships. A prophet is often not received in his home town (Mt. 13:57). It is easiest to hold back when we are with familiar relationships. She is willing to minister the truths of Jesus in the context of the people who knew her when she was just starting to walk with God.

L. She desires to bring the deep things of God to her mother's house or to those in the church.

M. Why does she want to stir up her old friends in the deep things of God? She has gratitude toward those who taught her in her beginning days. She does not forget her roots in a time of blessing. She honors the people that first trained her by seeking to serve them. She wants to return blessing to those who helped her. We must honor the heritage the Lord sovereignly gave us. We must not be critical of those we started with because they don't always grow into the deeper things of God.

N. The Bride longs to give her best to Him by praying, "I would cause You to drink of spiced wine, of the juices of my pomegranate (Song 5:1). One would mix wine with spices when hosting an honored guest because it a much more pleasant drink.

O. It was much more expensive but it was appropriate when seeking to honor a guest with their best. She longs to give her best to Jesus regardless of how much it costs her. In saying, "I would cause You to drink" she promises to attend to His every desire as she serves Him as her honored guest.

P. The juice of my pomegranate speaks of the sweet things of grace that she experiences in her inner life. The foundation of her ministry is what she experiences in the secret place with God.

## X. PARTNERSHIP EXPRESSED IN UNBROKEN UNION WITH JESUS (SONG 8:3-4)

*³ His <u>left hand</u> is under my head, and His <u>right hand</u> embraces me. 4 I charge you, O daughters of Jerusalem, do not stir up nor awaken love until it pleases. (Song 8:3-4)*

A.  Jesus answers her prayer to be close to her (8:1) and fulfills His promise to lay hold of her (7:8).

B.  The *left hand of God* speaks of the activity of God that we cannot see with our natural eyes. It is the hand that is under her head therefore, it is out of view. The Lord does many things for us that we do not see. He withholds and releases many things to bless, provide and protect us. He spares us from troubles that we are not ever aware of in this age.

C.  The *right hand of God* speaks of the visible or discernable activity of God. The idea is that Solomon stood in front of the Bride to embrace her. She can see and feel it. This speaks of the "sweet" manifest presence of God that can be felt and discerned. At times, we feel our heart tenderized by the working of God's right hand. A physical embrace is easy to discern thus it speaks of the manifest activity of God. The Lord allows Himself to be found by her (8:1) as He manifests His embrace to her. The embrace of God tenderizes her heart.

D.  The Holy Spirit guards us in strategic spiritual seasons (Song 8:4). The Spirit speaks here. He has ordained strategic seasons in each person's spiritual life. There are seasons, where He desires to establish our heart in new and deep revelations of His heart. The Spirit's agenda for the Bride in this season was to impart boldness and humility in her (Song 8:1-2).

E.  The daughters of Jerusalem represent believers who lack discernment of the various operations of the Spirit and the different seasons in God. The Spirit charges other believers to not disrupt or disturb the devoted ones with the Bride's heart in this season by their opinions and judgments.

F.  In the phrase, "Until <u>it</u> pleases", the Hebrew can be translated as <u>it</u>, <u>he</u> or <u>she.</u> The NAS accurately translates the phrase as "Don't awaken love until <u>she</u> pleases" instead of "until <u>it</u> pleases." If the Hebrew was translated "<u>He</u>" it would refer to the Lord being stirred to action by the daughters of Jerusalem. The Lord has no need for this nor does He need to be protected by the gentleness pictured by the gazelles. It is the Bride that must be protected from distraction.

G.  Three times Jesus speaks this phrase, "Don't arouse or awaken my love until it pleases." (2:7; 3:5; 8:4). In 2:7, He uses the same phrase "don't disturb her" but adds the phrase "by the gazelles of the field" because she was immature and lacked stability being easily tossed to and fro (Eph. 4:14).

# Session 23 The Bridal Seal Of Mature Love (Song 8:5-7)

## I. INTRODUCTION

A. Theme of Song 8:5-7: God's commitment to supernaturally seal our heart with His fiery love.

*⁶ Set Me (Jesus) as a <u>seal upon your heart</u>…its flames are flames of fire… (Song 8:6)*

B. This is the pinnacle of the Song and the New Covenant (Heb. 10:16). The Bride's journey begins with a cry for the kisses of God's Word (Song 1:2) and ends with a seal of fire on her heart.

*² Let Him (Jesus) kiss me with the <u>kisses of His mouth (Word)</u>… (Song 1:2)*

C. Review from Session 1: the Song of Solomon is an 8 chapter love song. It is interpreted 2 ways.

1. *Natural interpretation:* describes the love story between King Solomon and his bride, the Shulamite maiden. It emphasizes biblical principles that honor the beauty of married love.

2. *Spiritual interpretation:* the love story between King Solomon and his bride symbolizes the spiritual truths in the relationship between King Jesus and His Bride, the Church. This is the interpretation that has been used the most in the last 3,000 years since it was written.

D. Jesus spoke of Himself from <u>all</u> the Scriptures (including the Song) to the Emmaus disciples.

*²⁷ He (Jesus) expounded…in <u>all the Scriptures</u> the things <u>concerning Himself</u>. (Lk. 24:27)*

E. The Spirit inspired all Scripture (2 Tim. 3:16). He is loyal to exalt Jesus in all of Scripture.

*¹⁴ He will <u>glorify Me</u>, for He will take of <u>what is Mine</u> and declare it to you. (Jn. 16:14)*

F. Marriage will cease but the Word remains forever and will inspire us to love Jesus.

*³⁰ In the resurrection they <u>neither marry</u> nor are given in marriage… (Mt. 22:30)*

G. The context for understanding God's seal of fire is found in understanding the Father's commitment to bring forth an eternal companion for Jesus or a Bride equally yoked to Him in voluntary love. Obedience to Jesus is mandatory, yet love is always voluntary (Phil. 2:9-11).

H. Jesus prayed that His people would love Him in the way the Father loves Him.

*²⁶ I declared Your name…that <u>the love with which You loved Me</u> may be <u>in them</u>… (Jn. 17:26)*

I. It takes God to love God. We need the Spirit's supernatural help to love God with all our heart. The anointing to love God is the greatest gift that the Spirit imparts to a believer. The Holy Spirit is the "All Consuming Fire" and the "Living Flame of Love" that baptizes us with His fiery love.

*⁵ The love of God has been <u>poured out in our hearts</u> by the Holy Spirit… (Rom. 5:5)*

*¹⁶ He (Jesus) will <u>baptize</u> you with the <u>Holy Spirit and fire</u>. (Lk. 3:16)*

J.    The 120 believers in the Upper Room received a token of the baptism of God's fiery love.

*³ There appeared to them…tongues, as of fire, and sat upon each of them. (Acts 2:3)*

K.    The seal of God's love points to the same truth as the First Commandment and union with God's heart. God will help us to love Him in the way He loves us with all His heart and strength.

*³⁰ You shall love the LORD your God with all your heart, with all your soul, with all your mind, and with all your strength. This is the first commandment. (Mk. 12:30)*

L.    Jesus prayed that our hearts would be one with each other as we are one with His heart. This speaks of our mind and emotions coming into agreement with His in a supernatural way (glory). This happens in part in this age where unbelievers can witness it and in fullness in eternity.

*²¹ That they all may be one, as You, Father, are in Me, and I in You; that they also may be one in Us, that the world may believe that You sent Me. 22 The glory which You gave Me I have given them, that they may be one as We are one… (Jn. 17:21-22)*

M.    We must believe that it is the inheritance and destiny of the Church in this age to walk in the two great commandments that call us to love God with all our heart and our neighbor as ourselves. We must apply the principles of faith to grow in the anointing of love in our inner man to the full degree that God has determined to give the human spirit in this age.

*²³ Whoever says to this mountain, "Be…cast into the sea," and does not doubt in his heart, but believes that those things he says will come to pass, he will have whatever he says. (Mk. 11:23)*

N.    We cry, "Lord we want more of You." Jesus responds by saying, "I want more of you." This is the spiritual violence of love that Jesus said is required to take the Kingdom promises by force.

*¹² The kingdom of heaven suffers violence, and the violent take it by force. (Mt. 11:12)*

II.   **JESUS CALLS US TO INVITE HIM TO COME TO US AS THE JEALOUS BRIDEGROOM**

*⁶ Set Me (Jesus) as a seal upon your heart, as a seal upon your arm; for love (God's love in you) is as strong as death, (God's) jealousy as cruel (demanding) as the grave; its flames are flames of fire, a most vehement flame. 7 Many waters (sin, pressures) cannot quench love, nor can the floods drown it. If a man would give for love all the wealth of his house, it would be utterly despised. (Song 8:6-7)*

A.    The Lord spoke to me by His audible voice in July 1988. I was in my office reading Song 8:6 and began to pray, "Jesus seal my heart with Your seal of love." The Lord said that He would *release grace to walk in Song 8:6-7 across the Body of Christ worldwide* and that I was to focus on this theme throughout my ministry. (This was also a promise for the IHOP-KC movement).

B.    God's love in us is as strong as death: Nothing escapes its grasp. God's love in us is as strong or as comprehensive as death. Nothing in the natural realm escapes the power of death. *Its grasp is comprehensive*. So also, God's jealous love will not allow any areas of darkness to escape its grasp. It is "as cruel as the grave" or as demanding as death.

C.     Jesus as the Jealous God wants all of us. We walk with God according to the light He gives us. When we obey that light, the Spirit gives us more to show us how to increase in our love.

> *5 Do you think that the Scripture says in vain, "The Spirit who dwells in us __yearns jealously__"? (Jas 4:5)*

D.     We must earnestly ask Jesus to come to us as the God of Jealous Love who demands everything. This is the highest thing that God will give the human spirit in this age.

> *14 For the LORD, whose name is Jealous, is a jealous God… (Exod. 34:14)*

E.     Jesus wants to reveal Himself to us as more than our savior (forgiver), healer and master but as the jealous Bridegroom God who will not relent in His pursuit of us until He has all our heart.

## III.     GOD'S SEAL IS A FLAME OF DIVINE FIRE THAT CANNOT BE QUENCHED

> *6 Set Me (Jesus) as a seal upon your heart…__its flames are flames of fire__, a most vehement flame. 7 Many waters (sin, pressures) cannot __quench__ love, nor can the __floods__ drown it. (Song 8:6-7)*

A.     In the ancient world, kings put a "seal of wax" on important documents. They encased them with wax then stamped it with the king's signet ring. They were protected and authenticated by a royal seal. This wax seal spoke of the king's ownership, protection and authority. A king's seal spoke of his guarantee. It was backed up by all the power of his kingdom.

B.     Water always puts out fire (unless it is God's supernatural fire). The enemy will send the waters of temptation, apathy, disappointment, pain, etc. to put this fire out. God's love poured in our hearts (when continually yielded to) is more powerful than the dark floods of sin and temptation.

C.     The seal of fire is the progressive impartation of Spirit's power in pouring God's love into our heart (Rom. 5:5). The seal is our present tense experience in fellowshipping with the Spirit.

> *13 In whom, having believed, you were __sealed with the Holy Spirit__ of promise… (Eph. 1:13)*

## IV.     WE MUST SET JESUS AS THE SEAL ON OUR HEART BY INVITING HIS PRESENCE

A.     Jesus calls her to set Him as a seal on her heart. He urges us to cry out to know Him as the God of all consuming love. To set Jesus as the seal on our heart means to invite His fiery presence to touch or seal our heart. By the very definition of love, we must invite Him. He will not force us into a relationship of voluntary love. He waits until we invite Him in the matters of our heart.

B.     Some scholarly commentaries point out that there is uncertainty about the Hebrew pronouns in this passage. From theological point of view, it is impossible to interpret this passage as the Bride urging Jesus to set her on His heart so that He would begin to love her with fiery love. Jesus loves us with infinite everlasting love (that is not enhanced by us asking Him to do so).

> *3 The LORD has appeared…saying: "__I have loved you with an everlasting love.__" (Jer. 31:3)*

C.   God requires us to cooperate with Him in the grace of God. This is an expression of His desire for intimate partnership with us. <u>God will not do our part</u> and <u>we cannot do His part</u>. We set Jesus as the seal on our heart by putting on the Lord Jesus or by putting on the new man.

> *14 <u>Put on the Lord Jesus Christ</u>, and make no provision for the flesh… (Rom. 13:14)*

> *10 <u>Put on</u> the new man who is <u>renewed</u> in knowledge according to God's image. (Col. 3:10)*

> *24 <u>Put on</u> the new man which was <u>created</u>…in true righteousness and holiness. (Eph. 4:24)*

## V.   THE REWARD OF LOVE IS FOUND IN POSSESSING THE ABILITY TO LOVE

A.   We are the only one who can give God all our love. God will not force us to love Him. It is our gift to Him that we give voluntarily as we cooperate with the Spirit's work in our life. This is the work of the Spirit in her because it takes God to love God.

B.   The highest reward of true love is found in possessing the love itself. Those who are wealthy in love do not look at price tags. Anybody can quit except a person in love. When we are tempted to quit, the obstacle in our path is that we love God. God is raising up a people who will not quit.

> *7 If a man would <u>give for love</u> all the wealth of his house, it would be <u>utterly despised</u>. (Song 8:7)*

C.   Paul spoke of this love that will pay any price. He laid down his open doors of opportunity.

> *8 I count <u>all things</u> loss for the excellence of the knowledge of Christ…for whom I have suffered the loss of <u>all things</u>, and <u>count them as rubbish</u>, that I may gain Christ… (Phil. 3:8)*

D.   The Spirit is raising up many ministries in the earth who will also focus on making Jesus known as the Bridegroom and the Church as a fully devoted Bride fulfilling the First Commandment. Ministries with this focus will function as "friends of the Bridegroom" who prepare the Bride.

> *29 The <u>friend of the Bridegroom</u>…rejoices greatly because of the Bridegroom's voice. (Jn. 3:29)*

> *7 Rejoice…for the marriage of the Lamb…and <u>His wife has made herself ready</u>. (Rev. 19:7)*

## VI.   THE END-TIME CHURCH WILL BE VICTORIOUS IN LOVE

> *5 Who is this <u>coming up</u> (victory) from the wilderness (testing), <u>leaning</u> upon her Beloved? I awakened you under the apple tree. There your mother brought you forth…. (Song 8:5)*

The Bride is leaning upon Jesus as her Beloved empowered by love and gratitude. The Church ends natural history with a leaning and loving heart as she is victorious in love. The Spirit prophetically speaks as He declares the Bride's victory in the End-Times as she "comes up" in victory in the testing, temptations and difficulties in the wilderness in this fallen world.

> *2 Those who have <u>victory</u> (in love) over the Beast (Antichrist)…on the sea of glass… (Rev. 15:2)*

> *27 He might present…<u>glorious church</u>…that she should be holy and without blemish. (Eph. 5:27)*

# Session 24 The Bride's Final Intercession and Revelation (Song 8:8-14)

## I. OVERVIEW OF SONG 8:8-14

A. The Song tells the story of how the young maiden grew until she became a Bride filled with the fire of God. Now, she reveals how she sees herself in God. ***She knows who she is***. We can only be alive like the Bride as we walk in her revelation, confidence and radical obedience. The Bride offers her two final intercessory prayers, first for the church (8:8–9) then for Jesus' return (8:14).

B. In Song 8:8-9, we see her passion and intercession for the Church.

C. In Song 8:10, we see the Bride's confidence or the revelation of how God sees her (Song 8:10). Her 3-fold confidence is as a wall (selfless motives), as a tower (her supernatural abilities to nurture) and as one with peace (emotional hindrances removed). She enjoys living before His eyes. Her identity allows her to enjoy a radiant confidence to walk in her place before God.

D. In Song 8:11 she has revelation of her accountability before God.

E. In Song 8:12, she has confidence in her faithfulness to God.

F. In Song 8:13, Jesus gives His final commission to the Bride.

G. In Song 8:14, she intercedes with urgency for Jesus' coming.

## II. THE BRIDE'S PASSION AND INTERCESSION FOR THE CHURCH (SONG 8:8-9)

*⁸ We have a little sister, and she has no breasts. <u>What shall we do for our sister</u> in the day when she is spoken for? <u>If she is a wall</u>, we will build upon her a battlement of silver; and <u>if she is a door</u>, we will enclose her with boards of cedar (Song 8:8–9).*

A. In the overflow of having the seal of love renewed in her heart (Song 8:6-7), she is aware of the spiritual condition of others who have remained as babes in Christ. She intercedes for them.

B. The Bride speaks to Jesus saying, "we have a little sister" because she is working closely with Jesus. The Bride does not use the singular, saying, "What will 'I' do for my sister," but rather, she uses the plural, "we," indicating that she is in partnership with Jesus. Her original prayer in 1:4, *"Let us run together,"* is in the plural. All running in ministry is in the plural. We work together with the Lord and with others to help the lost and the immature.

C. The fact that she even "sees" the little sister's need is the work of the Spirit in her. She feels the same towards the little sister as Jesus does. He is ravished over them (4:9) and longs to see their face and hear their voice (2:14). She joins Jesus in mature partnership.

D.     The Bride remembers her little sister instead of forgetting her as she moves on to deeper things. Immature believers are under the responsibility the Bride. The "little" sister is little in faith and thus, easily loses her courage in difficulties. She quickly gives up in pressure. The daughters of Jerusalem were in this same condition as this little sister.

E.     The little sister has no breasts which means she is unwilling and unable to nurture others with the milk of the Word (1Cor. 3:1-2). She fellowships with those she hangs out with, but neglects to take responsibility for others being overwhelmed with her own problems and wants. She remains a spiritual babe who is focused on herself. The Bride is not offended by her but helps her.

F.     The Bride asks for the Lord's counsel and help concerning the little sister. She intercedes by saying, "What shall we do for <u>our</u> sister? How can we help bring her forth to maturity?"

G.     The Bride has a deep sense of responsibility for immature believers (Song 6:11; 7:11). This is the heart of a spiritual father (1 Thess. 2:11). She is not content to go on in the Lord without helping others follow Jesus.

H.     I had a life changing encounter with the Lord in the summer of 1983. I was very focused on my own spiritual development. I was seeking to grow in prayer and revelation of the Word. I didn't want to be burdened and distracted by others depending on me. In prayer, I was complaining to the Lord that I didn't want to be responsible for so many people (the church was 500 people). Suddenly, the Lord spoke to me powerfully from Josh. 1:2.

       *² Now therefore, arise, go over this Jordan, you <u>and all this people</u>, to the land which I am giving <u>to them</u> -- the children of Israel. (Josh. 1:2)*

I.     The Lord commanded Joshua to lead the people to their inheritance in the land. The Holy Spirit asked me a question in a strong way, "What is more important to the Lord than a holy man on the earth? I was perplexed by this question and could not imagine what the answer was. The Lord answered me, "a whole generation of holy people." Then the Spirit gave me Josh. 1:2, saying, "I want you ***and the people*** to inherit the land." This verse struck my heart like an arrow.

J.     As an immature believer, being holy was enough for me. But as I grew, the Lord began to say, "Where are your brothers? Where are your little sisters?" One significant sign of spiritual maturity is concern for the spiritual condition of others. "What shall we do for our sister?" This question was deeply rooted in the Bride's heart.

K.     The Bride knows that all will eventually stand before the Lord "in the day we are spoken for." The day a woman is spoken for is a reference to her wedding day. This refers to the time she attains to maturity in her bridal partnership with Jesus. For those who pursue the Lord with all their heart, the sense of being spoken for by Jesus for deep mature partnership happens in this life. To most believers, this happens on the day they stand before Jesus.

L.      She asks what she can do in partnership with Jesus to help bring her sister forth? Many believers miss out in partnering with Jesus in taking responsibility for others in the grace of God.

M.      The Bride presents her little sister's case before the Lord in intercession with two possibilities.

*⁹ If she is a wall, we will build upon her a battlement of silver; and if she is a door, we will enclose her with boards of cedar. (Song 8:9)*

N.      If the little sister is called to be a spiritual wall then the Bride and the Lord will build on her. A wall brings defense to a city and establishes a line of demarcation. "Wall ministries" either function in a pastoral way to protect the people from the enemy or they raise up God's prophetic standard. They establish God's line of demarcation for holiness to go forth in the land.

O.      In Song 8:10, the Bride speaks of herself as a wall ministry. This involves protecting others and being a prophetic standard bearer. There are pressures associated with being a wall. When the enemy shoots arrows, the wall stands in the path of the arrows meant for the young ones.

P.      If the little sister is called to be a spiritual door then the Bride and the Lord will enclose her. A door is the point of entry for others. The "door ministries" open doors of grace and salvation for others as an intercessor, evangelist, teacher or apostle. Intercessors open doors of opportunity for others. Evangelists open the door for unbelievers to come into the Kingdom. Teachers open the door for believers to go deeper in God. Apostles open doors to regions for new initiatives in God.

*³ Praying also for us, that God would open to us a door for the word to speak… (Col. 4:3)*

Q.      There are two directions the little sister might respond, to be a wall or a door. The Lord and the Bride respond to the little sister's response which is according to what God put into her heart. They will work to help her be effective according to her response to God's call in her life.

R.      The Bride says to Jesus, "We will build her into a battlement of silver." The battlement of a fortress was on the top of the tower where the archers shot through the indentations in the stone. They shot then stood behind the stone battlements for protection. The battlements provided places for the watchmen to spot and shoot the enemy and thus, defend the city.

*⁹ If she is a wall, we will build upon her a battlement of silver; and if she is a door, we will enclose her with boards of cedar… (Song 8:9)*

S.      Battlements speak of the ministries that provide safety from the enemy. Silver speaks of redemption. There was no such thing as a battlement of silver. They were usually made of stone. Battlements of silver speak of bringing redemption to others.

T.      If the grace on the little sister's life leads her to be an intercessor, evangelist, teacher, etc. then the Bride prays, "let us enclose her with boards of cedar."

U.      Boards of cedar or cedar panels were expensive, reliable, strong and scented. In the Tabernacle, wood was symbolic of humanity. The stately cedars of Lebanon were the most fragrant, strong, expensive building material. Jesus is the cedar of Lebanon (Song 3:9). The gospel chariot was made out of the cedar of Lebanon or the humanity of Jesus. The boards of cedar speak of the fragrance of Christ, as the cedars of Lebanon are fragrant. Cedars from Lebanon were used in building Solomon's Temple for the dwelling place of the Lord's presence (1 Kings 4:33; 5:6).

V.      To be enclosed with the cedars of Lebanon is to be clothed with the character and presence of Jesus. We are to be clothed in Jesus who is the cedar sent from the Father.

*14 Put on the Lord Jesus Christ, and make no provision for the flesh… (Rom. 13:14)*

W.      The Bride prayed, "We will enclose her…" Jesus and the Bride will work together with the little sister until she is enclosed by God.

## III.     THE BRIDE'S CONFIDENCE: REVELATION OF HOW GOD SEES HER (SONG 8:10)

*10 I am a __wall__, and my breasts like __towers__, then I became in His eyes as one who found __peace__. (8:10)*

A.      The fullness of the Bride's identity includes a 3-fold revelation that leaves her with confidence. She has revelation of her true spiritual stature. This is a rare yet powerful reality in the Church.

B.      She selflessly sees herself as a wall of protection that exists to help others. She does not see her life in context to pursuing earthly pleasures but sees herself as a source of protection for others. Her time, energy, finances and dreams are bound up in serving this high purpose in God. Paul saw himself as a wall of protection for others (I Thess.2:7-12; Gal. 2:11-14).

C.      Throughout the Song breasts speak of the ability to nurture the young. Breasts like towers speak of a supernatural ability to care for others. Her ministry is so abundant; it is as a tower of milk referring to her ability to nurture. Three times she has been compared to a tower (4:4; 7:4; 8:10).

D.      She has confidence in her effectiveness in ministry. Jesus commissioned her to let her __breasts__ be like clusters of the vine (Song 7:8). She knows that she skillfully uses the Word to help others. This is not arrogance. Paul, John the Baptist, David, Samuel and Moses has confidence like this.

E.      Paul wrote concerning himself, one of the boldest statements in the NT when he said, "imitate me just as I imitate Christ (1 Cor. 11:1; 2 Cor. 1:12, 15). Paul told the elders of Ephesus he served the Lord with all humility and did not count his life dear to myself and is therefore, innocent of the blood of all men (Acts 20:18-37).

F.      Enoch obtained a testimony he was pleasing to God before God took him (Heb. 11:5). John the Baptist said, "Jesus is even mightier than I…" (Lk. 3:16). Moses wrote about himself as being very humble more than any man on earth (Num. 12:3). Samuel at the end of his ministry proclaimed that he walked before the people from his childhood to that day with great integrity and that he would teach the nation the good and the right way (1 Sam. 12:1-5, 23).

G.      This confidence comes only by revelation (not pride) and fills her with great thanksgiving. She has confidence about her ministry and maturity because God spoke it to her. She can say before God that she lives to serve His people throughout her life because that is what the Lord thinks. She has the witness in her heart that is doing the will of God (Heb. 11:5).

H.      She has peace in her life and calling in God before God's eyes or before the Audience of One. She finds peace in Jesus' eyes which is not the same as finding peace in the eyes of others. This removes many emotional hindrances in her life.

I.      She enjoys living before His eyes. Her spiritual identity allows her to enjoy a radiant confidence to walk in her place before God.

J.      This confidence makes a believer powerful emotionally as they do their work in God. Consider how much emotional energy is expended on condemnation, fear, self-doubt and uncertainty. The fiery seal of love on her heart has produced this confidence and purity of motives (Song 8:6).

K.      Paul was criticized by many in the Church yet he had this peace and confidence (1 Cor. 4:3-5). How wonderful it is after 50 years of ministry to know you served Jesus with all of your heart.

L.      She came to peace with God's design for her life by knowing she lives to partner with Jesus. It is profound to understand our life and to have confidence that we accomplished God's will.

## IV.      THE BRIDE'S REVELATION OF HER ACCOUNTABILITY BEFORE GOD (SONG 8:11)

*[11] Solomon had a vineyard at Baal Hamon; he leased the vineyard to keepers; everyone was to bring for its fruit a thousand silver coins. (Song 8:11)*

A.      The outcome of living before His eyes is the understanding of the reality of our accountability and eternal reward before God (1 Cor. 3:11-15; 2 Cor. 5:10; Rom. 14:12-14). On the last day, every believer will give a full account of their earthly life to God. Her revelation of eternal rewards dignifies her smallest acts of obedience and gives every day a sense of importance.

B.      King Solomon owned a vineyard that he leased out to keepers. King Solomon throughout the Song is a picture of King Jesus. Jesus has a vineyard which speaks of His people (Isa. 5:1-7).

C.      King Jesus' vineyard at Baal Hamon has grown dynamically through history. There is no mention in Scripture or in Israel's history of Baal Hamon which may be translated as "the populous one." The word literally means in Hebrew, "the father of a multitude." Some Bible versions translate the meaning without trying to translate it as a city. King Jesus has a very large vineyard at Baal Hamon that reaches to the multitudes of the nations (Mt. 24:14; Rev. 7:9).

D.      King Jesus leased (entrusted) His vineyard to His Bride knowing she would keep it for Him. Jesus leasing His vineyard speaks of the Kingdom in this age as being entrusted to His people.

E.      In the parable in Matt. 21:33-44, Jesus made reference to Song 8:11-12, by teaching about a landowner who planted a vineyard, built a tower and "leased" it to keepers then went into a far country (Mt. 21:33). We are living in time when the Lord is in a "far country".

F.      The Lord entrusted the responsibility to cultivate His vineyard to keepers. Each believer is given a certain stewardship in His vineyard. You do not need to wait for an official job description or a title from a ministry organization to be faithful to your stewardship. Start serving people.

G.      She understands that "everyone" will give an account to the King for their assignment (Lk. 12:31-48). Each is responsible to cultivate the vineyard in such a way to bring forth fruit. The Lord rewards us based on the measure of our faithfulness, not giftedness or opportunity.

H.      The Lord desires a full return of fruitfulness from each keeper. Each must bring a thousand pieces of silver. The "thousand" is a complete number which speaks of fullness or the full measure that God requires according to what was entrusted to each person. The 1,000 pieces of silver was referred to by Isaiah to mean the fullness of the potential value of the vineyard.

*23 It shall happen in that day, that <u>wherever there could be a thousand vines worth a thousand shekels of silver</u>, it will be for briers and thorns (as a sign of God's judgment). (Isa. 7:23)*

## V.     THE BRIDE'S CONFIDENCE IN HER FAITHFULNESS TO GOD (SONG 8:12)

*12 My own vineyard is before me. You, O Solomon, <u>may have a thousand</u>, and those who tend its fruit two hundred. (Song 8:12)*

A.      The Bride's own vineyard is before her. In other words, she was aware that she will give an account of the responsibility given to her by Jesus. This includes her personal life and ministry assignment. At the beginning of her journey her vineyard was not kept but now it is (Song 1:6).

B.      The Bride is confident that she is able to give Jesus all that He expects from her by declaring that He may have the thousand pieces of silver that He requires from her in Song 8:11. Enoch before he was taken received the testimony that he was pleasing to God. She had this same confidence to say to God, "I lived to protect and nurture Your people" (Song 8:10).

*5 Enoch…before he was taken he <u>had this testimony</u>, that he pleased God. (Heb. 11:5)*

C.      She acknowledges that those who "keep its fruit" or her fellow workers will have a portion in her fruitfulness when they stand before God. She only fulfilled her mandate as she worked in team relationship with others. Each worker on the team will share in her reward in eternity. The 200 shekels of silver speak of the portion of reward that her co-workers will receive on the last day.

D.      The Philippians helped Paul financially and he reported that the fruit would be in their account.
        *¹⁷ Not that I seek the gift, but I seek the __fruit that abounds to your account__. (Phil. 4:17)*

E.      *Summary:* The Bride says before God, "I am a wall. I am a tower. I am at peace with You. I am ready to give account to You because I have given You the thousand that You asked for."

## VI.    JESUS' FINAL COMMISSION TO THE BRIDE (SONG 8:13)

*¹³ __You who dwell in the gardens__, the companions __listen__ for your voice—Let Me hear it! (8:13)*

A.      Jesus' last words to the Bride commend her effectiveness in serving the Church. Jesus names the Bride, "You who dwell in the gardens" to affirm that she is still dwelling in the midst of God's garden serving His people instead of retreating in selfish isolation. She did not quit. The gardens (plural) refer to the many parts of the Church as the beds of spices in Song 6:2 did.

B.      The Bride's continuing credibility and impact until the end is seen as Jesus affirms that the companions who she served still eagerly listen for her voice because there is a stature of maturity in her life that is obvious to them. They see reality in God in her, thus, they still receive from her. As the daughters wanted to hear her voice in Song 5:9; 6:1, 13 so others still listen for her voice.

C.      Jesus one more time calls the Bride to fervent worship and intercession by telling her that He still wants to hear her voice. Her voice was sweet to Him in her immaturity (Song 2:14). How much sweeter is her voice now that she walks in mature union with Him as His beloved partner.

D.      The Lord wants to continually hear our voice in 4 ways.

        1.      First, in *worship* as He forever wants to hear us declare our love to Him.

        2.      Second, in *intercession* as we join Jesus who makes intercession forever (Heb. 7:25).

        3.      Third, in *teaching* as we speak the Word to one another (Mt. 28:19-20; Col. 1:28).

        4.      Fourth, in *evangelism* as we share the gospel to unbelievers.

E.      The enemy wants to silence our voice.

## VII.   HER URGENT INTERCESSION IS FOR JESUS TO COME QUICKLY (SONG 8:14)

*[14] Make haste, My Beloved, and be like a gazelle or a young stag on the mountains of spices. (8:14)*

A.   The Bride immediately obeys Jesus' exhortation to let Him hear her voice by interceding for Jesus to come quickly. We see the urgency and longing of her heart to be with Jesus. She calls Jesus, "My beloved" because her love for Him is her strength to the end.

B.   Jesus was revealed as the gazelle and young stag who conquered the mountains in Song 2:8, 17. She asks Jesus to come quickly like a swift gazelle and a young stag to conquer all the mountains of opposition and to manifest Himself as the victorious King over all the obstacles of this age.

C.   She offers a 3-fold prayer that Jesus come **near her** personally in intimacy, **to her** city in revival and finally **for her** at the Second Coming. The End-Time Church has this same prayer.

*[17] The Spirit and the Bride say, "Come!"... 20 Surely, I am coming quickly. (Rev. 22:17, 20)*

1.   *Come* **NEAR US** *in intimacy* (individual breakthrough of our heart in God)
2.   *Come* **TO US** *in revival* (regional or national breakthrough of the Spirit in revival)
3.   *Come* **FOR US** *in the sky* (historical breakthrough by the Second Coming of Jesus)

D.   This will be the **first time** in history, that the Church worldwide will be in dynamic unity with the Spirit and therefore, the Spirit will be resting on and moving through the Church in great power.

E.   The 2-fold expression of the Bride's cry for Jesus to come (breakthrough)
1.   *Worship* – "We love You, we worship You, we beckon You to come by our love."
2.   *Intercession* – "We need You, we pray for You to come and release revival power."

F.   A two-dimensional cry: **upward** to God and **outward** to people (one billion new souls)
1.   *Vertical* – an upward **call to Jesus** to come to us in breakthrough power (near us/to us/for us)
2.   *Horizontal* – an outward **call to people** to come to Jesus as the Bridegroom King

G.   We call believers *(revival, discipleship)* and unbelievers *(evangelism)* to experience the Bridegroom God. The Church will "call out" in two directions. First, we will call out to Jesus in intercession to "come to us," and second we will call out to people who thirst to "come to Jesus."

H.   The Throne of God and the dwelling place of the Bride is a vast mountain of divine fragrance.

*[14] Make haste...and be like a gazelle or a young stag on the mountains of spices. (8:14)*

I.   The Bride describes the New Jerusalem as the mountains of spices. The individual believer is like a lily (Song 2:1) who has the fragrance of "**all the chief spices**" (Song 1:12; 4:10, 14). The corporate Church is spoken of as a "**garden of spices**" (Song 4:16, 5:1, 6:2).